MW01472439

THE DANGEROUS GAME

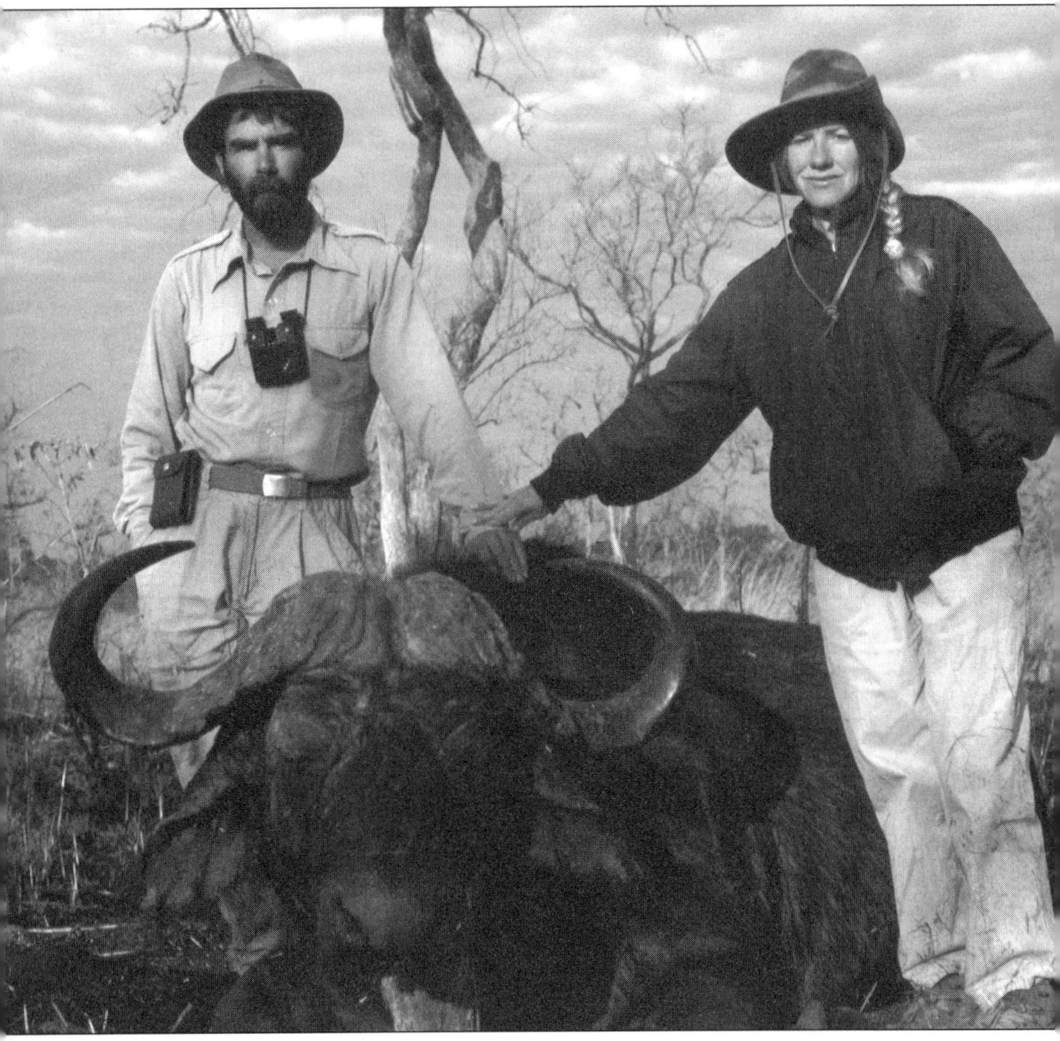

THE DANGEROUS GAME
TRUE STORIES OF DANGEROUS HUNTING ON THREE CONTINENTS

by

WALT PROTHERO

SAFARI PRESS

The Dangerous Game © 2006 by Walt Prothero. All rights reserved. No part of this publication may be used or reproduced in any form or by any means, electronic or mechanical reproduction, including photocopying, recording, or by any information storage and retrieval system, without permission from the publisher.

The trademark Safari Press ® is registered with the U.S. Patent and Trademark Office and in other countries.

Prothero, Walt

Second edition

Safari Press Inc.

2006, Long Beach, California

ISBN 1-57157-316-X

Library of Congress Catalog Card Number: 2004118130

10 9 8 7 6 5 4 3 2 1

Printed in the USA

Readers wishing to receive the Safari Press catalog, featuring many fine books on big-game hunting, wingshooting, and sporting firearms, should write to Safari Press Inc., P.O. Box 3095, Long Beach, CA 90803, USA. Tel: (714) 894-9080 or visit our Web site at www.safaripress.com.

To Cheri Flory, my better half, for patience and for dealing with the infernal computer technology while getting the manuscript written.

TABLE OF CONTENTS

Introduction x
Prologue: Questing xv

BOOK I AFRICA

Chapter 1   The Fear and the Lion 3
Chapter 2   The Last Step 10
Chapter 3   In a Leopard Blind 15
Chapter 4   Bulls in the Night 21
Chapter 5   For Adventure 30
Chapter 6   *M'bogo* 35
Chapter 7   Hippo—The "Accidental"
             Most Dangerous Game 44
Chapter 8   The Perfect Killer 50
Chapter 9   *Chui* 57

BOOK II ASIA

Chapter 10   Five Empty Chambers 68
Chapter 11   In Search of Marco Polo 72
Chapter 12   Bad Luck Bear 86
Chapter 13   A Russian Rides a Pale Horse 92
Chapter 14   The Hunt from Hell 100

BOOK III NORTH AMERICA

Chapter 15   Deadly Lesson 106
Chapter 16   Most Dangerous Hunt? 113
Chapter 17   More Horse Stories 119
Chapter 18   Trouble 124

Chapter	19	The Apache Puma	132
Chapter	20	Hunting with the Maya	138
Chapter	21	Lemon's Bear Chronicles	149
Chapter	22	Requiem for a Bush Pilot	153
Chapter	23	Incident in the Huachucas	156
Chapter	24	Kibler's Lion Scrapes	161
Chapter	25	Lost	168
Chapter	26	A Trophy Won and Lost	174
Chapter	27	Shoot-up on the Yukon	179
Chapter	28	In a Treeless Country	184
Chapter	29	The Old Woman's Gift	193
Chapter	30	Grizzlies	199
Chapter	31	The Last Bush Pilot	207
Chapter	32	Boreas's Stare	213

BOOK IV THE HAPPY HUNTING GROUNDS

Chapter	33	Home to a Place I've Never Been	222
Chapter	34	You *Can* Go Home Again	230
Chapter	35	Journey to the Dog Salmon	236
Chapter	36	Solitude	242
Chapter	37	More Solitude	254
Chapter	38	Call of the Sheenjek	262
Chapter	39	It Calls You Back	270
Chapter	40	Leaning Out	278
Chapter	41	Waiting for Christmas	289

Appendix 295

INTRODUCTION

The stories within this book fall entirely within the recognized genre of "creative nonfiction" (the other literary genres are poetry, fiction, and drama). If this sounds academic, I apologize, but I *am* an academic and teach various university writing courses, as well as English and zoology. I hope the reader won't hold this against me.

Simply put, creative nonfiction is putting real action and events into a fictional format, be it a novel or short story, complete with characterization, plot, theme, and the human aspect. Compared with straight journalism, where you get "only the facts, ma'am," creative nonfiction is livelier. Entertainment, not education, becomes the main reason for reading these stories. How many of us are in any way "entertained" by a journalist's account of the doings of the city commission in the evening newspaper?

Most hunters prefer the well-written true narrative to the essentially didactic how-to or technical article. And the more experienced the hunter, the truer this seems. The "Big Three" outdoor magazines—*Field & Stream, Outdoor Life,* and *Sports Afield*—have lost circulation during the last decade or so, largely because of their emphasis on teachy type articles (yes, yes, I know, another big reason is the proliferation of specialty magazines). Possibly, in desperation, they now include more hunting narratives within their covers. *Sports Afield* has entirely reinvented itself and now focuses on big-game tales, becoming the best magazine about hunting, bar none. *Gray's Sporting Journal* is almost entirely creative nonfiction and includes fishing, bird shooting, and big-game hunting stories, as well as essays that don't fall conveniently in any of these categories. Both the new *Sports Afield* and *Gray's Sporting Journal* are holding their own on the market.

Three of my last four hunting books—*The Hunting Adventures of Me & Joe; Safari: A Dangerous Affair;* and *Mule Deer Quest*—contain creative nonfiction. The first two are written entirely within the genre. Most of the last stories I wrote for *Field & Stream* and *Outdoor Life*, when I wrote regularly for them back in the '80s and '90s, were creative narratives, so I've had considerable experience writing such stories. As a result, I've formed opinions and philosophies about such writing. Of course, opinions differ among writers.

The first type is the story that's mainly fancy "wordsmithing." At first read, the story seems clever and the word use catchy, the kind of stuff you'd hear on TV talk shows or at an enjoyable cocktail party. Possibly the best wordsmithing comes from the late African hunting writer Peter Capstick. His stuff was and is popular because of sensationalism; it generally contained no human story or very little if any deep meaning. (Perhaps there's some sour grapes here, since I'd like to achieve his financial writing success.)

Russell Annabel was North America's premier wordsmith and I read him assiduously back in the "old" *Sports Afield*. Annabel, in my humble opinion, was the best outdoor writer going, not because of his excellent wordsmithing, but because his stories always contained a human element of some sort, however shallow it might have been. Ernest Hemingway agreed with my assessment of Annabel, by the way.

I've tried to avoid the rhetorical tricks like wordsmithing in my stories and focused on the truth of the action, the excitement inherent in real action presented simply. Of course, I wasn't always as successful as I'd have liked. I also avoided using the story and its action as merely a vehicle to transport a metaphoric, "deeper" theme, and let the event itself be reason enough for the telling. I've focused on dramatic events in this book because they are, well, dramatic. A Mozambique tracker getting tossed into a thorn tree by an enraged buffalo is sensational however you tell it, but I feel simple truth is often more sensational than anything we can construct with fancy words.

I've divided the book into four geographical areas. Book I handles Africa, Book II Asia, Book III is about North America, and Book IV deals with the Happy Hunting Grounds (a unique part of the far north wilderness). Some hunters have no interest whatsoever in the often artificial African hunting; therefore, they can skip right to what interests them. Likewise, other hunters have little interest in anything *but* Africa, so they can plunge right into Part I.

While the stories in this tome have the common thread of danger, real and potential, and mortality, immediate or not, not all stories focus on them in an obvious manner. Still, we hunters face danger at every turn. For example, in my polar bear story "In a Treeless Land," we faced no polar bear charges, we experienced little bad weather, and we weren't forced to swim open leads on the ice pack. Still, on the open ice pack in winter, frostbite, hypothermia, bear danger, storms, ice lead openings, and shifts were always potentially serious threats, to the extent the Inuit guides slept in their clothes. In other stories, people get killed or very nearly so. Elephant or grizzly charges often force you to face mortality, however they turn out, as does getting lost in a frozen British Columbia forest, or a rattlesnake bite, or a dunking in an Arctic river. True, few hunters think of the dangers we face climbing around after sheep or sitting on a saddle mule, but they are real and present, nevertheless. Perhaps, too, we'll find that the most dangerous beast isn't an African lion, Cape buffalo, elephant or grizzly, either.

Inevitably, I find bits of redundancy. Particularly dramatic events may be mentioned elsewhere, though I tried to avoid retelling the story in any detail. Parts of Book IV may "sound" like a few of the stories in Book III, North America, because they occur in the same locale.

So much for the analysis, dear reader, read on!

Behold a pale horse, and his name who sat on him was Death, and Hell followed with him.—Revelation 6:8

I have sworn an oath, to keep it, on the Horns of Ovis Poli, for the Red Gods call me out, and I must go.—Rudyard Kipling

QUESTING

"Nobody knows what's in those mountains. Maybe too many bears live there. No hunters go that way." Gwitchin caribou hunter, Strangle Woman Creek, 1983.

Pavement, hospitals and M*A*S*H* reruns were far away now, in miles four hundred to the south, in mindset thirty thousand years in the future. I'd stood on a tiny river bar beside a tangle of duffel scarcely larger than a big tussock long after the bush Cessna had disappeared into the leaden Arctic skies to the south, noticing first the surprising din of primeval silence and then feeling the familiar lump in the throat with the sudden and full understanding that I would not see or hear another human for at least eight weeks, if I was lucky and made no mistakes, and never if I screwed up.

Gradually apprehension disappeared, as it always does when I make this kind of expedition, replaced by the comfortable feel of becoming solitary but not alone (wolf, caribou and grizzly tracks crisscrossed the beach). But I had immediate concerns: Where could I camp where there'd be enough firewood? Was the big ram still alive? Keeping dry, well fed and alive was enough to think about, and they made petty the concerns of that other time.

As I pumped the inflatable raft, the memory of the broken-horn ram drifted up through river-bottom mists, and I saw him again on a high shale fin silhouetted against a swirling, wet-snow blizzard, one horn broken back six inches and the other pinching in close to the face then flaring straight out, forty-six inches around the curl at least.

Eventually the days ran together—I no longer cared if it was Tuesday or Sunday, August or September, 1984 or the Pleistocene—until all I knew was that I had floated a day downriver, cached raft and gear in steel drums to protect them from grizzlies and trekked up, first through the muskeg bogs in the bottoms then through stunted spruce forests and Arctic birch and dwarf willows and rushing streams and fractured glaciers, to the frost-shattered limestone and alpine tundra into the highest country that hid much of each day in the clouds. I couldn't remember how many days it had taken to get to the bare limestone peaks that had once been the bottom of a tropical sea, evidenced by the fossil coral and sponges. I continued upward, deeper into country where no civilized man had walked, toward the big ram's canyon. Wolves trotted alongside, fifty yards off, barking and howling in curiosity, predatory brotherhood, or something else. I climbed a narrow, steep canyon, thick with migrating caribou, and gazed into a prehistoric park.

Caribou grazed the already browning tundra between patches of early snow, and lower down two wolves ghosted like quicksilver beads across the tundra and rocks and through a milling then fleeing band of caribou, as the wolves cut out a big, crippled bull. The bull whirled and rushed, searching with velveted antlers for his tormentors. It was a last act of desperation, because within moments he was down, the wolves tearing into thin underbelly as the bull held his head as if to bellow in rage. Farther up the shoulder of a big, nameless peak I named Dark Mountain—still the modern man, I could not yet discipline myself *not* to label—a band of rams grazed dirty white against the black shale rock. A mastodon lumbering out of the swirling mists would have seemed completely natural (in earlier years, I'd found their fossils in a drainage forty miles east).

I pitched a tiny tent beside a rushing, garrulous stream, scrounged dead willow twigs from the knee-high scrub and built a fire as the sun dipped behind a bare ridge and the air chilled. In spite of a light techno-age sleeping bag and a synthetic wonder-parka, I belonged as I never had any place, and I understood all over that this was one reason I took the risk.

I stalked a band of rams the next morning, straining hands-and-feet up a seventy-degree ridge two thousand feet, into an avalanche channel, then over a rocky bench, and there they were. A dozen rams clattered about the cliffs like fat white insects on a dark wall. At least two went forty inches around the curl—exceptional trophies—but they weren't the holy grail, the broken-horn ram.

I didn't find him, but grizzlies, caribou, wolves, sheep and even moose were everywhere, like a *National Geographic* wall poster. Wolves often visited my camps, barking and howling from very close, too innocent to have had experience with man. Once, two big wolves, one very light and the other quite black, came in the twilight that passes for darkness (until September, when true night comes and gets longer and longer until by November there is no daylight), and sat and gazed as I boiled rice over a willow-wood fire, yipping like frustrated pets. It wasn't hard to see how humans had domesticated them. And without electronic stimulation, I had time to understand what I already knew.

I stalked and passed up rams often, living on rice, berries and grayling snagged with a nymph on a hand-held leader. Time meant nothing. Eventually, though, out of rice, above creeks and fish, I was forced to return to my cache on the river. I trekked back down canyons, over passes and across fractured glaciers until, as I staggered into a chasm, I glassed a ram on a ridge just as opaque clouds boiled over the divide and swallowed him. Was one horn broken? Had the other really flared out that much? Did I imagine the whole damned thing?

I turned away, from a place and time that seem a fantasy now, toward a thing that became more and more real with each step toward the cache. I drifted out, then, on the current of the Sheenjek toward the tiny fly-in Gwitchin village that represented it and where I could no longer hide from it. The expedition wasn't quite over, though the justification for it—the search for the big ram—was. I floated and spent weeks hunting caribou and moose—winter meat—and fly-fished for big grayling and shot ptarmigan. I lingered at familiar camps along the now-homey wilderness river and lounged away more nights atop pingos staring at the always-alien aurora shimmering and coiling in black silence.

I'd spend more seasons questing for the big ram despite the understanding that wolves had probably killed him in his old age or he'd slipped off an icy ledge. I was, after all, a modern man and had to have a concrete reason to justify going back, to make valid the risk. I couldn't even say to myself, let alone civilized man, that it was really the always-inexplicable aurora, the silence and the solitude (the most precious commodities on the planet), and the need to belong, to really go home and belong. I couldn't explain it in a way anybody could understand that it was the gory poetry of wolves killing caribou or the gooseflesh-raising wail of Arctic loons. I couldn't tell how it was the very blond grizzly facing me down over a caribou I'd killed and that I'd never, ever feel so intensely mortal as at that first growl.

So there must be a holy grail, a concrete object to quest for. Without that, it is merely abstraction. The object of the quest may change—in later years it became a big slickrock mule deer, then a sixty-inch Marco Polo sheep—but the real reasons for it never do.

BOOK I

AFRICA

THE FEAR AND THE LION

"He who has never been frightened by a lion must have missed half the sport of lion hunting. Where there is no fear, there can be no courage." Sir Alfred Pease, *The Book of the Lion*, 1913.

When hunting dangerous game, you should be prepared to shoot yourself out of whatever situation you shoot yourself into.

I thought about this as the head Masai tracker whispered "*Damu*" and pointed with a grass stem at a still-wet blood spatter in the dust. "*Eeh,*" the second tracker acknowledged without enthusiasm. We paused and stared into the donga. The thornbush was so thick you wouldn't see a wounded lion until you stepped on him. The trackers looked as happy as kittens in a bath. I'd really gotten us into trouble this time.

Earlier, we'd hunted lions in the first camp hundreds of miles to the west, but instead of lion, we had collected leopard, two buffalo, a probable world-record greater kudu, topi, waterbuck, bushbuck, roan, Lichtenstein hartebeest, and other beasts. But overshadowing the western Tanzania triumphs was our failure with lion. None roared in the night, none came to our baits, and we found no fresh spoor. The safari was beset with problems: The outfitter had relocated our safari to another area without notice; we had cleaned clogged fuel lines from the polluted gas drums when the Toyota quit in the bush each day; and the previous safari had shot out the local lion pride and sable, eaten most of the food, and drunk all the wine. Then, a camp transfer that should have taken half a day by air took two—two days of lost hunting time.

But on that first night in the new camp, two big male lions roared and grunted from half a mile down the donga. I lay awake as happy as I'd ever been and listened as the roaring crested in thunder, then descended into booming, guttural grunts that shook the cots and rustled the tent canvas. I tried to remember the Somali proverb I'd read, something to the effect that a brave man is frightened three times by a lion: when he first sees his track, when he first hears him roar, and when he first faces him.

We motored out of camp in the dawn and across the stream—the only water within forty miles—as buffalo stampeded into thornbush cover and small Masai boys trailed skinny dwarf cattle to water. We drove past the pleasant dung-and-wattle Masai *boma*, which smelled of wood smoke and cows, and down the cattle track, where leopard pugs wandered in the dust and Grant gazelle browsed the thornbush scrub.

"*Simba!*" the head tracker hissed and pointed. Lionesses slunk through the tawny long grass and two big, hairy male lions crouched behind a fresh buffalo kill. Finally!

The second tracker sucked in his breath and whispered, "*Doumi kubwa sana* (very big males)!"

The black-maned lion disappeared into the donga while the blond lion dragged the buffalo into the bush and rumbled an ominous warning you could feel through the ground. The professional hunter figured we could collect the black-maned lion, the most desirable of all African game animals.

We circled well away from the big blond lion and the lionesses threatening from the thornbush, cut the spoor, and followed Black Mane through the ravine, up out of the donga and across a dead-grass plain before we lost him. Our luck hadn't improved.

When we had hurried after Black Mane, certain we'd catch him within a few yards, we'd left Cheri alone in the open Land Cruiser. Now we were worried. Though a hundred yards away, the lion pride could easily have surrounded Cheri, and it would take no trick for one to hook her out of the doorless, topless Toyota. As we rushed back, a gunbearer pointed at the fever trees heavy with vultures. That meant the lions were feeding on the buffalo carcass—otherwise, the vultures would be feeding on the kill, not roosting in trees.

We hustled out of the donga when lions growled from the carcass hidden in the thickets. Two lionesses, then the big blond male, walked into the open, then into more bush. We followed, trying to get a shot, the big male moving ahead and staying in the cover. My mouth felt ashy and I had "a cold stone in the stomach," as the Masai say. The full-bellied lion became more reluctant to move ahead and more sullen in his rumbling threats. He stopped momentarily in the open eighty yards ahead, looked back over his shoulder, and snarled that throaty, guttural roar as the cross hairs settled low and solid behind the shoulder. I pressed the trigger.

The lion leaped at the blast and stumbled in the dust, then regained his feet and streaked for cover. I fired the .375 again and the lion faltered, but I knew the shot was too far back. The PH's double rifle cannoned in my ear and kicked up dust behind the lion, but the lion was gone.

Richards grimaced. "You gut-shot the S.O.B.," he half-shouted. "He's moved into that thick bush."

I saw again the sight picture in my mind, the cross hairs solid behind the shoulder. I'd never felt more sure of a shot. But the gun had traveled for two days in the back of a lorry, and a screw might have loosened.

Each time I replayed the shot in my mind, though, the cross hairs rested solidly behind the big lion's shoulder. Still, the .375 had bounced around the back of that lorry in the hard case for 200 miles of bush track during the camp transfer. The scope might have been jarred askew. I'd known crazier things to happen. I, too, began to believe I'd gut-shot the lion. The trackers, at first jubilant, had caught Richards's mood and now were the picture of gloom.

So now we stood on the edge of the ravine as the blood splatters darkened in the dust. Seeing lions from the safety of a safari vehicle is a world different from tracking them on foot, and even that is tame compared to spooring a wounded cat in impenetrable bush. We all shifted positions to peer into the thick thornbush from different angles, each hoping to see the lion. Trailing it into the dense wall of brush looked like a gory way to commit suicide.

It seemed unlikely that we'd be able to stop a quarter ton of feline chainsaw ripping through that tangle. If the lion was gut-shot, almost certainly someone would get mauled, quite probably killed. A lion is strong enough to puncture lungs and crush skulls

THE DANGEROUS GAME

with its heavy canines and massive jaws. If the first shot in isn't quickly fatal, odds shift to the cat's favor. This is even truer in thick bush.

The trackers threw stones into the thicket, hoping the lion would roar and give himself away, or better, charge into the open where we'd get a quick shot. Nothing. A francolin partridge *pa-tucked* from down the donga. Vultures dropped from the fever trees onto the buffalo carcass; the lion pride had moved off. The trackers whispered in Maa. I fiddled with the safety on the .375 and wished it had not come to this—us or the lion—with the odds all in favor of the enraged cat mauling someone. I worried about the unarmed trackers. After all, I'd gotten us into this *shauri*. I worried, too, that the lion would escape. I wanted him as badly as I had ever wanted anything.

"We've given him enough time to sicken," the professional hunter said. We started down into the ravine, the trackers crouching abreast and silently pointing at each drop of blood with a dry grass stem. Richards and I trailed immediately behind and five yards apart, with the trackers under our gun barrels. We could not see beyond our rifle muzzles in the thorny acacia. There'd be no chance of an aimed shot. We'd have to shoot in the direction of the commotion that came with the rush and hope for the best.

Before we'd eased into the dense thornbush, I had imagined how it might feel to face the charge, to hold fire until the lion was five or ten yards off, and then to aim for the open mouth or chest or shoulder. The reality of the dense bush made these plans absurd. We would not see the lion until he was on us. My legs felt leaden, and my mouth was parched. Richards looked pale. All of us were taut as piano wires, strung to the breaking point. I wanted the lion to charge, and the sooner the better. It's the suspense and the waiting that gives time to imagine everything that could happen and lets fear mushroom to unmanageable proportions. Once the action starts, we no longer have time to imagine consequences.

Estoni, the second tracker, crawled beneath some brush and pointed with a grass stem at a nearly dried clot of blood. Gabreli followed, and, once abreast again, they crouched and scanned beneath the undergrowth. They whispered in Maa. I followed, then the PH. We sat in a small opening in the thornbush three yards across. Each of us took apart the tangle ahead with our eyes. Each listened. I flicked the safety forward and back again out of nervousness. Richards cleared the sight of his double rifle again. The trackers crawled on again, and we followed at a crouch. Muscles fluttered in my thigh and something tasted brassy.

I marveled at the trackers' courage. It takes a special kind of bravery to follow a wounded lion unarmed into thick bush for a dollar a day. I wouldn't do it. I marveled, too, at their faith in two fallible men with rifles to protect them. Perhaps, too, they had confidence in their own abilities to get clear of the action when it came and let the shooters deal with the angry cat.

I admit the fear and the taste of bile. Any man who doesn't feel fear in a like situation is two eggs short of a dozen. I feared for the trackers getting mauled, and for myself. I was even more afraid that a tracker might jump into the line of fire and get his brains blown out when the lion finally charged.

Suddenly, the second tracker dived to the side and the other flattened, as both Richards and I fell to our butts at the same time and threw our rifles to our shoulders. A guinea fowl flushed somewhere ahead in a great squawking. I wanted to laugh out loud, but didn't dare. The trackers sat on their haunches and grinned in relief. While we grinned, we listened.

On again, the trackers mostly now on hands and knees, with the PH and me trying to follow in a crouch so we'd have time and space to swing a rifle. Standing upright to trail was out of the question in the intertwined thornbush. We all bled from thorn scratches, but we paid no attention, focusing instead on what we could see and hear ahead.

We came into another opening seven feet across, and sat and rested. It was a relief to get out of the crouch we had used to trail the spoor. I stretched out on my belly and peered ahead along the disappearing blood spoor. Still zero. The trackers crouched on their haunches and looked grim. We paid no attention to the irritating pepper ticks. All of us were tiring from the odd trailing positions and the tension. Then we were off again.

THE DANGEROUS GAME

The trackers suddenly stopped, rigid as pointers in a covey, then backed rapidly on their hands and knees, nearly upsetting me. I dropped to one knee and the .375 jumped to my shoulder. Five yards ahead something materialized in the deep shadows. The lion was crouched absolutely flat. Concentrating for the rush, the lion had its head turned slightly to one side. I shifted a millimeter for a clear shot, found the leading edge of the cat's heavy shoulder, and started to pull off when Gabreli hissed, "*Kufa!*" then again louder, "*Kufa! Kufa!*" Dead! Dead!

"Hit it!" the PH shouted at the trackers. Both hurled sticks at the lion to be sure. The sticks didn't make it through the brush. When Richards shouted again, I pressed the trigger. The lion rocked with the impact, but we knew from the reaction that it was already dead.

I felt let down. We'd trailed for what seemed hours, holding our bodies tautly to the point of snapping, expecting the charge at any moment, only to find the lion had died as it lay in wait for us. We all felt gypped, I think. We'd paid with anxiety for the charge that never came.

I shouted "*Kufa!*" I had to do something with the adrenaline coursing my veins. The trackers shouted "*Kufa!*" again, and then we were all chattering and laughing in English, Swahili, and Maa in a complete bursting of tension. I heard "*Doumi kubwa sana!*" (a very big male) and "*hatari!*" (danger), and "*simba,*" and other words I didn't know, but we all understood each other. The language we used was irrelevant. All hunters speak the same language, and it isn't taught in a phrase book. We'd all suffered through the same fear, and no one had been mauled. That first letdown was replaced by the jabbery elation that always comes with the collection of an exceptional trophy, but added to that was the relief that we had all crawled out of that tangle alive. No better feeling exists.

We dragged the big *simba* out of the thornbush and into the open. The first bullet—the one that counts—had hit precisely where I'd aimed, just behind the shoulder, had wrecked the heart, and lodged in the off shoulder. The big lion just didn't know it was dead.

THE FEAR AND THE LION

It took six of us to heft the big cat into the lorry. The trackers cut green boughs and festooned the Toyota. We drove back to camp and around the *boma* as small boys paraded behind and shouted "*Simba!*" *Morani* (warriors) trotted alongside, their spears glinting in the early sun.

In camp, the staff pushed me into a canvas chair, hoisted it, and then paraded around the tents, chanting "*SIMBA-A-A! SIMBA-A-A! SIMBA-A-A!*" Someone shoved a beer in my hand. The skinner said, "*M'uzuri, bwana,*" and pulled my thumb respectfully.

That night the local Masai streamed into the camp for the *ngoma*, or celebration. Slim, attractive Masai ladies placed beaded bracelets on my wrists. They named Cheri "Mama Simba." Elders held my arm and told of their encounters with the big, blond cow-killing lion in Maa. I answered in Swahili, "*N'dio*" (yes). A young *moran* lifted his bright red *shuka* and proudly displayed where the lion had mauled his buttocks.

Perhaps it's not written in any book on hunter ethics, but it's a given that a hunter, as Francis Macomber found out, must follow up wounded dangerous game if he wants to continue calling himself a hunter. Fear is part of the equation.

THE LAST STEP

Mahimba bush, Mozambique, 1993. The tracker did not know he was about to die. He followed the white professional hunter into the tangled thirteen-foot thatch-grass jungle. When they faltered, Domingo, the tracker, pointed over PH John Wambach's shoulder the correct direction to the Mercedes Unimog lorry parked under a thorn tree a mile on.

They could not see farther than the length of their arms as they pushed a path through the grass. In one place, vines fouled the rifle slung across Wambach's shoulder, pulling him back and down. Domingo pushed past the professional hunter so Wambach could pull himself up on the tracker's coveralls. Domingo leveraged Wambach to his feet and took the last step of his life.

Domingo knew without looking when he heard the buffalo grunt and rush from three feet. He felt the crashing ton of impact and the white-hot pain and the sudden, scalding rush deep inside as he cartwheeled through the air and the sky spun at his feet. When the spinning quit, he hung in a thorn tree eight feet from the ground. Something hot and wet hung against his bare leg and he screamed involuntarily at the pain. The enraged buffalo hooked again at the tracker dangling just out of reach. Domingo saw the tiny bloodshot eyes squinted in rage, and he felt the sudden sweep of the gaff-hooked horns inches from his back.

Wambach shoved the heavy barrel of the .458 Lott against the bull and yanked the trigger. The bull plunged and spun at the impact of five hundred grains of metal, slamming Wambach flat with the swipe of a hip. He threw the bolt of the .458 as he lay on his back, but the cartridge jammed. A second bull lunged from the grass jungle so close that saliva spattered Wambach's legs. Neither bull saw the hunter lying on his back, but the second bull

THE LAST STEP

got a snoutful of man stink and crashed off. The killer bull threw another hook at the dangling tracker, then followed.

Wambach sat up slowly and cleared the jammed rifle. He moved quietly so as not to trigger a charge. Domingo hung eight feet off the ground, the blue-gray coils of his intestines tangled in the thorns. Gouts of blood pulsed from the open gash. Domingo screamed in such agony that the hairs stood on John's arms.

Wambach struggled for twenty minutes to cut Domingo free and lower him to the ground. He slowly eased the spirals of intestine back into the gaping, gory gash in Domingo's side. The black, heavy, gaff-hooked horns had ripped in above the tracker's hip and torn upward, making hash of intestines, gut, and liver. The PH wondered how the tracker had enough strength to scream.

Wambach cut strips of canvas duck from his bush jacket, made rough incisions on either side of the gaping wound with the knife, then tied the flaps of muscle together as best he could with the strips. He wrapped a jacket around Domingo's waist for added support, then hoisted the tracker across his back. Within moments, Wambach's heavy shirt was saturated with Domingo's blood.

It took Wambach the best part of two hours to push through three hundred yards of grass jungle and stagger across the plain to the lorry. Domingo continued screaming, though with less vigor. Wambach arranged jackets and duffel in the lorry bed to cushion Domingo's ride.

Earlier Wambach, two clients, two trackers, and two helpers had trailed a buffalo herd into the grassy jungle, through a tangled *miombo* wood, and out onto another plain. From the spoor, the buffalo showed no sign of slowing, so Wambach had left the men to wait while he and Domingo started back for the lorry.

As the lorry slowly jarred out of a donga and across a plain toward where he'd left the men, Wambach tried not to listen to Domingo's weakening screams and moans. *Pain like that is supposed to make you pass out*, he thought. Now, he knew better. He marveled at the tracker's stamina.

When the two bulls had crashed off, they'd lunged in the direction of the men. *Bugger it*, Wambach thought, *if they kill a client, I might as well hang up the binocs.* Arriving at the spot where they'd last split up, Wambach found the men's rifles and walking sticks leaned neatly against a tree, but the men had disappeared. He slid from the lorry to look around, when he heard shouting from a sloping acacia tree. The bulls had broken from cover very near, and the men had raced for the tree and had not come down.

One of the clients, Smithie, practiced dentistry. He did what he could for Domingo. When he wiped his bloody hands, he'd given the tracker enough morphine to stagger a hippo, and most of the antibiotics, but the tracker continued screaming. Dental school hadn't prepared him for this. He gagged back the nausea, then walked away to clear his head.

"We've got to kill the bull," Wambach told the second tracker and helpers. In unison, they shook heads in the negative. They would not trail, and there was no discussing it.

"I'll go." The dentist shuddered when he spoke, and his complexion was ashen. Wambach nodded. He badly needed help.

Wambach and Smithie pushed into the grassy jungle until they found blood spoor. *Better to trail a wounded buff than listen to those screams,* Wambach thought. He looked at his watch—10:30 A.M. Normally, Wambach would let the tracker follow the spoor while he watched ahead and kept his thumb on the safety to answer the charge of an angry beast. But nothing about the day had been normal. Now, Wambach had to follow the spoor as well as watch ahead. Smithie followed two yards behind, his lips tight with fear. The PH consciously slowed himself. He was trailing too quickly to perform both the jobs of spooring and watching. That morning was as bad as it gets.

He stood from a crouch to ease the crick in his back. *Take it slowly,* he reminded himself. He drank from the canteen and handed it to Smithie. They spoored on, the sun a weight on their backs, through the thatch-grass jungle, into the open, and across the burned plain. They struggled through half a mile of *miombo* thicket into the open again and then into more thatch grass and mixed acacia thornbush. Wambach untangled the hours-old spoor slowly, the black, starry spatters becoming thinner and more difficult to find.

THE LAST STEP

The fiery orb of sun hung low in the northwest when the PH and his client pushed through the last thornbush tangle. They stood bloody from the thorns and swollen from mosquito bites and nettles. It was time to give it up—it was suicide to trail wounded buff in the dark. As Wambach scanned the pools of deep shade in the next thicket with the binoc one last time, he spotted a heavier shadow beneath the thornbush.

"Shhh!" he hissed, though Smithie had said nothing. "There he is."

The bull glared and waited in ambush as both men aimed carefully and fired simultaneously. The bull, already weakened from blood loss, staggered under the combined thousand grains of bullet impact and fell before either man could shoot again. They approached with rifles at the ready, but the bull was dead. Prepared for a charge and other drama, Wambach felt let down.

Heavy snare wire looped behind one horn and across the bull's muzzle. It had cut three inches deep into face hide, muscle, bone, and sinus. "Smells a bit, that." Wambach said, wrinkling his nose against the gangrenous stench as he examined the festering, maggoty wound. "Now we know why."

It was dark when the two hunters pushed through the last of the story-high thatch grass and out onto the burned-over plain. They could just see the lorry parked under the thorn tree in the moonlight. Their steps on fire-blackened clay raised puffs of ash that hung in the night like ghosts. The second tracker walked out to meet them. "He is dead now," the man said. Bloodied from the thorns and saw-edged grass, the two hunters were too tired to look relieved.

THE DANGEROUS GAME

EPILOGUE

"Why hadn't you rushed Domingo to the hospital instead of trailing the buffalo?" someone once asked Wambach.

Stung by the criticism, he replied, "It was two days downriver by dugout to the coast. From there, we would have had to flag down a plane or boat to get to Beira. Then, we'd have to charter a flight to Johannesburg, if we could find one. Just after the war, you couldn't count on anything. Domingo couldn't have survived that long. He couldn't have lived the day out." He added, "That buffalo had to be sorted out. He might have killed someone else."

Just after the Mozambique civil war, no agency existed where Wambach could report the incident. When a black man died in the bush, he simply ceased to exist. It had happened commonly and for many years. No one cared about another dead African.

IN A LEOPARD BLIND

It's hard to say if it's the immediate threat of death, exactly, but if it isn't, then it *is* the danger—tempting death and then skipping out of its way—that makes those gut-wrenching, pulse-pounding, sweaty encounters spring most easily to mind. Without half trying, I remember the grizzly I surprised at close range. After a cursory once-over from hind legs, he dropped to all fours and came on like those steam engines in silent movies. Very fortunately, he crumpled on the tundra after my bullet shattered his neck vertebrae. That one bullet was the only thing that kept me from a painful death on a very remote barren. There would have been no time for a second shot, I wasn't due to rendezvous with the bush pilot for a month, and the rendezvous point was two hundred miles downriver.

Then I picture the late-season, British Columbia goat hunt and remember working my way up to the dead billy wedged between boulders until the wet, heavy snow, thawed and rotten from an unseasonal Chinook, broke loose with a crack and I shot down the chute atop fifty tons of snow and ice and over a ledge. I landed in the tops of a clump of spruce as the avalanche thundered into the gorge a thousand feet below. I hate to recall that one, but it's there, too close to the surface.

Then there was the time we trailed the Cape buffalo at a trot across the immense, sandy islands of the Okavango, flushing bands of the scaly-black, Panzer-built buffs from either side as we spoored rapidly. When we rounded a thicket of wait-a-bit thorns, six bulls stood abreast, staring as if we'd insulted their politics before they whipped their tails angrily and disappeared. In the end, we didn't catch those bulls. Instead we found another herd, stalked into its midst, and hid in a clump of palms until the big bull profiled at fifteen yards. I stuck first one .375 slug through his heart, then another in the same place as he trotted by at ten yards. He didn't go far. Probably, there was no real close encounter with death for us there, but the potential was always too present, and that's danger, good or bad. It was that way with the leopard.

* * * * *

The arguable dean of latter-day professional hunters was J. A. Hunter. Hunter believed the leopard Africa's most dangerous game. Elephants and rhino he did not take seriously—they were big, slow targets that usually turned if hit. Lions and buffalo were more dangerous. They were faster, smaller targets and more determined when they came for you. The leopard was a smaller target and quicker yet; moreover, it didn't give its presence away with a warning growl and always pressed home the attack if at all able.

This ran through my mind as I shivered in the June cold that first night in a Zimbabwe leopard blind. Jackals wailed from out of the coal-mine dark, sounding like Wyoming coyotes, and owls and other night birds called and echoed from the immense, boulder hills called "kopjes" (pronounced "copies"). After buffalo, which I'd collected on my first safari the year before in Botswana, I wanted a leopard, but I wanted it fairly, in the traditional way of baiting. The largest safari company in Botswana at the time had good success on leopards, but they did it by trailing a leopard across the flat Kalahari in Land Rovers for days on end until the cat could go no farther, then they shot the cat from the car as it made its stand. The odds were all against the great felines, in spite of their courage (though I know of one PH who was mauled when a cat jumped into the car). I wanted none of that.

In my reading, leopards came to baits in the late afternoon. The concealed client picked a rosette just over the heart and potted the trophy spotted cat out of the tree. There was even time for photos before dark. Not so here. This was cattle country, and leopards had been shot at, trapped, and poisoned for more than a century. Those that survived were too cunning to show themselves before dark. So, Cheri, our professional hunter Russell Tarr, and I entered the blind at 4 P.M. and stayed until 10 P.M. June is winter in the southern hemisphere, and by dark we shivered beneath layers of clothing. I had reservations about hunting the big, spectacular cats after dark with a spotlight; in fact, I didn't know we'd be doing it until that first night in the blind but, once there, I understood the odds were all in favor of the leopard. (One of Russell's clients spent eighteen dusk-to-dawn vigils in a blind without luck.) This wasn't chasing them down in cars, thankfully, and it seemed sporting, and more than fair.

Hours after dark, the cold had penetrated into my bones and hung on like a honey badger. I heard something just outside the blind, and immediately all cold disappeared, and my heart jumped into my throat and throbbed so loudly I was sure anything out there could hear it. The tension from the others was heavy enough to feel.

Something walked across the dried leaves on my side of the blind toward the bait. I fingered the rifle, getting ready to slip it into the opening. Russell gripped my arm—our prearranged signal—then released it. I eased the .270 into position. The PH flipped on the spotlight, and something darted out of the beam. "Bushpig," Russell whispered, flicking off the light. I felt no cold the rest of the night, and I doubt my pulse returned to normal until we motored into camp. Even though it hadn't been a leopard, I couldn't imagine a more intense adrenaline rush.

I could hardly wait to get into the blind the next night. The animal sounds changed from the monotonous buzzing of insects and the croaks of hornbills feeding on the bait maggots when we first arrived, to the calls of exotic evening birds and the *OWRRrr-oooo* of a hyena somewhere beyond the immense kopje at dusk, to the faint whistlings of tiny owls and the occasional wail of a jackal in the darkness. I was mesmerized and absorbed by the African night sounds when, without warning, we all jumped.

Neither the word "sawing" nor the word "coughing" comes close to describing the deep, rasping, rumbling, coughing-growl of a leopard, a sound that vibrates through the air and earth and into your feet and through your skin and bones to your soul—you can, literally, feel the tremors in the air and ground. At close range, there's no other noise that can do those things to your gut. And even though I'd never heard it before, there was no mistaking the anger in it.

The tension in the blind almost crackled. Russell's hand trembled as he gripped my forearm. His breath came short and fast in the darkness, and I could feel Cheri's excitement. Then, the big cat roared again, this time from farther up the kopje—he knew we were there and he was angry about it—and we understood he would not come in that night.

"I heard him behind us," Cheri said, as we unfolded our cold and tension-stiff frames from the blind. Russell and I had heard nothing, though I'd sensed something at my back in the darkness, something that made the hackles stand on my neck. Cheri hadn't fired too many big guns, and her hearing was better. For proof we found the saucer-size pugs in the dust five yards from where we had sat behind a flimsy cover of burlap and grass.

"You can't beat that," I said, as the Rover rattled down the track toward camp. A black-and-white civet bounded out of the darkness and back into it again.

"You can't until a bloody spotted bushpuss jumps into the blind with you." Russell chuckled and downshifted to climb out of the ravine.

This was more exciting than hunting sable, kudu, waterbuck, reedbuck, wildebeest, and impala combined. That night in the blind was worth the price of the safari.

The next day we drove south six hours to another camp on the Bubi River, a tributary of the Limpopo that hadn't seen water in years, for waterbuck and bushbuck. We were also there for the leopard baits that Pierre Joubert, an apprentice PH, had been putting out.

When we arrived at the camp, Pierre told of the clients that had pulled out of a leopard blind on a whim at seven the evening before—much too early—so they could spend their last day chasing tsessebe. When Pierre had dismantled the blind that afternoon, he noticed that a pair of leopards had fed the night before. We rushed out and rebuilt the blind.

As it got dark, a civet trotted onto the sloping tree and began feeding. Later, after dark, a honey badger began to eat, standing on hind legs and reaching for a dangling impala leg. His claws scraping the bark kept me fingering the rifle.

The badger fed noisily for an hour, then suddenly it was quiet, and we knew from the thick silence that the leopard was there. As if to erase any doubt, the big cat started a deep, continuous, rumbling, purring growl. It was unlike the cough we'd heard in the first blind, but it, too, vibrated through the air and ground and into our guts. Russell's hand was on my arm, trembling with the excitement again, but I was strangely calm. The loud-feeding honey badger and the initial adrenaline rush from the leopard's first presence had drained the excitement and nervousness away. I was ready for whatever was next.

With hand pressure, Russell made me understand that it wasn't time since the leopard wasn't feeding yet. Then the purring growl moved off, and I felt sure it was over and that the cat was leaving. But then it came back, closer now, and I could feel it again inside me. At times I felt as if the deep purring surrounded me or as if there were two leopards. And then it was quiet again.

Russell's hand was on my arm a moment after I heard the faint crunching of the cat going to work on the impala. He held my arm for what seemed eons—whole worlds could have been created and destroyed by the time he released it.

I'd rehearsed it all in my mind. I slid automatically onto the .270 perched in the blind opening, my eye instinctively lining up with the scope. Even though I could see nothing in the dark, my thumb slid the safety forward as the rifle became part of me. The spotlight lit up the bush, suddenly turning night into day and illuminating the impalas hung in the tree, but there was no movement, no leopard. I eased the scope picture to the edge of the light—nothing—and back again. Then there *was* something, and a big spotted head came up out of the high grass, nose in the air and chewing, incredibly, still oblivious to the light. The cross hairs settled at the base of the neck without conscious thought, and my finger tightened on the trigger, and then there was the recoil I did not feel and the muzzle flash I do not remember—and no sign of the cat.

Russell hadn't seen the cat; in fact, he'd seen some movement out from the bait and thought it was something else. "Are you sure it wasn't a jackal?" he asked.

"A leopard," I said, preoccupied with watching through the scope in case the cat showed itself.

"You're sure you didn't shoot a jackal?"

"It was a leopard."

"You're sure?" he asked again. I didn't answer.

THE DANGEROUS GAME

Earlier, we'd agreed Russell would approach any downed leopard alone. At first I had insisted on going too, but that would have compromised things because then the PH would have to worry about a client as well as a leopard. It's professional death to have a client mauled.

So I covered Russell as he approached the bait, the cross hairs solid on the place where the leopard had disappeared. In the spotlight and through the scope, I watched Russell toss a stick into the grass, and another, and finally approach and lift a big spotted paw into the light so I could see it.

"Big jackal," I deadpanned after Cheri and I walked up to seven feet, two inches of spotted beauty stretched out in the tawny grass.

The trackers, Luka and Shorty, drove up in the Rover after hearing the shot, shook hands, and pulled thumbs, first respectfully, then jubilantly. Luka pulled a fist-size chunk of impala meat from the leopard's jaws.

Russell leaned on the "tooter" continuously on the drive to camp, often hooting himself, and once there he made a turn through the camp and then out to the game pole, honking all the time. The entire staff turned out, and we took photos by headlights, spotlight, and floodlights with the Polaroid and the SLRs. This *was* something special, an event more momentous than the big antelope we'd been bringing in. The cat had died instantly, had felt nothing, and that was important to me. Later, around the campfire, we relived and retold it all over Lion Lager beer.

Those nights are still strong in my mind. I see again the Southern Cross, feel the heavy cold and then the tension when the leopard comes, even hear that rumbling purring out there in the darkness. It's there, close to the surface. But why don't I recall the big antelope as clearly?

I now know the answer. The antelope weren't dangerous.

BULLS IN THE NIGHT

Why is it that some safaris collect a half-dozen dangerous beasts without anything more serious than a tick bite while others face sweaty close calls at every turn? Adventure—the kind that can kill you—is often the result of things gone wrong. I wasn't looking for adventure. I wanted a big elephant.

Probably it was an omen. The trip had gone too smoothly. The airlines kept their schedules and we made our connections. Our baggage, including the rifles, followed us faithfully from one hemisphere to the next. A side trip from Johannesburg to Victoria Falls up on the Zambezi River and back went off without a hitch. And, finally, Arthur Moore met us at the Zimbabwe border on schedule. Arthur is "Jumbo" Moore's father, and Jumbo owns Jumbo Safaris.

Then it started. Either we or the professional hunters weren't at the rendezvous; we found them twenty miles farther on an hour later. I've traveled a score of third-world countries, so I wasn't surprised.

Jumbo was the elephant expert and was to have guided me, but fate stepped in. He'd wrenched a knee a month earlier, and everyone knows elephant hunting normally involves walking, lots of it. Jim Mackie had just driven down from Harare and would guide Cheri and me, while Jumbo guided my friends Rick and Nikki Lovell on their first plains-game safari. Mackie hadn't expected the last minute job and was unfamiliar with the staff and the local elephant habits. No matter. If it was like other safaris, the professional hunter relies on the trackers and scouts for most of the expertise. The PH keeps the safari organized.

According to pre-hunt arrangements, the Lovells, Cheri, and I were to share the same tented camp. Instead we drove off in different directions. As I said, I should have known.

THE DANGEROUS GAME

Our camp was a rondavel—not the promised tented camp—in Gonarezhou ("place of the elephant," in Shangani) National Park. OK, so other hunts had started badly yet ended well. The international hunter must above all be flexible, be it in Tajikistan or Zimbabwe.

Bull elephants crossed the park roads as we drove through the dawn and paused in the headlights. Of course, you could not shoot them in the park. Gonarezhou can support thirty-five hundred elephants without serious range damage; it held five thousand. As a result, elephants raided neighboring Shangaan mealie fields. However, in the June drought the fields had been harvested, and the few elephants leaving the park did so sporadically.

The theory was we'd drive along the boundary fence and find fresh, large spoor leaving the park. We'd trail the big tusker—of course the local bush crawled with them—and dispatch him with a single shot. But the elephants hadn't studied the script. They left the park at night, traveled no more than a few hundred yards, then returned to the park, also at night.

* * * * *

"*Zhou!*" hissed Majara, the tracker, as the Land Cruiser jounced along the fence line that second dawn. Two bull elephants browsed on mopane scrub three hundred yards out. From the *bakkie* (truck) bed, you could just see their backs.

Mackie wheeled the Cruiser to a stop, we jammed cartridges into guns and grabbed binocs, and all seven of us marched off in the direction of the *zhou*. I wondered how so many—a PH and assistant PH, two game scouts, two clients, and one tracker—could possibly approach two elephants with keen senses of smell and hearing close enough for a shot in the thick scrub. We wandered through the scrub for forty minutes before Majara stopped suddenly. Then we all heard what sounded like a distant truck engine—the gut rumblings of a nervous elephant.

We stalked very cautiously toward the noise and closed to twenty-five yards until we spotted legs of the two bulls beneath the understory. One moved off and the other started to follow, then whirled suddenly and crashed toward us. Two stories of elephant stopped at eight yards and flared his ears, raised his head, and pushed out his shoulders to look larger and bluff us off. If we didn't push off, he'd charge. I kept my thumb on the safety and the .375 halfway to my shoulder.

"Thirty pounds a tusk," Mackie half-shouted when the bull had seen us off and then retreated. "Toothpicks. No hunter of mine will shoot toothpicks."

OK, not too bad. Only the second day and we'd already stalked bulls. I felt cautiously optimistic.

I shouldn't have. We didn't see another elephant for the next week. We became so obsessed, Mackie suggested we drive to a distant ranch to collect a nyala and get our minds off the *zhou*. So we drove three hours to find the place devoid of the game scouts, and then drove back without hunting. A wasted day.

We could see from the elephant spoor that each night bulls crossed the fence into the Shangaan campfire concession where we could legally shoot them. They browsed on acacia trees for hours then returned to the sanctuary of the park before light. The game scouts knew the whereabouts of the biggest elephant, a sixty-plus pounder. But it didn't help because the bulls stayed within the safety of the park during the day. So we tried the Limpopo River, three hours away by dirt road. Across the dry Limpopo was Kruger Park in the R.S.A., and occasionally elephants wandered out of Kruger to feed in the riverine bush and mealie fields on the Zimbabwe side. As we still-hunted through the riverine bush, Majara and the game scouts stopped and huddled for a conference.

The exclusion made Mackie angry. "I want in on any conference!" he yelled. Mackie's normal voice was loud enough, but when he raised it any game within three miles would have departed. The game scouts looked confused, and Majara shrugged and walked away. "I don't know what they've got against me," Mackie told Cheri. The incident underscored the problems.

We found tracks where elephants had dug into the mostly dry Limpopo sand. Clear water filled the excavations. One or two spoor belonged to decent bulls. We concentrated our efforts there during the day, driving six hours to and from camp. After those first tracks, apparently no more elephants came to that part of the river. So we returned to hunting the nocturnal bulls leaving Gonarezhou. I'd paid normal daytime safari rates, hundreds more per day than I would hunting crop raiders—problem-control elephants—yet here we were, stalking problem animals in the Shangaan concession.

Now, elephant hunting normally requires lots of walking. So far, we hadn't walked more than a few hundred yards. Instead of stretched hamstrings and calves, I had cramped knees and saddle sores from bouncing around the Toyota.

"Fifteen hundred kilometers on the odometer," Mackie said in wonder. "That's since the safari began." I prefer walking, and I hate riding in cars when we're supposed to be hunting. On safari, the less I see of machines, the better I like it.

We watched the fence line in the late afternoon, hoping to catch the big bull crossing before dark. Then we stalked into the bush in black night. These elephants were technically crop-raiders, even though no crops existed then, so we could legally hunt them at night. Days earlier, I'd rejected the idea of hunting at night. Spotlighting bulls didn't seem right, somehow. But we'd gotten desperate; days were running out and we hadn't even seen a good bull.

That first night we had heard elephants breaking branches a few yards into the concession. We had stalked toward the noise in the dark, all seven of us. We had heard splintering wood to our left, then to the right, with more in front, all within a few yards. We backed out. In the thick bush, we'd have been next to an elephant before we knew it. Cows with calves would have made it suicidal. Back at the end of the fence line, Mackie and Majara had words.

"Too bloody dangerous," Mackie said to Cheri as he returned to where we sat at a fire.

The Shangaan assistant PH waited half a mile down the fence with a two-way radio. If more elephants left the park, he'd let us know, and we'd stalk them.

"Too many people, too. We can't get out of the way if jumbo charges in the thick bush. Someone's apt to get killed, and it's my responsibility to see that doesn't happen." Mackie talked in a voice decibels louder than his normally loud speaking voice. Stalking at night through the thick bush had spooked him. It spooked me, too, but I loved the rush.

Mackie wanted Cheri to stay back where it was safe. It wasn't such a bad idea, but he didn't know Cheri. She thinks nothing of facing a charging grizzly at four yards or trailing wounded buffalo into heavy thornbush. And she has a mind of her own.

"We've got to leave some of us behind," Mackie said. His voice had risen again. He implied it was too dangerous for a woman, but what he said was, "Seven is too bloody many." He looked at Cheri when he said this. "I can't protect all of us."

Now, Cheri stands just over five feet and tips the scales at 102 pounds. Because she's petite, most people think she'll take it, so she catches them by surprise when she doesn't.

"I paid to observe, and I'm going to observe!" she bristled. "I've trailed wounded buff, hunted lions, and handled Egyptian cobras. I can take care of myself! And he can shoot." She aimed an index finger at me. My first inclination was to duck.

The argument raged across the fire. Fur flew, and from where I sat, most of it was Mackie's. The guys listened quietly from their own fire, with big grins. Mackie trailed off into . . . "I'm responsible, and if you don't like it, you can find yourself another PH."

Cheri replied with a one-syllable, "Fine!"

I tried to act as intermediary, but the combatants paid little attention. If there was any doubt about the winner, it was dispelled when the assistant PH clicked the radio twice, our signal, and Cheri joined us. Mackie fumed.

Mackie shouted something at the staff, and the game scouts stayed behind. They'd managed to get into the Shangaan "bottle store" that day and were still drunk. They were glad to stay back. Majara, the savvy, tough old tracker, grinned in the firelight and said something funny in Mashona to me; he was the one guy who fully knew what was going on here. Mackie was uncomfortable with that.

More bulls had left the park, and we heard them browsing the acacia. The assistant PH and Mackie whispered a conference. We stalked off again, finding a barren mealie field and sitting against a big acacia tree as the elephants fed toward us. I made myself comfortable in the night. From three directions we heard the melodious, distant chanting and drumming from Shangaan kraals. If I closed my eyes, I was back in a *Heart of Darkness* kind of Africa. An owl hooted from nearby. Mackie said something to Majara, and Majara hissed back. Mackie led us off toward the feeding elephants. Majara wanted to wait. We neared and heard the rumbling stomachs, the chewing, the flap of an ear against rough hide, the *plop-plop* of dropping dung. We could see nothing in the night forest, and the stars provided no light. Mackie occasionally stared through the night-vision scope. Suddenly, elephants crashed off on three sides. They'd caught our scent.

The following nights unfolded similarly, and the days ran slowly out. All seven of us stalked the thickets in the dark, returning to camp after midnight. We awoke in the black morning and drove along the fence. We drove back to camp to watch game drink at Buffalo Bend in the park at midday, returning again to the fence boundary in the evening. We'd become a grim group. Fewer elephants crossed into the concession, and those that did moved later at night. They knew we hunted them, and our hopes of ambushing one in the dusk vanished.

Mackie and the staff seemed less tense together. "I don't know what they have against me," Mackie told us again one morning. I did. Mackie often didn't take Majara's and the scouts' advice, and they resented it to the point they'd quit giving it.

We finally caught the big bull early one evening. From fifty yards into the park, he shook his head at us in annoyance as we cruised by. We drove three hundred yards on down the track and waited. Why we did this, I wasn't quite sure since I thought it wise to hurry up and ambush the bull when he crossed the fence into the acacia, rather than wait for the rapidly coming night. Everyone stayed put, quiet as snakes, until the big bull crossed the braided steel fence with a musical *sprong*. We could just see him in the dusk as he walked slowly into the concession. Had we stalked through the bush instead of stopping, the bull would be lying in the dust now. I couldn't figure it. The wind had been from him to us, and he wasn't alarmed. Now, we'd have to deal with the darkness again.

BULLS IN THE NIGHT

After Mackie collected a mountain of gear—spotlights, flashlights, night-vision scope, guns and ammo, this and that—it was fully dark. We hurried up the fence line and found fresh spoor in the flashlight's beam. We eased into the black tangles of thornbush without light, of course, Mackie looking through the night scope from time to time. "He's just ahead," he whispered in my ear.

We stalked through the black bush. Mackie and Majara whispered, and Majara pointed right, indicating we should stalk around the tree that way, and Mackie indicated left. We went left. Majara carried the spotlight. Tangled thornbush surrounded us. Majara switched on the floodlight, and the .375 nestled comfortably in my shoulder.

Behind the thickest of the thornbush, a white tusk flashed briefly. I momentarily found what might have been the crease behind the shoulder and nearly touched off, but thought better of it. The 300-grain Sledgehammer solid would have been deflected by brush, probably only wounding the big bull. I could not see his head at all. The bull moved off a few yards, stopped, and listened. Mackie led us out of the tangle. I wondered why we didn't wait to see what the bull would do. The wind was good, and we might have gotten another chance. Had we gone to the right around the tree, as Majara suggested, we'd have gotten a clear shot.

"I need a Coke!" Mackie half-shouted once back at the fire. His voice was unnaturally loud again. "I am eternally grateful you did not shoot," he said, "We had no shot."

Cheri had stalked silently through all of this, from time to time patting me on the butt to let me know just where she was when things got sticky. I admired her pluck, but her confidence in me made me nervous.

In spite of the bad luck, the poor planning, and the ego problems, tracking elephants into thickets at night was as adrenaline-pumping as anything I'd ever done. If nothing else, we had adventure, the kind that could kill.

The assistant PH clicked the radio twice, so we stalked back along the fence line in the night and again into the thick black bush. We got into more elephants, but of course you can't tell one from another in the dark. Eventually, they caught our scent in the shifty breeze, and that was it for the night.

THE DANGEROUS GAME

The next night only one bull crossed the fence, hours after dark. It kept very close to the boundary. Majara led us up on it until the bull chewed branches just feet away. Mackie whispered. I flicked off the safety.

Majara turned on the spotlight, illuminating impenetrable walls of the thickest kind of thornbush all around us. We had no escape if the elephant charged. Brush splintered toward us. Majara stood his ground, though once he faltered when the branches shook and it seemed the bull would burst out of the thornbush right over him. But he caught himself. We'd have been helpless without the light. The bull crashed off, to our intense relief.

"Bloody close, that," Mackie said in that loud voice.

Majara untensed visibly and grinned. I tried to wet my lips, and Cheri patted me on the butt.

The next dawn's spoor showed that no more elephants had crossed out of the park that night. We held a conference back at camp. The bulls came into the concession later each night, and fewer left the park each time. From the spoor, the bull that evening had been one of the smaller ones. Probably the big one had been frightened off permanently; he hadn't gotten big by taking chances in his forty or fifty years. Our chances seemed ninety-nine to one. I opted to give it up and spend the last two days up north, hunting eland, hippo, and croc. When I announced the decision, everyone grinned, and you could physically feel the relief. We joked for the first time in days.

Up on the Chiredzi River I brained a big bull hippo at 90 yards with a single 300-grain solid, double-lunged a good eland that Mackie also decided to shoot through the horn for reasons of his own, heart-shot a 56-inch kudu on the Mwakasine River, and missed a croc at 30 yards after Mackie bounced me to three locations before he'd let me shoot. In the end I had to shoot through brush, and a branch the size of my thumb deflected the bullet. At least that's my excuse, and I'm sticking to it. We were charged three times by elephants, and twice the backward-racing Toyota barely outran enraged cows on the thick bush track. We'd cut it pretty thin all safari.

Mackie said, "Nearly three thousand clicks on the odometer." He scratched his bald head.

BULLS IN THE NIGHT

The Lovells' plains-game safari had been productive and efficient. Our safari, on the other hand, had more close calls than a dozen previous safaris after dangerous game. As I said, you just don't get the kind of adventure that can kill you when events go as planned.

Still, I know how it is supposed to go—stalking up to an elephant dozing under a big mopane tree, aiming carefully between the eye and ear hole, then squeezing. The bull throws his head up and collapses backward in the dust, and I walk up as awed and pleased as it is possible to be. I hadn't wanted adventure; I wanted an elephant.

FOR ADVENTURE

The Mozambique civil war had officially ended, at least around the cities. For protection a convoy of twenty trucks started from Johannesburg and drove north through Zimbabwe, then northeasterly into Mozambique, and finally to the city of Beira. There, the convoy separated, each member driving off on his own business.

John Wambach headed up a smaller convoy of one lorry and four Toyota Land Cruisers, and they drove north to reopen the deep bush in safari concession Coutada 10, which had been closed to hunting, of course, during the war years. Wambach carried letters from both the Frelimo and Renamo factions of the war to allow him passage. And he'd brought along an old diamond miner from South Africa who spoke Fanagalo and Portuguese and knew the country. Wambach's first client was also part of the little platoon, wanting to help cut the bush tracks, make the bridges, and carve out the airstrip. For adventure.

They drove north from Beira through the grazed-over and burnt landscape and the dusty, dead-dog ghettos into the more sparsely populated bush, and then into small villages where all the men and boys had only one leg, or sometimes no legs, from the land mines still spread throughout the country. The people were Shangaan, but as they drove away from the city north, they became Chilozi.

The older roads and adjoining bush had not been cleared of the mines, and the party kept to the new road bulldozed through the red dust by the UN peacekeepers. Wambach took pains to keep the men on the new road, even when they answered nature's call. They even camped on the road; there wasn't enough traffic on the road for them to worry about blocking it.

The Land Cruiser *bakkies* (trucks) drove ahead, and Wambach followed in the larger lorry loaded with gear and supplies for the safari camp. Rounding a bend, he saw the logs across the road and the Cruisers surrounded by ragged men with AKs. He yanked the wheel and gunned the lorry through the borrow pit and mopane scrub, each moment expecting a land mine explosion. He ducked the thorn branches slapping his arms and shoulders until he felt cold steel against his neck—two rebels had jumped onto the lorry as it jounced through the brush. He saw the AK47 barrel against the client's skull, and he eased the lorry back onto the road and stopped.

Wambach showed the men the papers of passage from the two warring factions, but they threw them back at him and motioned for him to follow the men walking up the road. They drove slowly behind, all the while the AKs pointed at all of them. They drove down from the road and along a narrow foot track in the thick bush to a camp near a drying pan. The bandits shoved the men to a big fever tree and made them sit around it, then tied them to the tree, though they left their hands free. Toward evening, the captors brought a half plastic cup of water to each man. They slapped the captives in the face or slammed then with an AK butt and kicked them in the ribs.

When the United Nations had brokered the peace agreement between the warring Frelimo and Renamo factions, they'd promised to pay the fighters a salary for not fighting until they could reestablish themselves. This band had not been paid since the war's end months earlier and had taken to banditry. They stopped the local vehicles on the road, though they stole only enough to satisfy immediate needs so that the lorries would not quit using the road altogether. Wambach's convoy seemed too good to be true.

From what Wambach could tell, both factions of the war shared the potent gourd of sorghum beer around the fire that night. Then they started a second gourd, then a third. Within hours, they were shouting and staggering about the dancing shadows of the fire. A Frelimo fighter wobbled to the tree and pushed the AK barrel against Wambach's temple. "Die, white pig!" he said and laughed, then pulled the trigger. On an empty chamber. He staggered back to the fire and took a swig from the calabash. Before long, two more fighters approached. One kicked the client in the ribs. The other slammed a gun butt against a driver's head. They, too, staggered back to the fire.

"I didn't come for this," the client told Wambach. He had come to help open the country, for adventure. Now he had adventure.

"Me either," Wambach said, but what he thought was, *we're not getting out of this. It's getting too bad.*

The fighters continued drinking. One lunged across the fire and stabbed another in the shoulder. Another stood and fired a burst from the automatic AK into the air. Two others shoved each other out of the firelight, and the captives heard them fighting in the darkness. One returned with a bloodied mouth, and in a moment the other followed. Two other men staggered from the fire to the men tied at the tree.

"White, die!" one shouted. Both pointed the AKs at the white men's skulls and pulled the triggers on empty chambers. They laughed so hard they could barely stagger back to the fire. Another stood away from the fire and sprayed the bush with a burst of automatic rifle fire. The captives at the tree cringed as low as they could. Another fired into the air. They all kept drinking.

The captives dug deeper the depressions where they crouched and sat. They had to do something with the fear to keep it under control. The men at the fire sprayed the bush with bullets, once hitting the tree just above their heads. They hunkered into the depressions whenever a drunken fighter stood up with his AK. One slammed a black driver twice in the face with his AK's butt. Another kicked Wambach in the stomach and the client in the ribs. Wambach's men suffered through more Russian roulette. Once, two men stood simultaneously near the fire and pointed AKs at each other. Then two others staggered to the tree and held knives to the white men's throats until they drew blood, then wobbled back to the fire and laughed. Two fighters grappled with each other with knives, and one cut the other seriously on the forearm.

"You got us into this," the client told Wambach. He'd found his voice again. "This wasn't what I had wanted."

Wambach didn't answer.

Each time one of the fighters staggered to the tree, the old miner-turned-translator bargained and reasoned with them in

FOR ADVENTURE

Fanagalo. Sometimes it eased the situation. Sometimes he got a kick in the ribs for his trouble. You couldn't predict what the drunken men would do.

The next afternoon, they heard two vehicles drive down the track and then voices in Fanagalo and Portuguese. The translator paid close attention, but he could only just hear snatches of the bargaining. Then the vehicles drove away. They'd been UN trucks; the UN men had heard a rumor that had started in the Beira market, a rumor that whites were held hostage upcountry. When the lorries drove off, the captives' hopes dropped again.

The prisoners had been given two hunks of biltong and a plastic jug of water after the UN troops drove off. But the hope dimmed once more when the fighters started drinking. Again, Wambach and his men watched the fighting at the fire, the brandished knives, the random shooting into the sky and bush. Once bullets hit the tree so close to their heads that a bark fragment raised a welt on a driver's face. The fighters pushed AKs against the white men's heads and pulled triggers on empty chambers again. Wambach hoped the men didn't get too drunk to remember whether the chamber was empty or not. The captors cut them with knives and kicked everyone before the party sputtered out.

They heard the trucks grind down the dirt track in the midday. Voices again in Fanagalo. An hour later, a UN soldier armed with an automatic weapon walked down the path.

"We're negotiating your release," he said to the white men in English. "I think it will be successful." He chatted with the hostages for ten minutes, then walked back to the negotiations.

For the first time, Wambach felt they had a real chance to get out alive. The client became blustery. After what seemed half a day, three armed UN soldiers and the captors walked down the trail and cut the men loose.

"Get in your vehicles and drive out to the road and wait," a UN soldier said. "You are free." Their captors, the bandits, had not been paid since the cease-fire. They'd negotiated for the back pay and got it.

Wambach and company drove back to Beira, escorted by the UN soldiers. After three days of debriefing, they drove back

THE DANGEROUS GAME

toward Coutada 10. They kept to the new, bulldozed road. On the way they stopped at the bandit camp to let them know they were in the area. The bandits held them for two hours while they played cards, then waved them on. Whenever Wambach drove to or from Beira, they repeated the routine.

Each time Wambach's group made the trip, they had passed a stick jammed upright in the ground with a faded bit of plastic tied to the top. They got a flat tire nearby once, and while Wambach's men changed it, he asked a passing local about the marker. In Fanagalo, the local said that four mines were buried just beneath it.

Once, a Renamo general came to Wambach's safari camp. Wambach went out of his way to feed him well and to offer the best South African wine he had.

"Eat hearty," he told the general through the interpreter. The general ate simply, in small portions, and refused the wine.

"Please eat more," Wambach said, "we have plenty of food, and you are our guest."

"No," the general said, "I don't want to feel guilty if I have to kill you someday."

M'BOGO

"*M'bogo,*" the Masai tracker said. Just the sound of *m'bogo* does something to your guts. It's heavy, solid, threatening. I sat up top in the lorry bed with the trackers and game scouts. I saw them, a black phalanx, five hundred yards off in the *bundu*. The PH let the Toyota glide to a stop. Cheri sat in the passenger seat and strained to see the buffalo through the scrub.

"*M'bogo?*" the PH, Richards, questioned. He could not see them below because of the high bush.

"*N'dio,*" the second tracker said. Yes.

We drove behind the cover of a gray termite mound, and Richards switched off the engine. He slid the .577 double from its soft case, and I freed the .375. The trackers climbed down from the Cruiser bed, and Cheri unlimbered the video camera. The big herd had been grazing back into the heavy bush late from the drying pools of the Msima River.

We stalked to head off the grazing herd, using the scattered termite mounds and islands of bush as cover. The PH climbed a mound and glassed, then slid down, and we stalked off in a different direction. We finally crawled up behind a thicket surrounding a ten-foot termite mound and searched through the binoculars for a good bull.

"*Doumi m'uzuri,*" Gabreli, the tracker, said and pointed with his chin. A good bull. The bull grazed along the edge of the herd toward the heavier cover.

"*N'dio,*" Richards said, then looked at me to be certain I saw the same bull. I did. I eased around an acacia bush to get a clear shot.

The herd grazed unaware one hundred thirty yards away. I crabbed to a *mpingo* sapling to use as a rest, when the herd got our wind. They lumbered off through the grasses in that heavy, rocking-horse gallop they have. The bull disappeared behind lumbering black bodies and then came open again, as a calf

THE DANGEROUS GAME

sprinted from behind to catch up with its dam. Another cow raced up from behind the bull, leaving the window for a shot open for a second. I took it and heard the slap of three hundred grains of copper and lead, and then the bull was swallowed by the racing herd. Either the cow or the calf could have raced into the flight path of the bullet. The herd rumbled off, and the choking white dust swirled through scrub too thick to see through. More buff thundered through the bush right behind, then scented us then veered off. We all climbed the termite hill for safety.

"*Piga?*" Richards yelled at the trackers.

"*N'dio,*" both trackers said.

The game scout said, "*N'dio.*"

"*Piga m'uzuri?*" the PH asked. (Was it a good hit?)

"*N'dio,*" yes, a good hit.

I knew I'd hit something, but both the cow and calf were racing up just as I fired at the bull's shoulder. When the dust cleared, I saw the curl of black horn above the yellow-gold grass, and the horn was too big for the cow. It didn't move. I pointed it out to the PH. We all watched, then Richards relaxed. I'd shot buff before and had hit some through the heart on the first shot, but I'd never had one drop within thirty yards. It was too easy, and I didn't trust it.

We circled behind the bull in the waist-high grass and walked up; I kept the .375 butt against my hip and the thumb on the safety. Estoni twisted the bull's tail. No reaction. He was as dead as the finger-thick dried grasses.

The bull had good horn drop and extensive hooks, and though he only spread forty inches he'd score high because of the extensive hooking. His was a handsome head and my first Tanzania buffalo trophy.

"*M'uzuri, Bwana,*" Gabreli said, grasping my fingers in the Masai handshake. "*Kubwa.*" (Big) The second tracker, the game scout, and the rest offered their congrats.

That buffalo hunt was the exception, not the rule. Seldom do buffalo collapse from a single shot so quickly, even if the bullet pulverizes the heart. The 300-grain Sierra A-frame softpoint had slammed behind the shoulder, exploded the heart, and lodged in the off shoulder. The bull had galloped no more than thirty-five yards before collapsing. As a rule, you'll hit the bull well on the first shot, perhaps in the lungs or the heart or through the big veins above the heart, and he'll turn and gallop off as if nothing happened. If there's time, you'll put another in his stern as he races for the thickest bush he can find to wait for you to come and sort him out.

My first buff hunt went that way. We'd stalked through herds of Okavango buff for two days, getting close to good ones, including one that would have taped 45, but we couldn't get a safe shot. Finally, in the evening, we stalked to a clump of palm scrub, and when Willie Phillips, the PH, parted the fronds, the big bull and his harem stood at the edge of the water thirty yards away. I aimed the iron-sighted Brno 9.3 mm just behind the elbow, pressed the set trigger, then touched the second. At the blast, the bull whirled and the herd raced off. I jumped around Willie. "Don't move," he hissed. I aimed in the same place as the bull lumbered by ten yards off and fired again. The bull disappeared in the herd and the dust. I knew the second shot had hit where I wanted because I saw the sudden white hole in the black hide and the great gout of blood explode from the nostrils. I knew the bull would die. Willie didn't. The Bayei and River Bushmen trackers reassured him. The bull was indeed well hit.

"Watch," Willie said. I did, and when the dust cleared and the rest of the herd had lumbered off into the river bush, the bull walked very slowly toward the cover. I aimed well forward as the bull quartered away, pressed the trigger, and he dropped. Everyone chattered and laughed in the sudden bursting of tension and the ecstasy of collecting a good trophy. I wanted to make certain he was down for good, when we heard his sad and haunting death bellow.

"Always do that," Willie said. "It's the saddest sound I know, and it always does something to me." He'd been in on the killing of thousands of buffalo, too.

We butchered the bull on that Okavango island, and the guys hung the bloody chunks of meat in a big fever tree to keep it away from the hyenas and the lion pride we'd heard roaring earlier. Apparently, the first two shots both smashed the heart; all we could find of it were a few tatters of muscle. The trackers tied the

THE DANGEROUS GAME

42-inch head and cape to a pole. One took each end, and we trekked back to the *mekoro** (dugouts).

Even more typical was the bull I shot in Tanzania's south Masailand a decade ago. At least the first part of the shooting was typical. We'd followed a big herd of bulls into the thornbush thickets, at first in the Toyota and then on foot. We found a big bull in the tangle of animals, and we guessed he'd spread forty-six or forty-eight inches. He'd rolled in the white clay, so we kept him located by the dusty white of his back and rump. We trailed through the dark thornbush and heavy overcast. We'd almost get to where we might get a shot when the herd would lumber off again. And we'd repeat.

"That bull bringing up the rear is very good," the PH said, and then the herd whirled and galloped off again. I'd been concentrating on finding the white-rumped bull and had paid no attention to the others in the rear of the herd. "I'd collect the bull next time we get a chance," he said. "He'll go forty-five."

We were having no luck with the dust-covered bull, so when we closed again on the tail end of the herd and the bulls whirled again to glare, I settled the cross hairs of the .375 behind the second bull's shoulder as he stood quartering away slightly. I heard the slug hit the bull like a glove into the heavy bag and saw the dust puff just where it should. He whirled at the impact, pretty typical, and I hammered him again in the hip as he lumbered off. Richards's .577 cannoned in my ear, and I saw the black splinters of horn boss. The bulls were gone suddenly into the ash dust and *miombo*.

We followed the herd through the thicket, finding tiny splatters of frothy-orange lung blood, and trailed the bull into a donga so thick that it took us half an hour to cross. After moving into the open and then again into more thornbush, we spotted him standing in a small bush, silhouetted against the open plain beyond. As I was about to touch off, he spun and lumbered off

---

*Like other Bantu languages, Setswana, the official language of Botswana, uses *prefixes* to indicate singular and plural nouns. Thus, *mokoro* is singular and *mekoro* is plural. With the influence of English, there are people in Botswana nowdays who simply add an "s" to *mokoro* to form the plural.

again. Half a mile farther on, we saw him standing in a small tangle of thorn, glaring and waiting for us to come near enough to kill. I settled the cross hairs on his shoulder and squeezed off. He collapsed so suddenly and definitely that none of us had any doubt he was dead.

We walked up, jabbering in the relief and that soaring satisfaction of having collected a good trophy. Richards broke open the .577 and handed it to the tracker. I still had a slug up the rifle's throat and thought about jacking it out, but didn't. I smiled at the big bull stretched out in the dust. The horn bosses came solidly together, and he had good spread.

In the time it took to form that thought, the bull was on his feet and coming. Out of the corners of my eyes, I saw everyone disappearing. As I thought of vaulting out of the way, too, I felt the rifle butt against my hip. Instead, I yanked the rifle barrel up and slid the safety off, firing as I jumped out of the way. To my astonishment, the bull collapsed in the dust.

When we'd walked up on the bull moments earlier, he lay on his side with his legs stretched out to the side, bloody drool soaking into the dust. He had looked as dead as anything could. He came to as we stood there. Then he'd jumped up, quartering-on so fast I had a hard time believing what I was seeing. As he oriented head-on, the bullet broke his neck. The guys thought I did it on purpose, and I didn't disillusion them. The bull lay there with shattered neck vertebrae, and I shot him again to make sure. Someone said that it's the dead ones that kill you. The bull's snout lay three yards from my toes.

While charges aren't typical, the way the bull was initially shot was. Typically, it's one through the lights—the heart and lungs—then one aft, somewhere, as he lumbers off. Then you spoor him, and more likely than not he's either anchored or dead when you find him. Sometimes not, though.

* * * * *

Another time I'd hit an immense-bodied bull on the point of his shoulder as he stood quartering on. The bullet should have angled back through heart and lungs. Predictably, the bull whirled and raced into the bush before I could shoot again. We followed the dark, muscle blood spoor. We found no light, frothy lung blood. We gave it up when the equatorial night dropped faster than a thought.

We returned in the dawn and found the bull had moved a mile closer to the camp. "*M'bogo,*" the game scout said, and he said something else, and from its tone, it was profane.

I stepped from the Toyota and through the scope saw the caked blood and dust on the buff's shoulder. I kneeled as the bull glared at us from seventy-five yards, and just as he started to charge I drove three hundred grains of metal into his heavy chest. He staggered sideways at the impact, I hit him again and then once more, and he was down. He bawled that haunting death bawl, and as we walked up to him we heard the rattle of death.

The postmortem showed the first bullet, instead of raking back into heart and lungs, had been deflected outward along the outside plane of the shoulder blade and had gotten under the muscle aft, finally nicking a lung, but not enough to do much immediate damage. I'll always wonder if the bull, angry and vindictive from a night of pain, had caught our scent and was stalking the camp. After all, he was closer to the camp than the evening before, and he was still heading in that direction. In colonial Mozambique, a wounded bull had stalked into a hunters' camp and killed two men, or so the story goes. It could happen.

On a different safari, this one on the Masai Steppe in central Tanzania, we were returning to camp after an unsuccessful try for lesser kudu. We'd killed a dandy fringe-eared oryx instead. The sun was setting, and we were looking forward to a sundowner and a dinner of francolin partridge or buffalo tongue or bushbuck roast, whichever was on the menu that night, when I saw a buff silhouetted against the barren sand beyond the bush. He charged, with his nose raised and the spread of horns obvious, bursting from the thorny acacia in a shower of branches and twigs. The PH and trackers saw him coming at the same time. We raced off, easily outrunning the charge, but a little shaken by the surprise of it.

The tracker, a Masai elder, the PH, and the government game scout held a conference. "The game scout and the elder tracker say we should settle that bull's troubles for him," said the PH. "He's apt to murder someone, and the Masai herders water their cattle at the pan. Shoot it with the .577."

We turned around and motored back. I urged Cheri to climb up back on the high seat, where she'd be safe if the bull charged the open, doorless Toyota.

When the buff charged out of the bush on the opposite side of the track, Richards skidded to a stop. As I counterbalanced against the sudden braking, the buff veered broadside, and I touched one off. The buff nosedived into the dust and skidded to a stop with a raised head. I'd spined it just behind the shoulder. The second shot went through the nose and exploded the brain. What really surprised us was the buff wasn't a bull at all, even though it had a forty-inch spread. The cow was in bad temper because lions had chewed up its back and the wounds had festered. You never know.

Buffalo not only get injured by lions or other predators, but they also—frequently enough to make it scary—get into man-set snares. If a hunter spends enough time in the bush, he's eventually going to run across one of these aggressive potential man-killers. If the hunter's not ready, the last thing he'll see is the heavy, black horn bosses hooking up into his gut. (See "The Last Step" elsewhere in this tome.) It happens all the time.

* * * * *

Seems I've had more than my share of close encounters with *m'bogo*. I'm just lucky that way. On the other hand, I know of two men who have killed more than a hundred buffalo each without one sweaty encounter. They did it on official culling operations, and at least one of them was armed with an automatic AK.

Few hunters get charged by buffalo. Typically the hunter puts one through the boiler room as the buff stands broadside, another in the stern as he lumbers off, and maybe a finisher when he comes up to him. Since *m'bogo* is so big, solid, vindictive, vital and ornery and since it's the first one in that counts, your slug doesn't have to be too far off the mark to create what is

THE DANGEROUS GAME

euphemistically called an "incident." All that potential danger is what makes buffalo hunting so much fun.

And that's why few things are as satisfying as when the tracker walks up with that bleached-bone smile, grasps your thumb, and says, "*M'uzuri, Bwana. M'bogo kubwa sana!*" as you stare at a ton of the toughest, meanest beast in Africa stretched out in the sand.

Postscript: The following is quoted verbatim, so don't blame me for the grammar, mechanics, or organization:

BLACK DEATH FROM OUT OF NOWHERE

. . . An American client shot and wounded a large Buffalo Bull, which took off for parts unknown.

The South African Professional Hunter, a young man in his early twenties, was carrying a .375 H & H Magnum rifle. The two of them were following the blood spoor (blood trail) when the Huge Black Buffalo charged from behind a large anthill. Before they could fire, the wounded Cape buffalo gored the Professional Hunter to death, and was shot and killed by the American client. (*African Bowhunting Drumbeat*, 12/15/99)

The same source tells the story of a South African man and his two children who were visiting a game ranch. This is what happened to him:

From out of nowhere a Cape Buffalo came at him like a freight train and hit him, knocked him down and out. The bull returned and mauled him to death while his two children looked on from a pick up truck. They went and got help but the father was long dead, mashed by the hooves of the buff and ripped to shreds by the sharp horns, and squashed into the soil by the boss of the horns. . . .

Here's another from still the same source:

KwaZulu Natal, South Africa Game ranch manager Mr. Bertus van Niekerk, aged 50, was fixing a warthog hole in a game fence with several black assistants when he heard a noise behind him. He turned round and scrambled up the nearest tree to avoid a very angry Cape Buffalo, but the buffalo kept ramming the small tree until Bertus was knocked loose and fell out of the tree. The Black beast then gored the unarmed man several times with razor sharp hooked horns of death and mashed him with the boss. . . .

The Cape then stomped the man into the dirt, hammering him again and again.

. . . A Chopper then flew him to Durban's St. Augustines Hospital by Medical Rescue International.

. . . All his ribs were shattered and broken, and he had a bruised heart and two punctured lungs. . . . He had a huge gouge on his thigh, which went through to his hamstrings and a fractured cheekbone as well.

(Author's note: You can read more buff stories, some of them fatal, in my book *Safari: A Dangerous Affair* from Safari Press, 2000.)

HIPPO–THE "ACCIDENTAL" MOST DANGEROUS GAME

The statistics may be a little vague, but they indicate it's the hippo that kills more Africans than any other herbivore. Some evidence, again vague, says the crocodile kills more than the hippo; however, the croc is not an herbivore but, rather, a decided carnivore. The usual suspect in general missing-persons reports is the crocodile because the croc doesn't leave much evidence lying about, as will the hippo. Even so, my bet is on the hippo as the more dangerous of the two.

Back in the early '70s, my good friend and fellow wildlife biologist with the then U.S. Bureau of Sports Fisheries and Wildlife (later absorbed into the U.S. Fish and Wildlife Service), Malcolm "Mac" MacDonald, visited Uganda. The only story he brought back that I remember was that of a native boy killed by a hippo. Apparently the boy was herding the family cattle back to the kraal when he got between the river and hippos grazing onshore. Water means safety to a hippo, and if a person gets between the hippo and its comfort zone, he is in serious trouble. The boy was bitten in two, and Mac described the mess with relish and detail characteristic of a scientist. I'll spare the reader the gory details, but the scene repeats itself scores of times in Africa each year.

The hippo is rightly considered one of Africa's seven dangerous game animals. In truth, it's the most dangerous, if the main criterion for evaluation is the number of human kills. From a hunter's point of view, however, they are seldom dangerous. Humans usually get in trouble with hippos accidentally.

I know half a dozen fellow hunters who have collected hippos. The drill is for the hunter to sneak to the edge of the river or lake and to pot a big hippo through the brain as it dozes half submerged. The hippo seldom charges, partly because if done right it's unaware of the hunters, but even if it was aware, the

HIPPO—THE "ACCIDENTAL" MOST DANGEROUS GAME

bull would not leave its safety zone in the water to charge a hunter on land. None of these hunters killed a hippo with one shot. The brain's a tough target: It's the size of a large man's fist and it's located high in the head between the ear and eye when viewed from the side. Each hunter followed up with two to five more shots in the neck or body. If the water is deep enough, a dead hippo will sink and then float up an hour or two later, depending on the temperature of the water and the contents of the gut.

Though I'd had opportunities to shoot hippo several times in Tanzania and elsewhere, the proposition had never interested me for a couple of reasons. I'd never seen a mounted hippo trophy that looked half real.

In May 2002, after an unsuccessful elephant safari with Jumbo Safaris, I finally took the opportunity to hunt hippo in the Chiredzi River in eastern Zimbabwe. When we moved up from the southern elephant camp, I finally decided to try for the two dangerous animals in Africa that I hadn't hunted—crocodile and hippopotamus.

One morning, we drove out from the camp on the Mwakasine River onto the blacktop toward the town of Chiredzi. Then we motored down a dirt road through fifteen-foot sugar cane fields to the banks of the Chiredzi River. We walked down the bank, taking no particular advantage of the cover, and there they were. These hippos were used to farm workers wandering up and down the river, so they paid no attention to humans. The rumor was that this herd of hippos raided the cane fields at night, so at least some of them would be culled in the hope that the shooting and commotion would drive the rest out of the vicinity. The meat would go in its entirety to the village farming corporation. We could keep whatever we wanted for the trophy in exchange, of course, for the trophy fee. Majara the tracker, Jim Mackie the PH, and Cheri and I watched the herd with binocs to be certain which was the bull and to try to make sure he had complete, intact tusks.

"The cows have pink eyes," Mackie said.

I'd never heard that before, but then I'd never hunted hippos, either. We looked for the hippo where the flesh surrounding the eyes and ears was black, not the usual pink.

THE DANGEROUS GAME

"Second from the left," I opined. The bull, if that was what it was, lay mostly submerged on a sand bar. The rest of the herd stood in the shallows. They still paid us no attention.

"Let's wait till he yawns to be sure the tusks aren't broken," Mackie said, but the bull never did. I lay in the sand ninety yards away and watched through the riflescope. Finally, Mackie, not long on the waiting kind of patience, said, "Shoot him."

I'd studied the shot placement handbook I had in my kit and knew to put the cross hairs of the .375 one-third of the way between ear and eye. I squeezed off, and all hell broke loose. The bull, on his belly on the submerged sand bar, threw his head up, great spouts of blood gushing down his jaws, and the herd stampeded through the shallows and into deeper water. The bull rolled on his side and spouted pink froth a foot in the air.

I had my bull hippo. I can't say much for the hunt, if you can call it that. In truth, it was more like an assassination. I'd killed the hippo while we were in plain sight, and the hippos couldn't have cared less if we'd been there or not. Still, I had my hippo.

We'd hauled a small boat in the *bakkie* bed, and the guys rowed out to tie a rope around the bull so that we could tow him to shore. I covered them with the .375. I fired three times at cows approaching too closely, and I also kept an eye out for the crocs that were supposed to inhabit the river.

We hauled the big bull to the shore, but thirty-five men couldn't tow it up onto the sandy beach. Someone ran off and an hour later returned with an immense tractor owned by the farm co-op. Even it had problems getting the huge animal out of the water and up the bank; three tons of bacon was nearly too much for it. The tractor finally managed to haul the bull a few yards out of the water by gunning the engine and then popping the clutch, yanking the hippo forward a yard at a time.

As hippos go, the bull was good. The main trophies, the two lower canine teeth, were entire, though one of the long lower incisors had been broken off in a battle. The 300-grain Sledgehammer solid had entered in front of the ear and exited out of the off eye. The bull had died instantly. Though the hunt left something to be desired, I was pleased with the trophy. I now have the requisite golden-yellow hippo tusks and teeth filling

HIPPO—THE "ACCIDENTAL" MOST DANGEROUS GAME

three large Mashona baskets, so I'll never shoot another—unless it's in self-defense.

Though I never experienced the least danger on that hunt, hippos can be very dangerous depending on the circumstances. I'd had the pee frightened out of me while poling a *mokoro* through thick, lime-green papyrus channels in the Okavango in Botswana. We were hunting on the islands for buffalo, lechwe, and warthog. Few things are more pleasant than poling a cranky *mokoro* from island to island and hunting as you go. Twice, hippos bluff- charged us, but fortunately they didn't follow through.

Once, the trackers, professional hunter Willie Phillips, Cheri, and I poled through the green tangle in the dawn, with mist rising off the water in the near darkness. We heard hippos grunting and snorting not far in the distance from the channels. Nothing makes more noise than hippos when they want to. They wanted to. We poled the *mekoro* through the papyrus tangle along the channels, kept open largely through hippo activity. Willie, in the first *mokoro*, kept a close watch on the papyrus wall, the .460 Brno across his lap at the ready.

The sun hadn't yet hit the tops of the big river trees when something heavy rushed toward us through the papyrus and water. Willie pivoted toward the commotion and half brought the rifle up and I did the same, though what I would have done with the .270 I carried, I couldn't imagine. The hippo or hippos grunted and bellowed so loudly that it sounded like they were on top of us, and their wake rocked the *mekoro*. Fortunately, they stopped without showing themselves in the papyrus, but they were so close we heard their stomachs rumble between the snorting and hooting. We poled silently away, both Willie and I trying to stand in the shaky dugouts ready to shoot. I'm fairly certain the recoil, had we fired, would have knocked us out of the cranky little boats. We had a similar experience the next evening as we returned, and everyone grinned with relief when we climbed the bank onto our island camp.

Another time, we were crossing the Ugalla River in western Tanzania in a canoe that had been formed by hollowing out the trunk of a palm tree. The locals had cut the stern out of the canoe to let out fishing nets, and the water flowed into the

THE DANGEROUS GAME

canoe to the depth of half a foot or so. I was distracted, concerned with keeping my feet out of the water because it carried a microscopic blood fluke that caused inflammatory brain bilharziasis in humans unused to the parasite. The inflammation could kill you. The fishermen suddenly began shouting, and I pivoted to see a submerged hippo bulleting straight for the dugout. Both the PH and I fired in front of the hurtling hippo to deflect the charge. Fortunately, the bull dived deep and disappeared. I counted my blessings, as I definitely did not want to take a swim. That part of the Ugalla not only crawled with the dangerous fluke, but it also bristled with crocodiles (sixteen fishermen in the two villages nearby had been eaten by crocs in the previous seven months alone!).

Postscript: The following excerpts are verbatim:

SOUTH AFRICAN LOSES EYE AND NOSE IN HIPPO ATTACK

South Africa's *Saturday Star* reports the man also suffered crushed ribs and other internal injuries. (http://www.ananova.com/news/story/sm, 4/13/02)

I took this next story from an untitled article:

In one weekend, a pair of rogue hippos killed four people in the Malindi district of Kenya. A 20-year-old mother and her 8-month-old daughter were trampled to death while preparing the evening meal.... The other two victims were killed while crossing a makeshift bridge across the Sabaki River.
... In Mali, two men in town of Koulikoro were killed by hippos in separate incidents related to seasonal flooding.
The first victim was killed as he loaded sand into his dugout canoe. The other was killed when his dugout was overturned by a hippo. In both cases, the victim's bodies were not found....
(http://www.moray.ml.duke.edu/projects/hippos/Newsletter/new29.html, 10/15/01)

HIPPO—THE "ACCIDENTAL" MOST DANGEROUS GAME

Six killed in Zimbabwe Following Hippo Attack

On Saturday, November 24, five women and one man drowned in Zimbabwe after a hippo capsized their boat. The six were returning from a fishing trip at the time of the attack.

. . . According to many reports, hippos are responsible for more human death in African than any other mammal. (Associated Press, 11/26/01)

South African Woman Killed by Hippo

A South African woman . . . was killed in a hippos attack on February 2, at a private reserve in the Kruger National Park. . . . suffered several injuries to her side, arms, legs, and head but died as a result of a bite to the stomach. (Reuters, 2/16/02)

Hippo Flips Boat; Kills 11

. . . a hippo in Lake Malawi flipped a canoe causing eleven people to drown. (*Washington Post*, 5/25/02)

Four Drown in Three Unrelated Hippo Encounters in Zimbabwe

In two separate incidents over the course of one week, three people drowned as a result of run-ins with hippos. . . . Hippos are widely reported to be one of the most dangerous species in Africa. (Nhau Mangirazi of the *Zimbabwe Herald*, 7/24/02)

THE PERFECT KILLER

"That was the life," the professional hunter said to no one as he stared at the acacia embers, then out into the night. "I hired Joseph, then." Joseph was the Bayei tracker.

He yelled at the staff laughing around their own fire at the back of the kitchen hut. A moment later a tall, lean man drifted silently out of the shadows. The PH said something else in Setswana, and the man lifted a tattered gray jersey exposing the two neat rows of scars running diagonally across his abdomen. The tracker turned and showed identical raised scars across his back.

"Croc," the first man said. "Pulled him from the bank and carried him under to drown him, as they do. Once a big croc gets you, you're done for. Never heard of anyone escaping. Except Joseph, here. Joseph had the wits about him to jam both thumbs into the croc's eyes. The bugger released him." He stirred up the embers, then said something else, and the tracker dropped his jersey.

"Poaching, they call it now, but back then you were a hero for killing crocs. You'd hunt them at night. Hides brought a good price, then. You'd drift through the channels and use a torch looking for the big ones. If you were careful enough, you could drift right up to them at one or two meters. You had to brain them, though, or they'd submerge. If they thrashed about, you could get in another shot or get a spear into them. Even in the death fits they could upset a *mokoro*.

"That happened one night. We had a young man helping then. He held the torch. He had good eyes and spotted the crocs even before the light fell on them. In the light, the croc eyes reflected pink or red. I brained this big croc, a fourteen-footer, and we stood off as it thrashed about—often takes time before they know they're dead. I worried more about the hippos feeding beyond the papyrus in the channels, and we heard them grunting and threatening our intrusion. I'd worked a solid into the .303 in case of hippo difficulties, while Joseph and the new boy worked the *mokoro* up and secured the float to the croc's leg. We'd tie a float to them and let them sink, then come back for the skinning in the morning.

"I paid no attention to the croc. As I said, I half expected a hippo charge. They were the real dangers in crocodile hunting, not the crocs. Just as Joseph dropped the croc's leg, it convulsed, the tail knocking Joseph into the boy and off-balancing the *mokoro* so the whole bloody thing upset. I went down into the black water and held tight to the .303, thinking about the crocs and hippos. The torch went out, and I came up gagging and gasping for air in the pitch dark, still grasping the rifle, and in a panic sidestroked for the far bank, the one away from the hippos. I grasped a vine, tossed the rifle up onto the dry ground, pulled myself up, and coughed up a liter of water." He paused and stirred the embers.

"Later, Joseph walked down the bank. '*Baas*, it is me,' he said. In Setswana, I asked him about the boy. He didn't know.

"We found him the next morning when we came back for the skinning. The crocs had ripped a leg off, then stuffed the carcass into the reeds to rot.

"'Leave him, *Baas*,' Joseph said. We retrieved the dead crocs and skinned them, and by evening had thrown their carcasses in the main channel for their brothers to eat.

"Joseph left the camp the next morning and did not return for two days. I couldn't wait forever. As I shoved off the next evening to hunt, Joseph poled around the bend with something gray and green rolled up in front of him. '*Baas*,' he said, 'this is the devil that killed the boy. I waited at the boy's body and speared the devil when he came to finish.'"

* * * * *

Crocs haven't the innate intelligence to have the fear around man that the big cats have. Their brain is little more than a collection of ganglia—which makes them all the more frightening. It makes them cold and dispassionate, and you, the mighty human,

THE DANGEROUS GAME

are no more than a wildebeest or bushpig to a croc. It will grab a human at riverside with no more understanding than if it had caught a fish, and once a fair-size croc grasps any prey, it's done for. A big croc weighs more than a ton, and if one takes hold of you or a bull wildebeest, the conclusion is certain. Typically, crocs drown their prey, then stuff it underneath a root or submerged log until it rots enough that it can be pulled apart and the pieces swallowed whole; crocodiles cannot chew or rip.

I once watched crocodiles capturing migrating wildebeest on the Grumeti River in western Tanzania. The two big crocs I actually saw capture prey did it so suddenly and swiftly I wondered for a moment if it really had happened. They very literally exploded out of the muddy water as quickly as a Polaris missile bursts from the sea. Once they'd grabbed the wildebeest, they leisurely backed into the water until they and the wildebeest disappeared. One croc, which I guessed would go at least fifteen feet, grabbed a cow wildebeest and pulled her in. Crocs from elsewhere in the pool converged, and each grasped part of the wildebeest, all twisting and writhing to tear off chunks. The cow was torn apart in minutes.

Earlier, I'd been carelessly wandering around the river with my camera, but after I'd watched the big crocs capture wildebeest, I stayed well away from the water. I doubt I have ever been more astonished by anything than the speed the crocodiles attain when capturing prey.

At one time, crocodiles were considered endangered through most of their range. In Zimbabwe, crocodile farms that raised them for leather and meat were required to turn one crocodile loose into the wild for every one they killed for sale. This restocked the depleted wild waters for a time, but then it became counterproductive because it interfered with the natural behavior and territoriality of the species. Now crocodiles are no longer released into the wild, and the reestablished populations seem largely healthy, except where they interfere too seriously with man.

Though I'd seen crocs while hunting in Botswana, Tanzania, and Namibia, I'd never hunted them. I rectified the mistake in Zimbabwe, on a tributary of the Lundi River.

THE PERFECT KILLER

We still-hunted through the thorn trees above the river. Immediately, we spotted an eight-footer on a sandy beach across the water. We continued still-hunting farther along the river until the local guide crouched suddenly and motioned us down. We crawled along the edge and stared down at a good croc, thirty yards below. Through the riflescope, it looked like a dinosaur. The PH was so excited that he bounced me to three locations before he decided we were in the right position to shoot. In the thick brush, we couldn't see either end, only the back and legs. Mackie had me shooting through a tangle of branches, and a thumb-thick branch deflected the bullet. I thought he told me the head was toward the bank, but it was actually closer to the water. That's my story and I'm sticking to it. No one can miss a crocodile that close, and I found the bullet-shattered branch. As consolation, we noted it was probably only a ten-footer. I'm still looking for a legitimate crocodile, but I won't settle for one under thirteen feet.

On another safari, in the Okavango, an eight-foot croc crawled into the camp after the PH's mongrels. They were dear to the PH, Willie Phillips, since he didn't have a family. The croc didn't get one, and the cook chased it back into the gin-clear waters.

During the warmer safari months, after October and before April, baiting works well for hunting crocs. I watched a video where hunters staked and wired an impala carcass to the bank. The video showed the heads of at least a dozen crocs drifting into the carcass. Most of the crocs were small, but one or two had some size.

Crocs don't feed much during the cold safari months, roughly from May through August, in the south. They are ectothermic (not "cold-blooded")—that is, their body temperature is partially regulated by external conditions; humans, on the other hand, are endothermic, and body temperature is regulated from within the body. Crocs cannot digest food if it's too cold for their metabolisms; in fact, crocodiles die from eating when it's too cold. Big crocs, like those on the Grumeti River, may eat only once a year. Baiting is not the way to hunt crocs during the colder safari months. It's better to find them sunning themselves on the bank and then brain them.

THE DANGEROUS GAME

The brain shot is the best, but it's also the toughest. The brain sits just above the rear of the crocodile's "smile," and it's the size of a golf ball. I'm told by those who have hunted crocodiles a great deal that the body shot works and that even though the croc will submerge, it can't stay down long. If it dies, it eventually floats to the surface. This is fine in smaller, quiet bodies of water, but on big rivers, the croc will float off.

Crocodiles frighten me in an old place. It's their silence, it's their single-mindedness when drifting up on prey, and it's their speed when they lunge. They don't think about it, and we are no longer *Homo sapiens*, what we anthropocentrically think of as evolution's epitome. No, we are merely meat. The croc has absolutely no regard for our technology, our sophisticated weapons, or our philosophies. It thinks no more about a human entree than it does one of impala or tilapia.

Crocs are so perfectly adapted to circumnavigate their watery, equatorial habitats that they've hardly changed in nearly two hundred million years. They are one of the most successful vertebrate groups on the planet. As a comparison, the genus *Homo* has existed less than one percent of that time. Who would take a bet that *we* will survive for another two hundred million years?

Postscript: The following excerpts are quoted verbatim:

Look Out for Especially Aggressive Crocs

Two people were reported to have been attacked by crocodiles in the last two weeks. The body of 50-year-old farm worker Samuel Chauke, who was attacked while fishing on the banks of the Levhubu River in the Northern Province, was recovered at 4 P.M. on Sunday.

Thirteen-year-old Nsizwazonke Mthembu escaped with bites on his hand, thumb, thighs and abdomen after a crocodile attacked him while he was fishing at Lake Mzingazi in Richard's Bay. (South African Press Association, 2/25/02)

I took the next story from an untitled article:

THE PERFECT KILLER

Blantyre, Malawi—A businessman who was attacked by a crocodile in Malawi escaped by biting the reptile on its nose, police said Thursday, Dec. 12. Mac Bosco Chawinga, 43, went for a swim in a lake in the northern Nkhata Bay . . . when the crocodile grabbed him, said Bob Mtekama, a senior police officer in the area. "Both his arms were inside the full-size crocodile's jaws and the beast was dragging him into deeper water when he decide to fight back," Mtekama said. "Chawinga sunk his teeth in the crocodile's nose, one of the few soft places on its body, and the reptile let go of him. . . ." (Associated Press, 12/12/02)

CROCODILE ATTACKS MAN IN TENT

A man was attacked by a crocodile in his tent in Botswana's Moremi Game Reserve in Botswana last Tuesday. The incident took place in the same camp where an American boy was dragged from his ten and killed by hyenas recently. According to reports the crocodile dragged a safari company driver from his tent. However, he managed to grab hold of a steel pole, thereby saving his life. . . . (Associated Press, 8/13/00)

PROTECTED CROCODILES EAT MALAWIANS
BY RAPHAEL TENTHANI IN BLANTYRE

Crocodiles are killing at least two people every day in the Lower Shire Valley in southern Malawi, according to a survey carried out by a professional hunter.

The high death rate has been linked to Malawi's signing of the International Convention on Endangered Species (CITES), which limits the culling of crocodiles, among other animals . . . the reported attacks could be just the tip of the iceberg.

People in the area no longer report every death to police . . . because these attacks are happening every day. . . .

The issue of crocodiles in Lower Shire is so serious that parliament has become involved.

THE DANGEROUS GAME

George Ntafu, the neurosurgeon-turned wildlife minister, answering a question from an MP from the area on what government was doing to control the crocodile problem, said his ministry suspected witchcraft in the prolification of crocodile deaths. (www.news.bbc.co.uk/1/hi/world/africa, 4/27/03)

Postmortem on "Crocodile Death" Briton

A postmortem examination is being carried out on Tuesday on the body of a British woman who is believed to have been killed by a crocodile in Kenya.

According to friends who were swimming with Miss Nicholls on Friday, her last words were: "It's got my feet. It's a crocodile." (www.news.bbc.co.uk/1/hi/uk, 4/27/03)

Uganda Culls Man-Eating Crocs

The Uganda Wildlife Authority (UWA) says it has begun an operation to cull predatory crocodiles in Lake Victoria that have attacked and killed more than 40 people in the past seven months.

The authority said an armed patrol was hunting down the crocodiles, which waited for their victims in shallow waters before dragging them further offshore. (www.news.bbc.co.uk/1/hi/world/Africa, 4/25/02)

CHUI

The straightforward title of this chapter indicates something about the Swahili language: It's forceful, direct, and simple. Even though we may not understand a word's dictionary meaning, we immediately get a sense of it. *M'bogo* gives the sense of the power, danger, and determination of the buffalo. *Tembo* is just right for elephant. What's better than *simba* for lion? And so it is with *chui* for the leopard.

* * * * *

For reasons obscure to me but I suppose related to the earlier absence of biological information and antihunting pressures, the leopard is listed as endangered in the northern parts of its range and threatened in the southern African countries. Those listed as threatened are importable into the United States.

The irony of such listings is that, in all probability, the leopard, *Panthera pardus,* is what biologists call a "weed species," along with Norway rats, cockroaches, and humans. That is, we all occupy a variety of habitats and niches. In the case of humans we are found in the driest deserts, like the Namib, in the wettest rain forests on three continents, and from sea level to higher than sixteen thousand feet in the Andes. Weed species are tremendously successful because they are so adaptable. They are evolution's ultimate survivors. Calling such a species "endangered" is akin to calling Oprah "petite."

If leopard populations are vulnerable, it is those in deserts, simply because there's less food, and, therefore, individual territories must be larger to support a given animal. Leopards in deserts are always more vulnerable to human interference, be it from habitat destruction, elimination of critical prey species, or trapping and poisoning. There may also be less reproductive

THE DANGEROUS GAME

success because females must work harder to feed kittens, and fewer kittens will survive as a result. Those populations living in scrub or forest or other cover are less susceptible to drastic population declines. Take away readily available food and habitat, and humans become vulnerable in marginal areas, too.

That leopards are tremendously adaptable can't be doubted by any reasonable human, but then the protectionists are seldom reasonable. *Chui* is alive and well from the Kalahari Desert to the rain forests of Central Africa, and from sea level in the Zambezi Delta in Mozambique to the Himalayas in India. They live happily in game-filled wilderness or within the city limits of Nairobi, where they dine without compunction on dogs, cats, rats, and pigeons. Leopards live in places where they may never see a human, or in places where they may encounter man several times a day, the latter usually without man's knowledge. Leopard expert Dr. Randal Eaton called the leopard the "coyote of Africa," and predicted it would be the last major species to survive in Africa.

It's no secret to population scientists that human numbers in Africa are expanding exponentially (though the AIDS epidemic promises to slow things down), and, therefore, there are fewer wild places left on the continent. However, leopards are still abundant, and, in some places, more abundant than they've ever been. They continually come in contact with the burgeoning human population, yet they seldom eat *Homo sapiens*. That they do not indicates both their efficiency in killing tougher and faster game and their innate intelligence in understanding that killing human prey means big trouble.

Given both the numbers of humans and the density of leopards, it's amazing more leopards don't prey on humans. The most famous man-eating leopards lived in colonial India, where the Brits kept fairly accurate records. The legendary Jim Corbett killed several man-eating leopards that were credited with human-kill tallies in the hundreds. Leopard man-eaters in India ran up such horrific numbers for a couple of reasons: Indian human population densities were often much higher than those in Africa, and the basic nature of the Indian was more passive than that of the typical African native. The Indian would simply tolerate such depredations with resigned fatalism.

CHUI

The Rudraprayag man-eating leopard was credited with a hundred twenty-five human kills; however, Jim Corbett, who eventually ended the leopard's eight-year man-eating career, claimed that total was too low since some of the kills he reported to authorities did not show up on the tally sheets. While the Rudraprayag man-eating leopard was the most famous, Corbett also finished the human-dinner career of the Panar leopard, a cat with more than four hundred confirmed kills. That leopards haven't committed such astonishing inroads into African human populations is only for the reasons listed above.

Undoubtedly, African leopards eat people and do so efficiently (see the postscript of this chapter); however, it's their reputation for ferocity once wounded that's got most of the press.

Chui does strange things to people. A deadeye who thinks nothing of potting Mongolian ibex at six hundred yards turns into a drooling fool when faced with a leopard. A camp mate on a Tanzania safari missed a thirty-yard shot at a leopard profiling on a branch, then fired three more times into the empty tree long after the cat had departed for Lake Tanganyika. Another pal made three safaris for leopard without seeing one and now thinks the leopard is a haunt. An acquaintance spent nearly three weeks of dusk-to-dawn vigils in a leopard blind before he got a shot, which he missed. A PH I know hates leopard hunting because he has a recurring dream that a wounded cat rearranges his face—for no reason I can fathom, he is rather vain about his appearance.

You hunt leopards in a variety of ways. Hunts where the big spotted cat is chased miles and miles across the flat Kalahari Desert in Toyotas then blasted with shotguns when he refuses to run farther are the least attractive. Just as bad are the hunts where the leopard is chased across the desert by dogs, also mostly on the Kalahari. The "hunters" follow safely in the bed of the *bakkie,* and everyone cuts loose with shotguns and SSG buckshot loads when the dogs bay the cat. Both hunts offer little danger to the hunter and little chance to the cat. To me they are unethical. Trailing leopards with dogs trained for the purpose and doing it on foot offers a great deal more sport, danger, and adventure. Too often, leopards are still treated like vermin, and as a result there's more unethical hunting for leopards than probably any other game animal.

Baiting is the traditional way of collecting a leopard trophy. I'm a traditionalist, and I've been very lucky in my leopard hunting. Now, when hunting *chui*, also known as *ngwe*, I'm just slightly superstitious; my lucky number is three. I collected my two biggest cats on the third day of sitting in blinds. In Tanzania, we had three cats working three baits at the same time. On my first leopard safari in Zimbabwe back in the '80s, we had three baits out; I shot the leopard in the third blind we built. Mostly, I'm not superstitious. After all, I'm a practical-minded biologist and college professor. Superstition is not a factor in my persona. It can't be. But with *chui*, I'll take all the help I can get.

As I said, I'm a traditionalist. Where leopards have been persecuted by hunting, trapping, or poisoning, they become almost 100 percent nocturnal. This means they will not come to a bait until after dark. In Zimbabwe where I first hunted *ngwe* (also sometimes *ingwe*), they'd been persecuted by man for a century and a half, and no cat with half a brain would show itself during daylight. So we hunted at night.

When I booked the safari, I had no idea we'd hunt at night, but once in the blind the African night dropped like a coffin lid, and I understood the odds were all in favor of the big spotted cat. That first night, a bushpig came to the bait and cleaned up the maggots that had fallen from it. With the inborn tension that comes from strange noises in the night, the pig gave me such an adrenaline surge that I was immediately addicted to baiting leopards. The second night, an immense leopard stalked to within five yards of our blind and roared behind our flimsy burlap and grass structure, where we half-dozed in the dark. The PH Russell Tarr, Cheri, and I nearly jumped out the top of the blind. Then the leopard roared from up the kopje a few moments later, and we knew we wouldn't see that leopard again. We moved our efforts from western Zimbabwe south to the head of the Bubi River, where I killed the leopard I detailed in chapter four, "In a Leopard Blind."

Some years later in western Tanzania, we had three leopards feeding on three baits. The biggest cat, from its tracks, had appropriated an entire topi carcass we'd hung for lions. We let the big leopard feed for several days, and each afternoon we peeled back the mummified meat glaze so the cat would have easy and fresh picking. Each night he returned. We learned his routine from the tracks we'd find the next day. We built the blind several days before we actually sat in it, and it didn't disturb the tom in the least.

That first afternoon we crawled into the blind three hours before sunset. As I started to doze, I heard what I thought was a lorry engine coming closer. Larry Richards, our PH for that trip, Cheri, and I looked at each other with puzzled expressions. The "engine" came closer and closer until a huge swarm of bees flew directly overhead. I threw my coat over Cheri's head, since she's allergic to bee stings, but the swarm continued on toward Lake Victoria. The cat didn't come before dark, and shortly thereafter, the tracker picked us up in the Toyota Land Cruiser.

The second evening, a hyena circled the bait but was too timid to eat. He had neither scented nor seen us—he was more concerned about something deeper in the bush behind the bait, probably the leopard.

The third afternoon, we crawled into the blind, made ourselves comfortable in the aluminum lawn chairs, and both Richards and I almost immediately started to doze. Cheri stayed awake and elbowed us each time we snored. Once she elbowed me in the chest so solidly I choked. It was almost dark, and Richards and I were both fighting to stay awake when I fully came out of sleep to Cheri grasping my arm. She sat in the middle and held Richards's arm, too. He battled to wake up. Her expression said it was out there. I looked through the riflescope to see something pale standing next to the dark topi carcass, and, when my eyes adjusted, I made out the shape of the cat, its forearms grasping the carcass and tearing with those formidable jaws. The cross hairs settled nicely behind the *chui's* shoulder. Just then he twisted toward me, and the .375's bullet smashed low in the chest, angling up to clip the spine on exiting. The leopard crumpled on the spot. In the gloaming, Richards shined the torch on the cat, and I watched through the scope with my finger on the trigger and the safety off in case the tom twitched. We watched the green

THE DANGEROUS GAME

fire die out of the cat's eyes as the evening's full darkness dropped like a weight, and suddenly everyone was slapping me on the back and laughing. We climbed out of the blind and saw the carmine glow of the already set sun just as the Toyota drove up.

The trackers and government game scout festooned the Cruiser with the green boughs we'd used for the blind, and we drove off down the *vlei*, honking and hooting and as happy as it is possible to be. That memory is one of the many reasons I prefer the traditional method of hunting leopards.

Professional hunters of my acquaintance carry more scars from close encounters with wounded *chui* than from all other dangerous game combined. The reason is simple: A wounded leopard never gives itself away with a warning growl, as will a lion. Instead, it will wait until it's sure of getting you before launching an attack that's so quick and at such close range the human eye might not register it. And it will *always* charge if it's the least bit able. The late professional hunter John A. Hunter believed the leopard to be Africa's most dangerous animal and preferred many times over to follow a wounded buff or elephant rather than a leopard. True, your chances of getting killed by a leopard are slim when compared to a lion or buff, but a leopard can rearrange great portions of your anatomy—most often your face, throat, or scalp—in the time it takes to snap your fingers. No animal is more courageous. A leopard will drag itself toward you with a broken spine, and it'll charge and leap at a lorry with a foreleg shot away. If a leopard is wounded in such a way that does not hamper its movement, say a gut-shot or muscle wound, it'll come so fast you may only be aware of a slight blur.

Professional hunter Russell Tarr had a German client who wounded a leopard that eventually escaped into the rocks of a big kopje in southern Zimbabwe. Tarr, PH Pierre Joubert, and one tracker followed the tiny black stars of blood down the kopje and toward a cave opening. The cat rushed from the cave before anyone could bring his gun up, grazed Tarr's chest, and hit Joubert. Both the leopard and Joubert plunged off the ledge and onto the rocks below, and Joubert broke both ankles seriously. By the time Tarr and the clients got Joubert to the hospital just across the border in Messina in the R.S.A. hours later, Joubert was lapsing in and out of consciousness from blood loss. (See the detailed story of this incident in my book *Safari: A Dangerous Affair*, Safari Press Inc., 2000.)

Tarr hired Peter Brookman and his hounds to follow up the injured *ngwe*. "No-theeng to it," Brookman said later in his heavy Afrikaans accent. "Just pull ze trigger undt choot." He killed the cat with a load of buckshot at three feet.

Professional hunters John Wambach and Japie Schoeman partnered with father-son clients in the R.S.A.. Japie's client, Mauro Rossi, wounded a big leopard just before dark. Japie requested Wambach's help, and they both followed the blood spoor into ever-thickening bush in the night until they both got a sudden "prickly sensation." They backed out and returned to camp.

They returned in the dawn to sort out the spoor. They saw from the tracks that the wounded cat had waited less than ten yards from where they had stopped and backed away. From the blood in the sand, they saw that the tom had been wounded through the wrist and would have been little hampered had it attacked. That it *would* have attacked, both Wambach and Japie were sure; it was obvious the cat had been waiting the night before to try.

To make a long story shorter, they trailed the cat all day, used up two packs of dogs—of which the leopard killed two—and survived an ambush and then another charge at close quarters. In the end, they both crawled into a grassy "cave," formed when rains had swept dead vegetation over the trunk of a dead thorn tree spanning a wash. The cat charged when both PHs crawled into the temporary hideout, and they both fired their shotguns simultaneously. When the dust and cordite settled, the cat was down, and they backed out to congratulate themselves and let the client know all was well.

Wambach crawled back in to pull out the dead leopard when, just as he was about the grasp the tom, he got nervous. He yanked his .44 Magnum revolver free and pushed it ahead. The leopard stood suddenly, and Wambach thumbed the hammer, pulling off at a very literal point-blank range, fortunately, this time, for keeps. That leopard truly did have nine lives. Wambach and Japie were both pleased at their luck. They both knew they should have been mauled at least twice.

THE DANGEROUS GAME

"Perhaps we should visit the casino," Wambach joked, when he'd skidded the big leopard into the open.

While I do not consider my spectacular leopard trophies my most valuable big-game mounts—a 228-point Marco Polo sheep, a 10-foot polar bear and a 40-inch snow sheep take those honors—I do consider the leopard the most beautiful, courageous, and, generally, admirable animal on the planet. He's a loner, afraid of little or nothing, and smart enough to leave man alone unless he's pushed too far. The black-rosetted, golden coat is simply so stunning that it takes your breath away, especially as he profiles on a thorntree branch in the last rays of the sun. He is only slightly less stunning in the trophy room. Each time I gaze at either the rugs or the full mounts, I consider myself fortunate, indeed, that those leopards collapsed on the spot and that I did not have to follow them into thick bush.

Postscript: The following are but a few articles on leopard attacks I've come across in various published sources; I have deleted some superfluous portions but have otherwise not changed the accounts in any manner.

Leopard Attack Four Men in Broad Daylight in KwaZulu, Natal, South Africa

A Zulu man was walking his dog outside the Mkuze Game Reserve, near the Unbombo Mountains, in KwaZulu, Natal and heard what he thought was a goat making a noise in the bush. He sent in his dog to investigate and was attacked by a huge male leopard.

. . . The local Zulu men formed a classic Zulu hunting party, which included a policeman armed with an R-5 rifle and with spears, knives, guns and whatever weapons they could find, they hunted, located and they ran the leopard down and surrounded him.

. . . In the melee, three more Zulus were attacked and bitten, and five shots were fired from a 9mm pistol and the leopard was destroyed. The injured men are expected to survive and recover, except for the one who lost his eye. (www.vivamos.com/bhn/tink.nsf, 9/9/99)

Enraged African Leopard Mauls Six People
Hand-To-Hand Fight To The Death With Enraged Crazed Leopard That Claws Out His Victim's Eyes!

... Santos got off his bike and was pushing it through the water with his brother when from out of nowhere a large Adult Male African leopard attacked him and grabbed him by the neck.

The leopard started killing Santos and had him down on the ground and Reason was unarmed, so he picked up some stone from the creek bed and attacked the leopard with the rocks and stones, smashing them against the cat's head.

At once, the killer cat attacked him, leaving the brother dying of blood loss and bit Reason through the left thigh, and started dragging and carrying Reason away into the thick bush to finish him off. Reason beat on the predator with fists to no avail and he knew he would die when the cat returned to the business at hand.

"It kept trying to get me by the throat and neck, so I screamed to my brother to get a small knife from my bag," said Reason.

Santos . . . managed to stab the leopard in the hindquarter, but was too injured to fight when the cat jumped on him again.

"I grabbed whatever I could find and threw stones, sticks and even sand at the thing, while screaming as loudly as possible," said Reason.

"I don't know why, but it turned and ran off into the bush." Reason stopped the bleeding of his brother . . .

. . . 49 year old Tinos M'Kansi drove by the scene of the attack minutes later, his small pickup truck loaded with eight local villagers in the back. . . .

That's when the fur hit the fan.

THE DANGEROUS GAME

... "The bloody (covered with human blood) animal leapt onto my windscreen (windshield) as I came to a halt in the road. It then jumped into the back of the bakkie right in the middle of the passengers" said Tinos.

The wounded spotted cat mauled Lawrence Sihlangu and then turned to attack the other terrified and howling passengers who started to flee the truck. Sihlangu was mauled seriously as he fought off the huge cat with his bare hands.

... "I cold not find any weapon except the screwdriver, so I used it to stab the leopard from behind" said M'Kansi. "I had to stab it repeatedly in the neck and ribs before it collapsed and died."

... Lawrence's face was badly mauled and he lost both of his eyes and is now blind.

The spotted killer cat mauled a total of 6 men. (www.vivamos.com/bhn/tink.nsf, 12/9/98)

Here's another report:

The [leopard] attack was only 6 miles from the edge of Kruger Park where . . . male leopard attacked, killed and ate an armed Kruger Park Game ranger, Charles Swart in front of 11 people on August, 1998.

And here's one more:

"I once knew an experienced leopard trapper who killed leopards that were cattle killers for the government who found a female leopard with her foot caught in a steel trap attached to a steel chain to a 200# log as a drag. In the . . . hunt, the leopard killed his armed tracker, who was an armed South African Police Officer and attacked and killed 2 of the 5 dogs, mauled 2 members of the hunting party and escaped from the trap and was never seen again!" (These last two are both from www.vivamos.com/bhn/tink.nsf)

BOOK II

ASIA

FIVE EMPTY CHAMBERS

Sheep hunting has inherent dangers: cliffs, avalanches, twisted ankles, and cardiac or pulmonary edema from altitude. Food is typically Spartan, and you might drink bad water from a mountain bog because you're too thirsty to wait until you get back to camp. If you aren't in condition, you may well have a heart attack.

I'm a sheep-hunting fanatic. I love the giddy heights and the treacherous scree slopes where a misstep might mean a broken ankle. Altitude sickness doesn't frighten me. I don't mind the Spartan food, and, in Russia, Spartan means *very* Spartan. I'll chance beaver fever, or worse, from imbibing from mountain rivulets.

What really scares me, though, are the Russian helicopters. I've yet to ride in one that looked well-maintained. Most are exhaust-blackened from the turbo exhaust pipes aft, and that's half the length. Most have bad tires—everything from the cords showing through what little is left of the rubber to being completely flat. One had bullet holes through the rotor blades. "Afghanistan," the translator said by way of explanation. Afghan liberation forces had shot at the bird on its retreat to Tajikistan, a story that did not reassure me in the least. Still, we took off and had a good sheep hunt in spite of the bullet holes.

On a hunt that took place on the Kamchatka Peninsula, the 'copter took off into the wind on a beach bordering the Bering Sea. The bird was badly overloaded, and as we swung out over the breakers of the sea it began losing power and altitude until we were only feet above the nearly frigid waves. It finally found some strength. I never did find out what the problem was, but apparently it didn't worry the fatalistic flight crew because we ratcheted over steaming fumaroles and smoking volcanoes and jagged glacier valleys until we finally made it to the city of Petropavlovsk two hours later.

FIVE EMPTY CHAMBERS

A hunt out of Nelkan, in north-central Khabarovsk Krai, proved successful when I finally killed two good rams, after six days without seeing a single ram. I felt very pleased with myself and was in a magnanimous mood, so I thought we might try to get back to the city of Khabarovsk so Cheri could shop, something I detest. The guides radioed Sergei, the outfitter, in the bush-village of Nelkan, and arranged for a helicopter pickup flight the next day. It didn't happen because the weather was bad. They tried the following day, but this time the downdrafts literally forced the 'copter down in the next valley. We heard them finally get off again and scramble back to the village. They got to us the next day.

Riding in a helicopter means riding in "unsupported flight," unlike an airplane, which is supported flight, because the wings create lift. Riding in a 'copter feels completely different from taking a flight in a plane, and I am never at home in one. I am even more worried in air turbulence, which always seems to exist when flying in sheep country.

On one sheep hunt a hundred fifty miles west of the coastal town of Okhotsk, on the Sea of Okhotsk in northern Khabarovsk Krai, we flew to the camp in very rough air. Olga Parfenova, the hunt manager and translator for Spartak Company (she speaks better English than most of my university students), looked decidedly green. The immense, yellow, begrimed turbo-copter wailed and screamed and vibrated as it ascended and descended suddenly in the down- and updrafts. We had to shout to make ourselves heard, and we had to hang onto the seat to keep from getting thrown about the cabin. I vowed never to ride in a helicopter again, a vow I unfortunately broke.

The spot where we were to have camped was impossible to reach because of the winds. The flight crew finally put the helicopter down on a volcanic plateau two miles away, just barely clearing the ridge when it flew back toward Okhotsk. We went in style on this hunt because it was the first hunt Yuri Chernyschevich, the outfitter, had conducted commercially in many years. (He had not paid the authorities the trophy fees and other charges five years earlier.) Our party included a real professional cook, two guides, Olga the translator, and a second

THE DANGEROUS GAME

translator and gofer, along with Pete Spear, a college buddy of mine and fellow hunt fanatic, Cheri, and me. We had more food than I was used to on any Russian hunt; in the past, the guides cooked, and did it terribly. (The next year we got a hooker to work as the cook, and she was even worse than the worst of Russian guides.)

After six days of hunting, I finally stalked to within thirty yards of a band of bedded rams and collected a heavy-based forty-incher. Even though we had spotted rams every day, Pete unfortunately didn't kill a sheep.

We waited for the 'copter to retrieve us. First, the pilot radioed that the weather was bad, though it was sunny in camp. Then Okhotsk was fogged in. Then another excuse. By that time, I'd hunted in Russia enough to know about the wheel within a wheel and to intuit that something else was afloat. Finally, the helicopter pitched into the camp and in the worst weather we'd had since we'd got there. We loaded up and took off, flying low into the river valley and along the twisting Ulya River. At some point, we landed on a big gravel-and-sand bar ten feet above the water, where Pete, Yuri, the second translator, the guide Vladimir, and the cook got off with a mountain of duffel to float-hunt for brown bears.

The helicopter lifted off again, and we hammered down the river valley. The scud tangling the peaks began to drop until we flew through it, the cliffs on either side only meters from the giant rotor blades. We did this more than once, too, and it was only blind luck we survived.

Occasionally, the mists dropped to river level, and we flew through the fog and towering cliff passes and somehow made it. I was more happy to step out onto the Okhotsk mud than I was when I had shot the big ram.

On a different hunt but one also based out of Okhotsk, we 'coptered north along the coast to search out spring brown bear. The 'copter danced and screeched and struggled into the strong north wind. The wind was so violent that we couldn't get all the way to our destination and had to put down and offload miles short of the place where we'd planned to hunt. The flight crew was worried about having enough fuel to make it back to the

FIVE EMPTY CHAMBERS

village, but with typical Russian fatalism, they took off with a grin and a shot of vodka. They made it, largely because the headwind became a tailwind on the way back.

I've hunted sheep since then, including the famed Marco Polo argali in the highest sheep country in the world where fatal altitude sickness, known as edema, is a real possibility. (One outfitter told me that three of the thirty clients he had taken out for *poli* the season before had died of altitude sickness—that's 10 percent!) It is also the coldest sheep country on the planet (minus-thirty-five degrees, with winds of fifty-plus knots in December). I've hunted mid-Asian ibex and all North American sheep, and I was always extremely relieved that I didn't have to ride in one of the behemoth Russian helicopters.

Instead of the hammer-and-sickle Soviet insignia still adorning most of the helicopters, they should stencil a skull and crossbones. I'd like to believe that I am through riding those 'copters and through hunting in eastern Siberia. For me, the averages say to quit. Riding in the big, ugly, Russian helicopters into the backcountry is a form of Russian roulette, and I've already heard the hammer click on five empty chambers. Do anything dangerous for too long, and the law of averages is bound to catch up to you.

IN SEARCH OF MARCO POLO

Author's preface: I originally wrote this story to publish in a nonhunting adventure magazine, in the defense of hunting as a legitimate adventurous pursuit. I think that defense here is subtle, takes up little enough space, and is different enough so that hunters won't yawn. I know we've all heard enough of these types of essays to grow sick of them, but this approach is, I think, unique. Besides, the story is concerned with the quest for the greatest game animal on the planet, the Marco Polo argali, which I hunted in the unique country of Tajikistan in central Asia, a very third-world area.

"How," they ask, "can you, a compassionate man, a reasonable man, a university professor, do this thing, this killing?"

I look at their eyes. If they are baiting or challenging, I am to the point. "The only difference between us," I say, "is I do my own killing." I gesture at their belts and their leather shoes. "The difference," I say again, "is I'm not the hypocrite." If they are still sanctimonious, I point to their paunches that have likely digested too many black Angus tenderloins.

If they are friends or colleagues, they accept this thing because they accept me on other levels and terms. They are truly struggling to understand. If they are sincere, I make the point about the leather shoes—after all, nothing lives after conversion to shoe leather. Perhaps I mention the turkey clubs they bolted at their two-highball lunches. I say we are involved at all levels—physically, of course, but spiritually beyond mere religiosity; mentally in the manner of a tough chess match; and emotionally in a goulash of soaring anticipation, plummeting disappointment, lust, and sorrow. Yes, sorrow, and often it is intense; I have seen combat vets who watched comrades die in battle weep at the death of their quarry. But there is no question they will hunt again. Too, it's an excuse to escape from the freeways and from computer screen trivialities to a place where we see fully our niche on the planet.

At this point, slipping into the old clichés, trying again to give substance to the intangible, I feel the same foolishness. "These are all very fine thoughts," I say ironically, "but I do it because I must. If my passion is politically incorrect, so be it." I understand again Mallory's retort to the question of why he climbed Everest: "Because it is there." What he really was saying was that if you have to ask, you cannot understand the compulsion. At this point, I refer them to Kipling (after all, any man who quotes poetry in the twenty-first century must be sensitive): "I have sworn an oath to keep it, on the Horns of Ovis Poli, *For the Red Gods call me out, and I must go.*"

* * * * *

Westerners first heard of the great, central Asian sheep of the high Pamirs from Marco Polo. This immense wild sheep, with horns that could measure six feet around the curl, became a myth of the exotic and a symbol of Polo's exaggeration. "It's a Marco Polo!" were the shouts of the crowd soon after the publication of Polo's *The Description of the World*, their jeers aimed at the buffoon on the stage whose sole purpose was to entertain through rough exaggeration. Thirteenth-century schoolboys used the same phrase to describe a falsehood. Marco Polo sheep remained in a mythological netherworld of unicorns and rocs until Lieutenant John Wood killed one six centuries later. Still, naysayers were convinced it was a hoax.

The great sheep of high central Asia is still almost mythological, first because of its size but also because it ranges the most remote part of the most enigmatic continent on Earth. Most zoologists have never heard of this great, wild argali sheep, *Ovis ammon poli*. To the devout, it's a quarry too wonderful to contemplate. It's a high school buddy's big sister, the state lottery, Nirvana. It could never happen to a mere mortal.

And so it was with me. I heard of the mythological beast first from the late outdoor writer Jack O'Connor, who wrote of

THE DANGEROUS GAME

several 1950s and '60s millionaires who had lubricated enough fists to hunt on the northern frontiers of Afghanistan or Pakistan. Then I read Roosevelt's *East of the Sun and West of the Moon*. In 1925, Teddy and his son Kermit justified collecting the family group in the then-Soviet (Tajik) Pamirs, in the name of science, for Chicago's Field Museum of Natural History. These fabled sheep did exist after all. As a starry-eyed college freshman, I made the pilgrimage at great financial sacrifice to worship at the shrine of *Ovis ammon poli*. The rams, ewes, and lambs in their dusty diorama didn't match my Technicolor vision of burnished glaciers beneath twenty-thousand-foot peaks, but the myth became tangible.

Glasnost made the tangible seem possible. Then the resulting ethnic warfare in Tajikistan didn't. Neighboring Kyrgyzstan was in less political turmoil, but the biggest sheep weren't in Kyrgyzstan. They ranged the Tajik Pamirs, where Teddy killed his group, and into eastern China, with populations in northern Pakistan and Afghanistan. But either the U.S. Fish & Wildlife Service wasn't allowing importation until more information on population sizes and management practices became available, or ethnic war made it too dangerous.

The best chance in the 1990s for collecting a Marco Polo sheep was in Kyrgyzstan. The first Kyrgyz sheep making it to the West scarcely taped four feet. But I'd seen a photo of a pickup ram from Tajikistan measuring six. Better to keep the dream, I reasoned, than shoot a smaller Kyrgyz sheep and ruin it. Why settle for a Camry when there was a chance, however remote, at a Carrera? It seemed as ethereal as ever, a fantasy as unattainable as those in my fifteen-year-old brain of my pal's seventeen-year-old cheerleader sister.

When ethnic war subsided in Tajikistan, in 1997, the USFWS decided that sheep populations were sufficient, and photos of the first rams showed up here and there. The Trophy Connection arranged the first trips. Still, the first rams were scarcely larger than their Kyrgyz counterparts. It took time, but the odd photos of Tajik rams became larger, with one or two reaching the West with curls of fifty-seven inches. Then a sixty-incher. Now, a sixty-inch Marco Polo ram is the hunter's equivalent of a grand-slam homer in the last game of the World Series. It's the top-end Porsche, with Catherine Zeta-Jones as copilot. It's too wonderful to believe it could happen to you.

I began the inquisition. Yuri Matison was rumored to be the outfitter who collected the biggest *polis*. I questioned hunt brokers in the U.S., and it took more time for Matison's and my schedules to jibe. When they did, the fantasy seemed almost tangible. *Almost* . . . because inside I was certain this was still too wonderful to happen. Something had to go wrong.

It did. The State Department issued travel advisories for Tajikistan: Armed Islamic fundamentalists out of Uzbekistan and Afghanistan were making things hot for the Russian-backed Tajik army. Four U.N. workers had been murdered. American climbers were kidnapped in Kyrgyzstan. The travel agency misbooked our flights. Then, Dad died peacefully of a heart attack. Six weeks later, Mom joined Dad, ten days before we were scheduled to leave. When my brain cleared enough to think coherently a week later, I realized our Russian double-entry travel visas hadn't arrived; they didn't come until the night before we were to depart. After the complications and tragedies, I was surprised when the jetliner lifted off from Salt Lake International. How, I wondered, could it become airborne with my heart so heavy?

Finally, my body broke free, and in a dream—mixed up with a gargantuan Marco Polo ram—on the Delta nonstop from New York to Moscow, Mom lectured me: "Life goes on," she said. Dad stood behind her in a nineteenth-century-style portrait pose, smiling in agreement. They were right, of course.

My heart eased as the sky lightened over Finland. Eventually, I realized, grief ends. To live *is* to grieve. Death is part of life, and it happens to all families and to everyone. Hunters should know this better than anyone.

Things improved. Another Yuri met us at the Moscow airport, whisked us through customs and the paperwork of bringing a rifle into the country, purchased our tickets to Bishkek, then Osh, Kyrgyzstan, hurried us to the Tajikistan Embassy for visas, and then out on the town before we caught our flight to central Asia. We visited Red Square, and though I loathe tourist attractions, Cheri photographed with glee. In spite of the dismal Moscow December

THE DANGEROUS GAME

gloom and filthy snow (why did Hitler and Napoleon want the place?), my heart was buoyant. When we boarded the Aeroflot flight to Bishkek, I wondered if all pilgrims felt so ebullient.

In Bishkek, five hours later, we were escorted out of the debarking crowd and into the glowing VIP lounge by Matison's people. They handled customs and firearms formalities, while we dined and dozed until the next flight to Osh, the expedition's starting point.

When we stepped off the Kyrgyzstan Air Yak 40, former Soviet Officer Boris Popov, another of Matison's vast retinue, grabbed our gear, and he and Sulli, our Kyrgyz driver for the remainder of the expedition, loaded it onto a Russian four-wheel-drive van. One step closer to Mecca.

Sulli drove intelligently through the heavy foot, horse, and truck traffic of downtown Osh, and then up a broad valley and along rushing streams like Montana trout water, then through naked apricot and pistachio orchards older than Christianity, and eventually up the never-ending Kyzyl-Art Pass of ice and snow that didn't top out until fourteen thousand feet. We entered the Tajikistan Pamirs, glowing in the low sun like Hemingway's Kilimanjaro. We were intensely alive.

Mid-December in the Pamirs is frigid enough that the entire inside of the van was rimed with ice in spite of the heater grinding at full bore. Cheri and I pulled on down sleeping bags. In Tajikistan, the term "highway" is a euphemism. The Pamir Highway (Highway M41) hasn't been repaired since the Soviets pulled out of Afghanistan. It's one lane, bucked heartily by frost heaves, cratered in places deep enough to lose a small yak, paved only infrequently, and plowed not at all in winter. You would pay serious money for the ride in an American amusement park, and it would put to shame the "extreme thrill" rides found there today. You would not find overturned trucks and bloodied, frozen bodies on the ice in an amusement park.

In spite of the sudden launchings and crash landings of the tough Russian van, and regardless of finding ourselves hurtled to the floor or heaped into the gear, we fell asleep. It helped to have had no sleep in three previous days of travel. Cheri and I awoke only long enough to climb back onto the seat or whenever one of the tattered CIS guards at one of the roadblocks climbed in to shake the hands of the first Americans he'd seen, his ancient Kalashnikov pointed carelessly at our chests. At each roadblock, Boris or Sulli bribed our way through with the vodka and fruit we'd brought for such purposes. You had to understand the routine to make it through. The tattered guards survived by institutionalized extortion, and neither side resented the other. It was all very good-natured.

Somewhere late in a High-Pamir night, we clattered to the thirteen thousand-foot base camp. I had only felt cold like this once before, when traveling by dogsled in full winter on the polar ice pack. Thirty-five below is only a reading on a thermometer or words on a page; it has to be felt to be believed, especially when you are not dressed for it.

Cheri was ill during the night, a result, probably, of the lukewarm eggs in the Bishkek VIP lounge, or one of the vendor stops on the way out of Osh. Except for hurried forays to the loo, she slept the next day. No matter, the first day is used to begin to acclimate to the altitude, anyway.

Layered in extreme-weather gear, we were up and out into the frozen dawn and into the icy 4x4s, jolting along yak trails and across frozen marshes and up broad, bare glacier valleys. Later, we left the yak trails behind and climbed the pathless and steep talus slope onto a wind-blasted pass two thousand feet higher. We climbed from 4x4s, frosted inside and out, into the arid, cutting cold.

The hunt party consisted of Yuri Matison, the outfitter; Dovelat (a Dushanbe Tajik) and Taktamat (a Pamiri Tajik), the guides; and Cheri and me. We labored up the ridge for a mile, and another, until we crested a pass and stared into the broad, U-shape glacial valley beyond. And we gazed into Valhalla. To the devout, the true believer, this was Mecca, the Happy Hunting Grounds. No place could be more sacred.

Six hundred Marco Polo sheep grazed and rutted within a mile. I had never expected this, not in my wildest fantasies. Nothing Polo or Roosevelt or anyone else ever wrote even remotely prepared me for the spectacle. A sun too gory to be earthly climbed above the icy-blue Chinese Pamirs and bled over the ridges into the valleys. The scene glowed in air too clear and colors too vivid to come from this world. I'd never seen snow so white. Possibly it was the altitude, but for a moment, I wondered if I had died and gone to Nirvana.

I heard a distant voice through the ether, then archangel Taktamat led me to the spotting scope. Yuri had it trained on a ram a mile below. Until that day, I'd never seen a live Marco Polo sheep. The horns dropped well below the jaw line, pinched into the cheek, flared out, and then curved back downward for ten inches. The Red Gods spoke. I wanted the ram more than I had wanted the high school cheerleader.

"How big?" I asked Yuri. It seemed the thing to ask. Yuri had been outfitting and guiding since Glasnost, his clients were nearly 100 percent successful, and together they'd collected the top heads in anyone's record book, including the world record, a 68-inch behemoth, arguably the top big-game head on the planet. If I could trust anyone's judgment, it was his.

"Fifty-eight," he replied, "perhaps fifty-nine." Yuri is a man of few words.

Previously I'd made up my mind not to shoot anything under fifty-five inches around the curl, even if I went home without a ram. I'd studied photos of such rams, and they were plenty good enough for me; anything larger was too good to hope for.

Across the valley, another mastodon of a ram chased a smaller ram away from a ewe he was tending as she approached estrus. Smaller rams drifted in and out of ewe herds, searching urgently for breeding opportunities. On the cliffs above, bands of sheep stood or lay in the sun, watching us below. Fantasies prepare the holder for the letdown of reality. This was the reverse—the fantasy didn't live up to the reality.

In much of the Pamirs, shots are, by necessity, long-range affairs. No stalking cover taller than six-inch grass exists. The mountains are vast and rounded and the valleys broad and U-shape from glaciation, making stalking to close range tough. Matison is often faced with another problem that makes long-range shooting inevitable: Most of his clients are overweight financiers and physicians from sea-level cities who don't bat an eye at the thirty-five-thousand-dollar price tag but who cannot

Cheri with the big simba. *We had to trail him through the thick thornbush behind her. (Book I "The Fear and the Lion")*

This is the hippo bull on the bank. PH Mackie is on the left, and I am on the other side with Majara, the tracker. (Book I "Bulls in the Night") (Photo by Cheri Flory)

I'm aiming at the bull, the one second from the left and mostly submerged. At this angle, shoot between the ear and eye. (Book I "Bulls in the Night") (Photo by Cheri Flory)

A 56-inch kudu I collected toward the end of the safari. (Book I "Bulls in the Night")

*The guys with my 7'3"-*chui *taken over a topi bait along the Msima River in Tanzania. (Book I "Chui")*

These are the kind of Tanzanian buff few will pass up! (Book I "M'bogo")

This is the hairy lion we wanted; it really got the adrenaline pumping. (Book I "The Fear and the Lion")

The guys with my western Tanzania chui. (Book I "Chui")

Cheri and PH Willie Phillips with my first Botswana buff in the Okavango. (Book I "M'bogo")

Cheri and I mugging it up with our Zimbabwe trophies. (Book I "Chui")

The Masai trackers and a government game scout with another Tanzania buff. (Book I "M'bogo")

This jumbo resents our presence and is about to bluff charge. (Book I "Bulls in the Night")

Hunting by mokoro *in the Okavango is productive and very pleasant. (Book I "Hippo—The 'Accidental' Most Dangerous Game")*

Cheri at a remote Masai boma *on the Masai Steppe in central Tanzania. (Book I "M'bogo")*

Three elephants visit a Botswana pan for an evening drink. (Book I "Bulls in the Night")

This big bull is truly standing up in the tall and aptly named elephant grass in Tanzania. Try hunting them in this stuff! (Book I "Bulls in the Night")

Glassing distant sheep in the Pamirs. Left to right: Yuri Matison, Taktamat, and the author. (Book II "In Search of Marco Polo") (Photo by Cheri Flory)

Dragging the big ram to the valley floor. You can tell it's cold! (Book II "In Search of Marco Polo") (Photo by Cheri Flory)

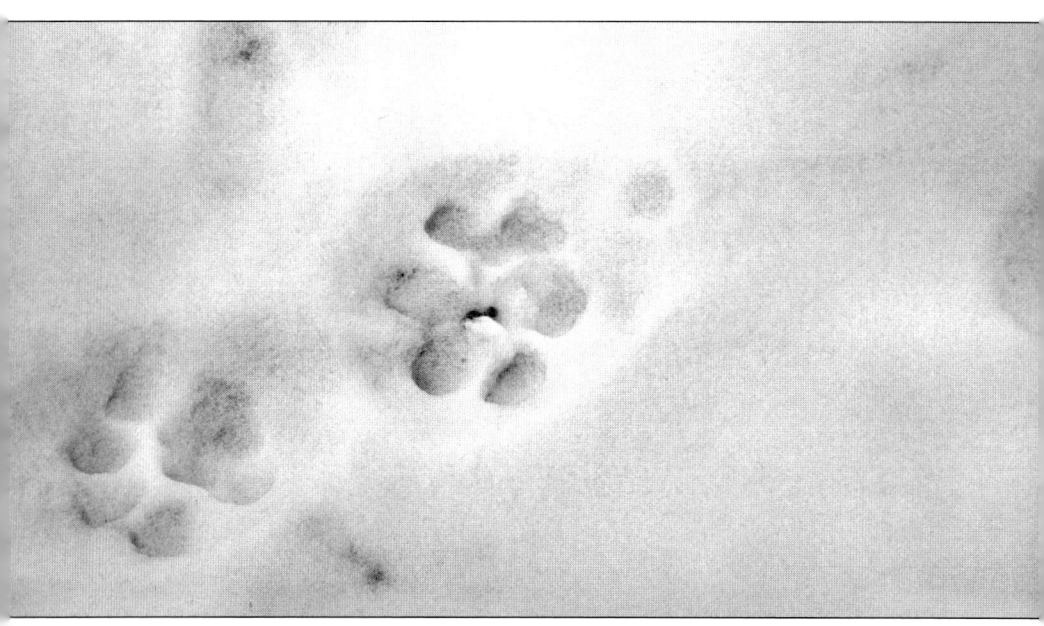

Snow leopard tracks in the Tajik Pamirs. We found them everywhere. (Book II "In Search of Marco Polo") (Photo by Cheri Flory)

My pal Taktamat, the Pamiri guide, and my nice mid-Asian ibex. (Book II "In Search of Marco Polo") (Photo by Cheri Flory)

My big, 62-inch Marco Polo ram back at base camp. Taktamat is on the right. (Book II "In Search of Marco Polo")

Cheri and a nicely furred Kamchatka fall brown bear. (Book II "Bad Luck Bear")

Here's another of those infamous Russian helicopters, with me trying to pretend I'm looking forward to the ride to the sheep camp. (Book II "Five Empty Chambers")

The stunning south Kamchatka Peninsula coast. (Book II "Bad Luck Bear")

We're glassing for snow sheep in the Dzug Dzur Mountains and enjoying the sun. (Book II "Five Empty Chambers")

This was our snow sheep camp in the Dzug Dzur Mountains of the Khabarovsk Territory. I collected two fine rams there. (Book II "Five Empty Chambers")

Guide "Cola" posing with his ancient rifle and my book The Hunting Adventures of Me & Joe *in the Dzug Dzur sheep camp. (Book II "Five Empty Chambers")*

Cheri on an alarming boat we dubbed the Siberian Queen, *near Sakhalin Island on the west coast of Khabarovsk and on the way to the Koppi River to hunt isubra stag. (Book II "The Hunt from Hell")*

Cheri on skirt ice along the cliffs bordering the Sea of Okhotsk. The next day the ice collapsed. (Book II "The Hunt from Hell")

walk more than a few yards in the extreme altitude without gasping for breath. Seven-figure incomes don't buy health. Any serious climbing is out of the question, and, as a result, five-hundred-plus-yard shots are common.

We glassed the sheep for an hour before Taktamat and I stalked the big ram and his harem. All of us wore white anoraks, but as soon as we crossed a slope blown bare of snow, we stood out to the sheep as if we'd worn neon. The ram and his harem cantered two miles down the valley and over a distant col.

Temporarily defeated, Yuri, Dovelat, and I hiked rapidly across a side slope in the direction of the sheep. We crossed a ridge, then another, and another. Cheri waited with Taktamat and watched the sheep below.

I live at six thousand feet above sea level. I run trails in good weather, snowshoe in winter, and slug a heavy bag, so I didn't expect altitude problems. As we sidehilled, hiking mostly on level lines with few inclines, I felt no shortness of breath. But then the serious climbing began, and, while I kept up with the guides, I gasped to do it. Hours later we rounded a knoll, and Yuri, in the lead, crouched suddenly. I slid off the pack and pushed it ahead, resting the rifle across it. The big *poli* stood broadside at a scant two hundred yards, as close as you could hope for. When the cross hairs settled nicely on the ram's shoulder, I pressed the trigger. But it was the squeeze from a nightmare. I pressed the trigger until my knuckle turned white. I pushed again at the safety, but it wouldn't budge. The ram trotted to the ridgeline while I fought with the .300 magnum's safety. It snapped free just as the ram silhouetted against the cobalt stratosphere and evaporated. I'd had a chance at the holiest of holies and blew it. Dovelat stalked away, shaking his head and clucking his tongue at my mere mortality.

We stumbled down the ridge feeling the altitude and the failed stalk. Cheri and Taktamat met us in the bottoms. Bands of *poli* on the slopes above raced into the valley bottom ahead, congregating into one huge host of argali sheep. Seven hundred Marco Polo sheep moiled momentarily and then in one mass raced up the opposite wall toward China. At least forty trophy rams flew above the snow in a mist of their own body heat. The sheep concentration explained the snow leopard tracks; we couldn't walk through the country without finding fresh cat prints.

I'd been convinced that I would not need acclimating to the altitude—after all, I'd been running for years at elevations to nine thousand feet without ill effects—and I tried that day to prove it. I'd kept up with the altitude-acclimated guides, though gasping in the rarified, intensely cold and dry air had freeze-burned my bronchi. By nightfall I'd developed a cough whenever I stepped out into the polar-cold air or exerted myself. A physician had warned me that high-altitude exertion could cause bronchitis and had prescribed a respiratory anti-inflammatory inhalant. Though the cough would last for months, the inhalant kept it from worsening.

Three hours before the next dawn, we bounced through a particularly rough glacial moraine, then over a high pass. By dawn, we had clattered into another trailless valley and watched goatlike ibex scaling the cliffs, and then we descended into yet another valley and through a herd of yaks.

Small herds of *poli*, all with at least one harem-master ram, raced off ahead of us. We debarked and climbed a steep shale slope toward a pass a thousand feet above. I took my time climbing, nursing the cough in the thin, frigid, and mummifying air. I was in no hurry and had little faith that Yuri could predict that the monster ram would come to this valley, miles away from where we'd spooked him the day before.

On the ridge, Cheri and I waited while the guides, by unspoken agreement, climbed farther, leaning twenty degrees into a fifty-knot blast. We all wore three layers of extreme-weather gear under saintly-white, windproof anoraks. The wind buffeted the anoraks like mainsails in a gale. While I reduced as much of my body to the force of the blasts as I could, I wondered how it had been when Genghis Khan's horde swarmed west in the thirteenth century, just below where I stood. Dovelat, the Dushanbe western Tajik guide, claimed direct descendency from Alexander the Great, and he was indistinguishable from the Balkans I'd met. Alexander and his men must have been remarkably prolific, if you could believe the Central Asian peoples. Dovelat bore absolutely no resemblance to Taktamat, the Mongolian-looking, sixty-two-year-old Pamiri guide. Taktamat was born and raised within a day's walk.

Snow plumed from the ground and into the wind, and visibility was limited to five yards. Wind ripping across the rocks literally howled like a live thing in agony. As I watched the snow sweep past in opaque sheets, Dovelat materialized out of the blizzard and gestured. At last, action.

Cheri and I followed Dovelat up the ridge in the blizzard. Farther along, Yuri and Taktamat huddled in a depression as the snow eddied and drifted around them. As we hunkered down half out of the blast, it occurred to me that I was hunting with the three high priests of Marco Polo sheep guides. Look at a photo of the top heads ever taken, and you will see either Yuri, Taktamat, or Dovelat. How could I be so blessed?

"Your ram is on the other side of the valley," Yuri said calmly in my ear over the winds now shrieking like the Mongol horde hurtling out of the Chinese Pamirs.

Yuri took the pack, Dovelat handed me the rifle, and I worked the bolt to feed a cartridge into the chamber, then checked the safety. Twice. Out into the blast again, we formed a single file, with me in the number two spot behind Yuri, followed by Dovelat, Cheri, and Taktamat. Yuri crouched as we neared the ridgeline, and everyone else did the same. We lay in the snow and watched the grazing sheep, tiny motes at five hundred yards. I thought again of Kipling: *Do you know the long day's patience, belly down on frozen drift, while the head of heads is feeding out of range?* When the blowing snow obscured the sheep, we crabbed rapidly across the frost-shattered shale. When the snow cleared, we stopped again. Eventually, we could go no farther without spooking the sheep, and a running shot at five hundred yards is too risky. No one wants a wounded animal.

"Be aware of wind," Yuri warned as he slid the pack forward for a rifle rest. Mostly, the wind raged at forty knots, but occasionally it quieted. Still, no one could guarantee it had quieted on the opposite slope of the valley. This would be the trickiest shot I'd ever attempted. At that range, I'd have to hold twenty inches above where I hoped the bullet would hit and compensate for the typhoonlike wind. The ram stood with his rump to the gale. I settled the cross hairs a foot above the hip and wondered

THE DANGEROUS GAME

if I was estimating right. I hoped the wind would drift the bullet three feet downwind and into the chest cavity.

When the plumes of wind-driven snow thinned, I slid the safety forward, said a prayer to the Red Gods, let my heart quiet and the cross hairs settle, and gently squeezed the trigger. The sheep burst into a run and plunged through a drifted nullah. I barked a Russian obscenity I'd picked up in a Russian bar. Then the ram slowed, and the other sheep passed him. He *was* hit. And he stopped. Through the riflescope, I calculated wind drift and bullet drop and touched the trigger again. The ram collapsed.

Someone shouted above the wind. Someone else slammed me on the back as I lay still watching through the riflescope, and someone squeezed my shoulder and shouted a very good thing in Tajik. Then strong hands yanked me to my feet and pounded my back and hugged me, and I felt again that best of sensations. This was reason enough to obey the Red Gods.

We plunged through the drifted snow and ground blizzard and into the bottoms, laboring up the opposite slope in the gale. As I wheezed to catch my breath at sixteen thousand feet, I knew the ram was everything I'd fantasized. More. It was the high school cheerleader, Catherine and the Porsche, the state lotto. To a hunter, nothing better could ever happen. I could never journey to a more sacred place.

No one minded thirty-below gales as we photographed then skidded the four hundred-pound ram down the steep, drifted slope. We shouted jokes above the wind. No matter they were in four languages; all hunters speak the same language.

Hours later, we'd skidded the ram to a place where we could drive the 4x4s. We horsed the vehicles down the valley, dug them out every forty yards when they floundered in a drift, and finally forced them to the valley floor. Then we banged through the moraines until we hit what was left of the ancient Silk Road as it disappeared in a vast washout. We ground in low gear through that, into another valley, and around scattered yak-dung-and-stone Pamiri huts. Men emerged. They finally waved, each armed with a Kalashnikov, just in case.

*****

IN SEARCH OF MARCO POLO

My heart wasn't really in the hunt for a mid-Asian ibex, a wild goat inhabiting the rougher and rockier part of the Pamirs. After the great *poli* ram, I was too content to care. It was still too wonderful to have happened. But before dawn we were out in the frigid 4x4s again, beyond the Karakol marshes, following the Red Gods and skidding up the overflow ice of a glacial river in the direction of twenty-five thousand-foot Communist Peak, where we pulled on anoraks and trekked up the ice.

Cheri stopped for another photo of the ubiquitous snow leopard tracks. The snow leopard is supposedly one of the most endangered predators on the planet, yet we'd seen fresh tracks everywhere we'd hunted. The Pamirs were snow leopard heaven, too. A rangy, reddish wolf trotted down the river ice, scented us, and loped off toward China. We weren't the only ones hunting ibex.

Three miles upriver we found three billy ibex through the glasses and stalked them. Before we could get as close as I wanted to, they scented us and bounded up the boulders.

"The second is best," Yuri said calmly. Dolat hissed, "Shoot!" then more urgently, "Shoot!"

I did not want another long shot. With the naked eye, I could barely see the ibex. I held high as they bounded the house-size boulders, cursed the distance, and pressed the trigger. I didn't have to worry about gales this time, and the Red Gods smiled. The ibex tumbled off the cliff and skidded to a stop in the scree.

I'd be lying if I said I felt the same level of elation as with the collection of the great Marco Polo ram, and I'd be lying if I said the guides did. Still, the rounded-fat, chocolate-brown ibex, with the knurled horns that curved back like heavy Arabian scimitars, was highly impressive. But a ten-carat emerald compares poorly with the Hope diamond. We did, all of us, feel the satisfaction of a long and successful stalk, a very long shot, and the collection of a rare and exceptional head. After the elation of the kill, after the tension of the stalk, after the sorrow and mulligan stew of emotions and camaraderie that come with success, that level of satisfaction is a deep breath after the strain of holding it too long. Feeling it, you understand all is right.

Andrei, the Estonian skinner, had thus far been invisible. But with the trophies, he came into his own. He began the ritual of steel and stone, then fleshed the hide and deftly removed the ungual bones from the foot as quickly as it takes me to think about it. He spent the next day immersed in the rites of skinning, fleshing, salting, and drying the hides of the ram and ibex.

Later, Boris, the retired Soviet officer, the briber at roadblocks, the secretary with papers to get trophies out of the country, the soon-to-be-arranger of celebrations, the cook for foreign hunters, and finally the raconteur, announced that the ram horns measured so many centimeters around the curl, which he translated to mean sixty-two inches. I do not like to measure trophies in camp; no need to spoil the experience. But I'd wondered. Now, I knew. This was better than decades of fantasies. The extra inches were an unexpected windfall. I would not have been less happy if the ram only measured the fifty-eight inches we'd assumed. Too many hunters place too much emphasis on an inch or three of horn, making hunting a competition with other men. Still, a "Top Ten" head was a thing to consider.

The next day, Cheri and I hiked the mountains around base camp and above the lake. When we topped out, we saw the thickly frozen lake stretching nearly to the Chinese border. Beyond the mountains to the southwest was the Afghan Hindu Kush, and just on the other side of the lake to the south was the ancient Silk Road. Within view, Marco Polo had explored, Teddy Roosevelt had hunted, and Genghis Khan and Temur Lang (Tamerlane) had marched, each with his own fantasy.

* * * * *

I could rationalize as I stared out over the frozen blue lake and history that my thirteen thousand dollars in trophy fees would finance Marco Polo sheep and ibex conservation projects. I could also rationalize that the considerable sum I'd spent would stay in one of the poorest, most backward countries on the globe and that the willingness of hunters to spend that kind of money made the sheep and ibex here worth government protection from Tajik yak herders armed, now, with neo-revolution Kalashnikovs that could wipe out a herd of *poli* with the bursts of two clips. I could, but I won't. If you still have to ask, then you can't understand. I obey the Red Gods because I must.

EPILOGUE

We made the trip out in a raging blizzard a few days later. Sulli drove well but took too many chances in his rush. We saw double the accidents as coming in, though fewer were on the road in the storm. Considering the few driving and the number that crashed in nullahs, I calculated we had a fifty-fifty chance of making it. I was thankful to debark in the relative civilization of Osh, thirteen hours later.

The ram scored nearly 228 points, for whatever that is worth.

BAD LUCK BEAR

A Tepecano Indian guide down in Old Mexico once told me that the world was full of omens if we just knew what to look for. For instance, he said, if a raven circled your house twice, there'd be a death in the family. When a magpie crashed through the kitchen window and broke its neck that June, I didn't think of the incident as an omen.

There were other portents that summer, but I never noticed them at the time. A neighbor's mare foaled a two-headed colt. Bishop Stone, at the age of ninety-six, had to be physically restrained from groping nurse Brooks. The spring rains lasted into July, and large fungi sprouted on the walls of the Mormon church. Whiskey Bill Stoker caught a twenty-two-pound pike with a kitten in its stomach. Afternoon clouds formed the letters G-O-P in the sky over Huntsville, and county Democrats accused Republicans of skywriting. Doc Petersen removed an eighteen-inch appendix from Mabel Callahan shaped like a coiled snake, a rattler. Possibly this all meant nothing; no one notices such things until afterward.

If I failed to place proper relevance on the omens that were all about, I should have relied on the doubt that gnawed at me when the booking agent and outfitter misbooked our flights to the Russian Far East. Twice. But I'd been impressed with the glitzy, red brochure with gold letters, the photos of Marco Polo sheep, ibex, and stag on its pages, and the owner who talked the talk in military precision. I was equally impressed by office addresses both in the East and in Germany.

Then the booking agent postponed the hunt for some reason he could never decide on. My anxiety increased as the hunt drew near. Suspicion became conviction. A flying squirrel got into the storage room and electrocuted itself in the innards of the freezer, and I didn't notice the spoiled food for a week.

BAD LUCK BEAR

When we arrived in Khabarovsk in the Russian Far East, on Alaska Airlines, my baggage, including the rifle, had stayed in Anchorage. Alaska Airlines couldn't locate it, either. Then the visa the stateside agent had procured didn't include a stop on Kamchatka, our actual hunting destination. It took days and thousands of rubles to straighten that one out. On the flight across the Sea of Okhotsk to the Kamchatka Peninsula, I got airsick for the first time in hundreds of flights around the globe; the odorous wolfhound on the next seat might have had something to do with it. Once on Kamchatka, the customs official gave my passport to the wrong passenger, who was just disappearing into the crowd. I ran him down.

Then, in spite of a contract with the stateside agent saying we could hunt in Tigil, a destination noted for the largest brown bears, we found we couldn't hunt within five hundred miles of the place. The stateside agent's representative said it was fogged in, the hunting cooperative was on strike, the bears had a disease, and then, finally, the guides had quit because the stateside agent hadn't paid them. When the subcontracting outfitter, Valeri, put us up in a country hotel, we found it barricaded with armed guards to keep out the local mafia.

If only we paid attention to omens and portents. Our worlds would orbit smoothly. We would undertake important events only when the omens said the time was right. When they were bad, we'd stay home.

Leaves had begun to drop in the early autumn, and the air had a chill to it. Subtly, things changed. A yellow rose sprouted from an apparently dead twig. In the morning, the rumbling, spewing volcano about Petropavlovsk-Kamchatsky quieted, and the smoke drifted out to sea. Cheri found a tiny pearl in a steamed clam. But we didn't attach importance to those things at the time.

Valeri had rented clothes for us and a Russian "Tiger" assault rifle for me to shoot bear. We climbed aboard an immense and decrepit ex-military helicopter and drummed down valleys beneath smoking volcanoes, over steaming fumaroles, and above salmon streams choked with fish. We flew out over the craggy North Pacific coast, and an hour later we swung into a broad estuary. As we hovered to land, a brown bear broke from the alder cover and sprinted down the beach.

THE DANGEROUS GAME

Anatoli Ratushny, a bear of a man with a broad, gold-filled grin and the profile of a Roman bust, hugged me with apparent and genuine warmth. We greeted Ivan, the cook; Rashiid, our second guide; and Andrei Konovalov, the interpreter. Everyone was happy to see us, in spite of the fact that no one had notified the outfitter we were coming until the day before.

The scenery staggered our senses. Down the beach, the North Pacific crashed against towering, jagged cliffs. Upriver, immense volcanoes loomed on the horizon. Sea-run char rolled on the river's surface as they hurried upriver. The vegetation was thick and green, and sea birds circled and cried. Anatoli said something that, when translated, meant we were the first foreigners in his camp, and that this would bring luck.

In camp, a recently completed cedar cabin on the beach, we dined on smoked salmon, salmon caviar, shrimp, crab, home-brewed beer, and fresh vegetables and strawberries from the garden. I'd heard horror stories about Russian food, most of them from that stateside booking agent, but this was the best fare I'd eaten in a hunting camp, anywhere. Finally, things were looking up. The Russians, exceptionally friendly and curious about Americans, kept Andrei the interpreter and me busy with questions.

That night, heavy clouds rolled in from the sea and the rain started. Sheets of rain and sleet pelted the windows the next morning. The bad luck had returned. I must have looked glum when we sat down to our salmon steak and Russian champagne breakfast, because Anatoli said something like, "Not to vorry. Ve choot bearz in rain!" With Anatoli's cheery disposition, my gloom soon evaporated.

We motorboated upriver in the deluge. The week before, bears had lined the river, capturing the last of the salmon run upriver. But the run had passed, and the bear had followed them up into feeder streams where the salmon spawned themselves out. We hiked immense, boggy tundra flats, searching for bears feeding on blueberries. We climbed hills and glassed for bears browsing on pine nuts. We motored along the seashore looking for beachcombing bears. We didn't see one bear in the downpour.

BAD LUCK BEAR

The next morning, the rain continued as steady and hard as ever. We didn't find bears on the berry flats. None on the pine nut slopes. Only old tracks on the river bars. Nothing along the ocean beaches. When Anatoli didn't know I was watching, I caught him frowning. Back at camp, I slipped in the mud. By that time, I'd begun to recognize the omens. I avoided looking into a cracked mirror in the sauna hut.

The next day, we motored farther upriver. We searched new and distant berry flats and found a herd of caribou. The clouds lifted late in the morning. We climbed onto pine scrub slopes and found where bears had stripped the scrub of cones days earlier. We flushed a flock of ptarmigan. We picked blueberries and ate pine nuts. The sun came out. Volcanoes upriver appeared as if by magic. But no bears.

Back at camp, I took special care stepping out of the boat in the mud. In the cabin, a floorboard cracked under my modest weight. I hurried into the dining room and tossed salt over my shoulder.

Days passed, and even Anatoli looked discouraged. He tried not to show it, but he wasn't smiling. Andrei confided that Anatoli had vowed to throw himself off the cliffs into the foaming breakers below if he didn't find us a bear. Anatoli knocked against the door jam three times whenever he left a room.

Day dawned clear and frosty. Anatoli had a new idea. Now that he'd found we could hike, he proposed backpacking into the higher country above the rivers and staying at an isolated government weather station. We agreed. After all, the hunting couldn't get worse.

We trekked along a slippery and narrow bear trail atop four hundred-foot cliffs. A misstep meant a plunge onto rock and breaking surf forty stories below. Cormorants, puffins, and half a dozen shorebird species whirled and screamed at us. The trail worked its way down a treacherous, steep slope to the beach. We trekked through kelp and saw fur seals that heaved themselves off the rocks and into the surf. No sky could be bluer. Then we climbed another bear trail along a waterfall and up into a lush valley thick with orange berries and scrub pines, both good bear feed. I slipped in fresh bear scat. It was bright orange with the berries the bear had eaten. Soon, bear scat lined the trail winding its way through brush so thick that visibility was limited to two feet. I shoved the clip into the assault rifle and flicked the lever to full-automatic. Rashiid jacked a round into the chamber of his bolt-action. We'd seen more bear sign in half a mile of trail than in the previous five days. Anatoli plucked a fern sprig and put it in his lapel for luck. We all felt the change.

Late in the afternoon we climbed the last slope to the weather station. A couple manned the station, and they immediately vacated the bedroom to Cheri and me, in spite of our protests. Their only contact with the outside world was the helicopter that delivered coal and food twice a year. During the summer, they lived on garden vegetables, berries, salmon, and caribou. They very literally gave us the best they had, though they were poor as street urchins. And they assured us that the bears had moved into the valley upstream. Anatoli's gold-filled grin flashed, and he gave a thumbs-up.

We hiked up the canyon. The cloudless skies promised good weather for days. We climbed a hill and glassed the valley, spotting a bear grazing on pine nuts on the opposite slope. Anatoli gave a thumbs-down, his way of saying too small. He smiled and patted the fern sprig in his lapel, though, indicating that our luck had changed. After days of hunting, we'd seen our first bear. We hiked back along the bear trail in the dark. Something crashed off through the alders. Every gun worked a cartridge into its chamber.

We set out again at dawn, climbing slopes and glassing. Rashiid spotted a bear that afternoon. It fed in the pine scrub, then disappeared, then reappeared farther down the slope. Anatoli, after studying the bruin through his binocular for an hour, gave a thumbs-up. I knew the bear wasn't one of the legendary Kamchatka giants, but time was running out fast, and this was the first decent bear we'd seen.

Anatoli and I set off through the scrub pine and alder tangle. We measured progress in feet. Two hours and four hundred yards later, we arrived at where we'd last seen the bear. Anatoli put two hands to his cheek and tilted his head, indicating the bear was napping. Though our interpreter was back at the main camp, we four hunters had no communication problems. Tactics, discussions, and plans were as clear to all as if we spoke the same language. In truth, we did—the language of the hunt.

We eased forward. Suddenly the bear stood. Anatoli busily climbed through the scrub, but didn't see the bear, and my mouth was too dry to whistle and alert him. The bear started our way, then changed its mind and galloped off. I made a quick decision, brought the assault rifle up, and aimed at the back of the bouncing head and neck as the bear ran quartering away. The bruin dropped as if poleaxed.

Cheri and Rashiid hooted and hollered from the valley below, where they'd been watching through binoculars. Anatoli grabbed me in a bear hug that popped three ribs, kissed both cheeks, then hugged me again and pounded me on the back. He shook my hand and then hugged me once more. Now he wouldn't have to jump from that cliff. I put the bear between us so he wouldn't hug me again. At the weather station that night, we celebrated with salmon sushi and a vodka concoction made from wild cranberries.

In the morning, we trekked back to the main camp through drifting fog. Through a rent in the mist, an immense bear browsed on a nearby ridge. Undoubtedly, he was one of the Kamchatka giants. We all felt as if we'd been kicked in the gut. No one looked at anyone else. Anatoli tossed the fern sprig over the cliff. Luck is like that.

A RUSSIAN RIDES A PALE HORSE

Each remote Siberian village has at least one surplus military helicopter given it after Glasnost. Okhotsk's 'copter had been dissected and its parts strewn about the mud airstrip. Just three miles east, ice cakes choked the Sea of Okhotsk in the Siberian Far East. We'd waited four days for the mechanics to reassemble the helicopter so we could fly north along the coast and above the sea ice and cliffs to hunt spring bear.

The guides, outfitter, and translator had been drinking the vodka and eating the food for the hunt while we waited. As we paced, I wondered what was really going on. In Russia, things are seldom as they appear, and something is always going on beneath the surface that you would not know of unless you spoke the language fluently, and maybe not even then. We neither spoke the language nor understood the Russian mind.

I was on my sixth hunt in the Russian Far East. We'd had some good ones and some incredibly bad ones. The latest had been the August before with the same outfitter for snow sheep in the mountains a hundred miles west. This trip I was escorting a Greek Texas A&M rocket scientist (literally!), a New Jersey jeweler, a New York lawyer, and Cheri. But so far we had been stuck in Okhotsk, doing nothing as our days ran out except eating and drinking the supplies for our hunt.

Finally, I got Andrei, the translator, to contact the organizer, Spartak Company in the capital city of Khabarovsk. They could get nothing going until I threatened to board the next Aeroflot flight south and leave the country with my group.

As they say, events transpired. Fast. Spartak promised a helicopter out of Magadan, to the north, by morning. Okhotsk, seeing they were about to lose the charter fee, reassembled their helicopter in what must have been record time. By the time Magadan's chopper hammered over Okhotsk the next morning,

A RUSSIAN RIDES A PALE HORSE

Okhotsk had theirs taped back together and ready to fly—or so they claimed—and they refused Magadan's helicopter permission to land. After the outfitter, Yuri Chernyschevich, was dragged through the coals because of his outstanding bills at the airport, and after he'd bribed the appropriate airport officials, and after an angry call from the woman that ramrods Spartak back in Khabarovsk, we got under way. Finally.

The monstrous yellow, black-begrimed helicopter lifted from the mud slowly, with all the grace of an airborne tank, and oriented into the heavy north wind. The 'copter ratcheted north over the log cabins, mud, and dead-dog slum of Okhotsk and out over the broken ice of the Sea of Okhotsk. As it banked, empty vodka bottles rattled and rolled out of the flight cabin. Flying in the big, decrepit, and largely neglected helicopters was a consistent danger in hunting the Russian Far East. Often, Cheri and I had to front extra money to buy the fuel to get the craft off the ground. Tires were beyond dangerously worn or out-and-out flat. Once, I pointed to obvious bullet holes in the rotor blades. The translator shrugged and said, "Afghanistan," in explanation. "Don't vorry!"

The tidal flats gave way to towering black cliffs dropping straight to the sea. The snow was heavier, and broken ice became solid pack ice, with black open water here and there. Rivers dumping into the sea were still frozen in early May. I worried the bears might not be out of hibernation. Then I saw bear tracks along the top of the cliff just off our port blades, then more, and I began to worry that they'd been out too long, had wandered back into the interior, and had begun to rub. Nothing had gone according to plan yet, as so often happens in the Russian Far East.

We bounced and screamed into the bullying north headwind toward the Lisyanskogo Peninsula. There, I'd been assured, we'd find big bears, perhaps the ten-footer I wanted, and the snow sheep would still be low along the sea cliffs where they wintered. (In much of Asia, you can hunt sheep in the spring, but with snow sheep, the capes were worthless.)

Yuri, the outfitter, returned from a conference with the flight crew. He talked with Andrei, the interpreter, and Andrei shouted in my ear. "Ve can't make it to Lisjanskogo. The vind is too strong and there isn't enough fuel. Ve haff to land very soon."

THE DANGEROUS GAME

I should have expected it. In my experience, Russians seldom plan ahead, so hearing that they hadn't brought any surplus fuel was not a surprise.

The lumbering yellow helicopter swung into a bay and landed, then belched out the New York lawyer, his guide, and a pile of gear. In a moment we were off again, flying along the ice shelves along the black cliffs, out beyond the peninsula, and then into another, bigger bay, where the 'copter hovered over a wood shack and log cabin ruins. We could see from the rusted metal conveyers, steel vats, and other debris that the place was a failed fishing village and cannery.

We literally heaved the gear out the hatch so the helicopter could get back into the air as soon as possible. I was happy to be out of the 'copter and onto solid ground. Though I'd survived forty takeoffs and landings in those old transports, they all looked and felt like deathtraps.

Yuri and his son, Nikolai, and my guide, Vladimir, tried to make the few still-standing structures livable. The rest of us hustled gear to shelter to beat the curtain of wet snow blowing down the fjord. The guides had chosen the big sauna for sleeping quarters. All of us slept there—the three guides, the three hunters, Cheri, and the hooker-on-holiday cook. I always carry my own gear on Russian hunts, and after two days, Cheri and I pitched our own tent for privacy and quiet. We had no worries that bears would invade the camp with all the snoring.

In the morning Tom, the jeweler, and Nikolai hunted to the west across the rotten but still solid sea ice in the fjord. Cheri, Vladimir, and I hunted toward the eastward point, then along the ice skirting the cliffs. The Greek engineer and very overweight Yuri puttered around camp, trying to inflate the boat. The Greek wasn't happy.

Near the mouth of the fjord, the water was open, with big cakes of ice floating in its black frigidness. An ice skirt clung to the dark cliffs, ten feet above the water crashing against them. The skirt was seldom more than nine feet wide, but Vladimir led along the ice skirt with confidence.

"This looks bad," I told Cheri, "but Vladimir seems sure enough." Later, I said to her, "Keep twenty feet ahead of me to spread out the weight so we don't break through."

A RUSSIAN RIDES A PALE HORSE

If the ice did break and drop us into the thirty-degree sea water below, the cliff was so sheer that we'd have no way to get out, and we'd last only minutes in the frigid water. The water was so clear we could see big, long-legged crabs on the bottom, twenty feet under. They'd eat us if we went down. No one had a rope, and I doubt we could have pulled anyone straight up with all his clothing and gear if he did fall through. Even if we could, the ice would undoubtedly give way with the strain.

Despite the inherent danger, the going was easy on the ice skirt. We edged along the cliffs, while sea birds glided into the open water and baby seals floated by on ice chunks a hundred yards out. Sea fog hung at the top of the cliffs. We walked into a cove, then hunted along the beach dunes and searched for bears feeding on the shrimplike crustaceans in the rocks and kelp. We found old tracks.

We left the first bay and hiked out along the skirt ice again, farther south and east and into another big bay, where we found no fresh sign. We did see that bears had excavated in the beach rocks searching for the crustaceans, which skittered away by the hundreds when I rolled away the rocks. We hiked along the skirt ice until we found where it had collapsed into the sea. At that point we could go no farther, so we turned around and hunted back the way we came.

The jeweler and his guide had hiked across the fjord sea ice and overnighted with a game warden stranded there in a tiny log cabin all winter. In the Russian Far East, game wardens are often poachers—they live off the land and pretty well shoot whatever they want. Pay is little or none, and they get resupplied once or twice during the long Siberian winter by helicopter, whenever one happens along that remote part of coast. Mostly their supplies are cases of vodka.

Yuri and the Greek didn't get out at all the first day. The second day, Vladimir and I elected to make a spike camp in the bay along the skirt ice where we had walked the day before. Cheri stayed behind in base camp.

The two of us trekked out along the skirt ice for about a mile but couldn't go farther. The day before, Cheri had stopped at one place on the skirt ice, which resembled a natural ice bridge. The

THE DANGEROUS GAME

frigid sea water slammed the cliff ten feet below and spumed through the six-inch gap between the ice and the cliff face. The "bridge" was only six inches thick at that spot. Cheri, full of wonder, said, "Look at that!" as she stared down at the ocean below.

"Move!" I'd said, as I came up. "Don't stop."

That night the entire thirty-foot span of ice bridge had collapsed, stopping Vladimir and me where we stood. We could see for two miles along the ice that skirted the cliffs to where it turned into the bay. All along, sections of ice had collapsed. I couldn't believe the luck we'd had the previous day. Apparently, we'd weakened the skirt ice enough to make it collapse. If just one of the sections had collapsed after we'd crossed it, we'd have been stranded. And at least one of us would have died. Too often, the country is the danger, not the animal being hunted.

Vladimir and I backtracked, found a narrow break in the cliffs, and climbed the better part of the morning until we topped out and stared over the Sea of Okhotsk, its broken pack ice, and the Lisjanskogo Peninsula in the distance to the northeast. By late afternoon, we'd trekked down into the first bay we'd reached the previous day. We pitched the tent, and Vladimir built a small smoky fire while I glassed the beach for bears.

In the morning, one small bear came to the beach, and by afternoon we'd elected to trek back over the top to the base camp to figure something else out. While crossing over the saddle into the canyon, we found immense bear tracks that were two days old.

Yuri and the Greek had hunted that day, motoring the inflatable boat south along the coast. He'd killed a six-and-a-half-foot bear with a luxurious coat. We heard by radio that the lawyer had shot and wounded a bear, and it had got away. Later, the lawyer killed a six-footer, but he wasn't happy about it.

The next day the Greek, Yuri, Vladimir, and I motored out through the broken pack ice, trying to reach the Lisjanskogo Peninsula. The tiny inflatable was badly overloaded and overpowered with the 175-hp Yamaha outboard. We didn't make it through the pack ice; in fact, the wind pushing the ice cakes into the fjord closed us off from reaching the peninsula, and it nearly closed us off from getting back. In the sea fog, Yuri ran the inflatable up onto jagged ice at full speed. That the ice didn't eviscerate the inflatable rubber boat is one of those miracles far beyond my comprehension. Of course, we'd have frozen in the icy water, and getting back to land across the ice was out of the question. We had a very near thing of getting back to the mainland.

In May, this far north, there's very little darkness, so once we finally worked the boat back to the shoreline, we motored south looking for bears. Almost immediately, we spotted a good bear on a rocky outcrop. I was certain the bear would "square" eight feet (calculated by taking the measurement from tip of nose to root of tail, adding it to the measurement between forepaws, and dividing this sum by two). And even if it wasn't as large as I wanted, I felt I should collect it . . . given the way things were going. You're allowed two bears in the Russian Far East. If a bigger one came along later, I'd kill it.

In the overburdened inflatable boat, I found no room to maneuver for the shot, and the swells made the shooting platform unsteady at best. I sat on a duffel bag, my knees jammed into my chin, and I tried to steady the cross hairs behind the bear's shoulder, two hundred yards away. I tried to time the trigger squeeze with the swells; the trough of the swell seemed to last longer than the crest and was less disturbing to the inflatable boat, so I tried to shoot in the trough. Then a fog descended from the cliffs and partly obscured the bear. The bullet skimmed the brisket of the bear as he stood broadside. We found a pinch of hair and a tiny strip of hide, and though we tracked him for a mile, we found no other sign he'd been hit.

Later, we motored south again, passing up half a dozen bears in the six- to seven-foot range. Once, we ground the raft onto the gravel beach, and I stalked to within thirty yards of a very dark bear, but he would square no more than seven and a half feet. I let him go.

Yuri gunned the too-big outboard on the way back, and the raft shimmied and nearly flipped. Only then did he back off. Again he rammed it onto an ice cake in the fog, and again I marveled that the sharp ice didn't puncture at least one bladder. It just wasn't our time.

I nearly kissed the ice on the shore when we beached and began unloading the gear. I can think of at least two thousand

THE DANGEROUS GAME

ways I'd rather die than in the frozen waters of the Sea of Okhotsk, with my carcass feeding the giant crabs.

We hung around the base camp for a day or two more, hunting, without luck, in the surrounding mountains. The helicopter decided to pick us up early because of some scheduling conflict. Later, we figured we had got less than three full days of hunting out of a two-week hunt. Of course, we were all disgusted, but I, at least, was glad to have survived it. The icy sea is no place to die. Along the shore of the Sea of Okhotsk, the rider of the pale horse grins with gold teeth and speaks Russian.

EPILOGUE

Later, Olga Parfenova, the hunting manager for Spartak Tours, told me she had got the job as manager because the preceding manager had been lost at sea with the translator while boating north out of Okhotsk. The guide and client had left in the first boat, and the translator and hunt manager had followed in the second. Both boats were standard skiffs, fifteen or sixteen feet long. They got separated in fog in the rough seas, and when the fog lifted, the second boat had disappeared. The event got big press in the capital city of Khabarovsk and around Okhotsk. In spite of a massive search, no trace was ever found of the second boat. Olga wouldn't tell me the entire story because she didn't want it to reflect badly on Spartak. (By the way, Spartak organizes hunts as efficiently as is possible to do in the Russian Far East, and their forte is arranging the reams of paperwork. Sometimes their choice of outfitters leaves something to be desired, but then it's tough to find good ones in that part of the world.)

THE HUNT FROM HELL

We've all had them, those hunts where nothing works out. The hunts that you spend a small fortune on and that fail miserably. The hunts from hell.

I'd hunted in the Russian Far East before, and there always seemed to be some problem. I'd booked my first hunt on Kamchatka Peninsula to hunt the legendary brown bear, but when we got to the city of Khabarovsk, the stateside booking agent with the offices in Virginia and in Germany and the very glitzy brochures had sent a representative to meet us. Anatoli, in decidedly careful English, said, "Ze guidz in Tigil von't guide no more for K—. He doze not pay ze money." That story eventually changed to the bears all had caught a disease, and then the country was fogged in. But from what we later pieced together after talking to two other outfitters, the first story was closer to the truth. We eventually got hooked up with Nikolai and Olga Parfenova, outfitters in Khabarovsk, and they arranged a hunt with another outfitter on the Kamchatka Peninsula.

That outfitter and the guides did all they could for us; in fact, they couldn't do enough. The food was exceptional (crab, ocean fish, salmon, caviar), in spite of warnings by the stateside agent that Russian food was terrible. They did everything humanly possible to get us a bear. Unfortunately, we had to hunt to the south of Kamchatka, not in the famed big-bear area of Tigil, in the west, where we'd originally booked. The crew was the most enjoyable of any outfit I'd hunted with in Russia.

Another time our gear didn't get on the Alaska Airlines flight out of Anchorage, even though we got to the airport three hours early to make sure it did. The Russians loaned us clothes and an assault rifle, and that hunt did turn out reasonably well. But the worst hunt was yet to come.

THE HUNT FROM HELL

We'd just flown down from the Ayansky-Nelkan region of north Khabarovsk Krai from a successful snow sheep hunt where I'd bagged two exceptional rams. I rode on a hunter's high without a care in the world. It was a good thing, too, because I think otherwise I might have shot the outfitter.

We flew the typically dismal Aeroflot flight out of Khabarovsk City, east to Sovetskaya Gavan, just across from Sakhalin Island in the western Sea of Japan. Sovetskaya Gavan was a dirty, failed, industrial and seaport city. We stayed overnight in the only hotel available to tourists at the time. When they built the hotel, they had high aspirations and lined the entrance halls and lobby with marble. The rest of the hotel was an appalling mess of peeling wallpaper, cheap paneling pulling free from the walls, carpeting torn up and begrimed, exposed plumbing leaking down the walls, and wiring hanging out of the ceilings. Cockroaches skittered noisily under the dresser and bed when we turned on the light in the room. Water stains streaked the walls and stained the ceiling, and rusted water pipes poked through the walls. The toilet would not flush. The entire floor stank of urine and vodka. Single men lived in the rooms; each had his door open, and all seemed to wander about in their underwear. Since the hunt manager and interpreter, Olga Parfenova, escorted us, and, of course, Cheri was along, this led to some embarrassment, though mostly on my part. The women handled it well.

To my great relief, the next dawn we left. We climbed aboard a more decrepit version of the *African Queen* and motored out of the badly polluted harbor, into the sea, and south along the coast. Before long, the stretched swells turned to ten-foot waves. Olga got seasick and spent much of the trip hanging over the side, with me clutching her belt so she wouldn't fall overboard. Six hours later, we turned into the mouth of the Kopi River, motoring past the fishing village of Kopi, up the river, and around a big bend to a cedar cabin set back in the conifer trees.

We planned to hunt isubra stag, a smaller version of North American elk, in the thick birch, pine, and larch forests along the salmon-choked Kopi River. I worried, because the hunt had been scheduled in early September. I'd studied elk biology for eight years while working on a graduate degree in wildlife biology, and

THE DANGEROUS GAME

I knew that North American wapiti rutted in late September and early October. Any way I looked at it, we were too early for the rut, and the thick foliage still clinging to the trees would make it impossible to see much of anything in the thick forests. It was so warm that the stag would be off somewhere in the high country, away from the clouds of gnats and mosquitoes.

The outfitter had been an up-and-coming star in the Communist party before *perestroika*, and so, without any experience, but logically enough in the Russian mind, he'd decided to be a hunting outfitter to avoid being unemployed. The guide knew this and had no faith in the outfitter, the timing of the hunt, or the prospect of any stag in the vicinity. To his credit, the guide went through the motions and tried. Usually, Russian guides work hard, often for no other reason than they don't get paid unless the client gets game. It's the outfitters you must watch out for. On this trip, the outfitter brought his brothers and pals along for a big party at my expense.

The first day my guide, the boatman, Cheri, and I motored upriver through the rock-strewn rapids in a moss-slimy, cranky, and ancient skiff, bailing as we went. I have videotape of the event, and each time the boat hit a wave, a spout of water shot three feet straight up through the floor of the boat; otherwise, it only spouted six inches. We'd taken a turn in the boat the evening before, and it was so dilapidated I talked Cheri into staying behind at the base camp with Olga, while the guide and I motored upriver to a likewise dismal fishing shack in a swamp. (It was only ten minutes from the base camp, so I couldn't figure why we planned to camp there in the first place.) Rats hopped across our bedrolls in the night as we tried to sleep on smelly fish-drying racks; it was one of the most uncomfortable nights I've spent.

We hunted out in the dawn and found absolutely no stag sign. We did find the pugs of a Siberian tiger, and we could see from the way they wandered that he was as confused about the hunting as we were. The temperature climbed to near eighty, and the gnats and mosquitoes dined on us with what I thought was far too much relish. By evening we'd had enough.

We floated down the river in the evening, the pilot avoiding the rocks in the rapids by cutting the motor and poling us through.

THE HUNT FROM HELL

As we floated, we watched the dense, junglelike shoreline but did not see an animal. Long after dark, we poled into the big, quiet slough in front of the base cabin, fired up the motor, and sped to the dock. A half-dozen boats were moored, and I could see the concern on the guide's face. I felt it myself.

Fifteen or twenty men from the entirely male, Kopi fishing village had congregated on the camp, apparently extremely interested in both Cheri and Olga. The outfitter and his party had motored back to Sovetskaya Gavan earlier in the day. The men passed bottles of vodka around, and you could see the worry on the women's faces. When we walked into the clearing with the rifles, the men began leaving. I don't know what would have happened had we not roared into camp when we did, but I prefer not to think of it.

A cabin perched across the river from ours, and, when we motored upriver the next morning, two Japanese fly-fishermen, a guide, and another man stood on the shore. One of the men motioned us ashore, but the guide merely waved and indicated we were motoring upriver. Predictably, we did not see a thing, not even an old track.

At dinner in the cabin that night, the man that had motioned us ashore earlier that day burst into the cabin. He ranted and gestured, and the guide shouted back. Olga tried to reason with them all, all totally unintelligible to me. As it unfolded, the man was a game warden, and our outfitter hadn't purchased any of the licenses or tags we'd paid for. We'd been hunting illegally. The warden said we could not leave the grounds, or he would confiscate my rifle and arrest both of us. Olga, in her excellent English, explained the situation to Cheri and me.

"Don't vorry," the guide tried in his best English, "No problem. Ve go hunt."

"*Nyet!*" I said in my best Russian, shaking my head no for emphasis. I wasn't about to land in a Russian gulag. Sometimes, especially in Russia, you got to know when to fold 'em. I knew.

Days later, we motored back along the coast to Sovetskaya Gavan, with me fuming and the outfitter knowing it and keeping to the opposite end of the boat. Then we had problems boarding the plane, first because of the rifle and then because Cheri insisted on tripping the metal detector even though she nearly stripped. In the end, they had her sprint through the detector so fast it wouldn't sound the bells.

Throughout Russia, at least in the more remote parts, you carried your gear to the plane and loaded it yourself. I'd used the drill throughout Siberia and Kamchatka, but suddenly the local authorities wouldn't let me carry the gun. The airport officials were extremely cautious. They searched the hard case several times, examining every item in it. Finally, an official indicated that *he'd* carry the case on board. We climbed on, enduring the glares from the passengers who had been held up an hour and a half. A moment later, the official climbed aboard and slid the rifle case in the seat behind me. Apparently, once the plane left the ground, he was free from responsibility.

Back in Khabarovsk that night, we haggled over payment with the hunt manager. Predictably, he wanted full payment. The hunt manager couldn't understand English, fortunately, because Olga was urging us in asides not to pay the full amount. I'm glad she did, because being in a foreign country, I'd have eventually felt compelled to pay it. In the end, we paid for the airline tickets and some basic expenses.

Later, after shots of vodka, salmon sushi hors d'oeuvres, the ubiquitous caviar, then dinner with the hunt manager and Olga, I did not feel too bad about it. After all, I still had the great sheep trophies from the earlier hunt. Live and learn. I felt thankful we lived through the boat rides on the Kopi River and along the rough coastal waters in the equally frightening *Siberian Queen*.

And I learned not to do that again.

BOOK III

NORTH AMERICA

DEADLY LESSON

Sarge Brown was a former cavalry trooper who'd chased the last Apaches into Mexico, and only quit the army when they phased out horses and mules after the first World War. He'd built a simple stone house on the south slope of the Huachuca Mountains, a long spit from the Mexican border. For some reason, he'd taken a liking to me, an adolescent wannabe hunter and mountain man, and my old man, an infantry officer stationed at Fort Huachuca on the north slope of the Sierra, had taken a liking to Sarge. It was all highly convenient for a kid who ate, slept, and dreamt guns, hunting, and horses. No one in that part of the borderlands knew more about any of them than Sarge. On top of that, Sarge was a top houndsman, and ranchers from Bisbee to Sonoita paid Sarge to chase cow-killing lions.

"Damn cow dies and the rancher right away blames lions," Sarge said. "If there was any wolves left, they'd blame it on them, too. Doesn't occur to the buckaroo that the cow ate loco weed or got hisself snakebit or jes died of old age.

"Rancher's happy when I kill a lion, and he's convinced he's got no more problems, and chances are that cat ain't been within half a mile o' his damn cow."

I rode along on those lion hunts, and as often as not I got to shoot the cat when Sarge's half-breed hounds treed it. From those chases, I've never been able to get the rush of dry-ground lion hunts out of my blood. Even today, I dream of those chases with Sarge at least once a month.

When Christmas break rolled around, I raced through the doors of the junior high school, and before long, Sarge and I were packing the mules for a trip south into Mexico to hunt Coues whitetails, javelinas, and lion, and maybe turkeys up in the pines in the Sierra Madre. I swung onto the pale little

DEADLY LESSON

buckskin gelding Sarge reserved for me. I'd already cinched down the saddle, stuffed the saddlebags with jerky and a canteen, and slid the Model '94 into the thorn-torn saddle scabbard. I'd ridden down into Old Mex with Sarge before, but this time we planned to push far enough in to climb into the high mountains to a place Sarge knew from the Apache Wars.

"Damn buck behind every piñon," Sarge said, as he yanked on a mule's pack to test it, "and plenty of lions and even jaguar. Lots of turkeys. Scrape some of that slate down there against yer knife, and they come a runnin'."

From the way Sarge swung onto the big bay mare, you wouldn't guess he was over seventy-five. You wouldn't guess it from his fluid step, either, or from his sunburned face.

We rode down Bear Creek and crossed the dirt road between Nogales and Hereford, then headed down the slope toward the border. In half a mile, we came to a two-strand barbed-wire fence. Sarge swung down, yanked a rotted juniper post out of the ground, and laid the wire on the ground. We rode across the Mexican border, and Sarge replaced the post, lifting the wire back into place.

We jumped javelinas and deer as we rode down the arroyo, and deer, and we saw the odd lion track. We could hunt right there, but Sarge had the urge for a trip. And he'd gotten into a bit of hot water with the local game warden, the Cochise County Sheriff, and the commander on Fort Huachuca because his hounds had run a big tom lion over the top of the Sierra and onto the army base. Everyone was a bit jumpy because of the Cuban missile crisis.

When the base commander raised hell, Sarge told him where to go, and the MPs collared Sarge and called in the county sheriff to get him off their hands. The sheriff called in the game warden to see if they could charge him with something. They couldn't, but all three warned Sarge against having too much fun with his hounds.

"Gettin' too growed up 'round here," Sarge said, as we trailed deeper into Mexico. "Used to be the time when a man could ride a horse where he wanted. The cops wouldn't bother a man, lessen he shot someone or robbed a train."

THE DANGEROUS GAME

We camped at a *tanque*—a water hole vaqueros had dug for cows—and spitted a jack rabbit I'd shot earlier. We listened to coyotes yelp out in the desert.

"Some wolves left up in that Sierra," Sarge said and pointed with his chin at the mountains in the distance to the south. "'Bout the only place left, too."

We hit the Sierra Madre foothills the next afternoon and camped. I shot a desert pig for meat, and we ate javelina saddles broiled over mesquite coals that night.

In those days, no one had heard of high cholesterol, and not much was said about high blood pressure or about how red meat causes cancer. We polished off two javelina quarters a night, if we had them.

The next day, we trailed up a big, sycamore-thick cañon tangled with trees of all kinds. Clear, cold water ran over the gray, mossy boulders, and it seemed we were in a different world after trailing through the desert for two days.

We camped at a flat meadow at the base of a big, snow-dusted volcano. We raised the wall tent and staked the horses on good feed, and then I gathered oak deadfall for the little stove. After Sarge had fried javelina steaks in onions and bacon, had beaten out the bread dough, and had put a can of beans to boiling, we sat back.

"Damn best camp in the Sierra," Sarge said. "If a fella wanted, he could shoot a buck at the bottom of the meadow at first light. If a fella wanted, that is. The big ones are up top, though.

"Fella owns this land made me promise to kill a coupla lion. Got notions they're eatin' his cows, so first thing tomorrow we'll ride up the peak with the hounds and see if we can jump a cat."

Though I'd already run lions with Sarge, I absolutely could think of nothing else in the world I'd rather do. Not even hunting lions in East Africa like I'd read about in that Hemingway book, or shooting the Marco Polo sheep in the Wakhan Corridor I'd read about in *Outdoor Life*. Well, maybe hunt a polar bear, but I'd want to do it with Eskimos by dogsled, not hunt them with airplanes like they were doing now.

DEADLY LESSON

We ran a lion the next morning and treed him three hours later. "That kitty never killed no cow," Sarge said as he leashed up the hounds. We swung onto the horses and rode off, leaving the cat alive and more than a little confused. We ran another lion the next day, a big, aggressive female that chewed up two dogs. We let her go, too. "We gotta 'ventually shoot one to make the rancher happy, though," Sarge said, "so let's make it a big tom so you kin keep the hide fer a rug."

As we warmed ourselves around the cookstove, red hot with the good blackjack wood before dawn, Sarge said, "Let's you an' me ride up fer a look. Might get a big buck today or a turkey or two. Once saw a jaguar up there in the pines."

We topped out before noon and rode through the big ponderosa pines, the mounts quickstepping silently on the pine needle carpet. Each time we rode up on a sapling, we saw the bark strips lying on the ground from a rutting whitetail starting to feel his oats.

"Bucks just startin' t' rut," Sarge said. "Keep yer shootin' eye peeled, 'cause when they're a ruttin' they git dumb and wander 'bout in broad day."

Just then, a hound opened. The other three hounds, mostly a mix of Walker and bluetick, caught the scent, and the chase was on. At first it was good going, the horses loping easily behind the hounds across the mesa top between nicely spaced pines, but then the hounds plunged off the bluffs and down through the cliffs and rocky scree slopes. We sat on the horses and watched the hounds sorting out the scent trail in the rocks below.

"Worth a man's life to ride down that," Sarge said, then spat.

The chase angled across the steep slope and through more boulder slides, the hounds taking a long time to sift through the scent trail, and then out of sight into a deep cut in the flank of the mesa. We rode along the mesa edge and tried to keep up, above the chase and within earshot.

"Treed!" Sarge laughed when the bawling changed to a more hysterical yelping. We couldn't see the melee half a mile below, but the yelp and bark of hounds floated up in the warming air. "Gotta walk," Sarge said, "an' bring yer carbine."

THE DANGEROUS GAME

We unspurred because the long Mexican rowels would trip us up in the rocks, and unlaced our chaps. We tossed our canvas coats under a piñon, then slid off the mesa and down slides where the big rocks would roll if a fellow just looked at them. Sarge led and was usually below.

"Don't roll one of them boulders on me," he said, "'cause it'll mush me flat, and I don't aim to be dinner for them vultures circling yonder.

"Nice tom," Sarge said when we worked close to the lion perched on a boulder as the hounds tried to get up and tear him apart. "He's your meat."

Shooting a bayed lion isn't much, really. The real fun is the chase. I jacked a round into the chamber of the Model '94, and when the .30-30 barked, the tom leapt straight up and came down in the middle of the pack, dead as last spring's peonies. We let the dogs worry the cat a bit, then Sarge and I bent to skin it with our pocket knives. We cut bits of meat from the carcass and tossed them to the hounds. Back on top, we stuffed the skin into one of Sarge's oversize saddlebags and the lion backstraps into mine.

"That there's real good meat," Sarge said. "The ol' mountain men used to say nothin' tasted better than painter meat. Mebbe it's prejudice, but I can't bring myself to eat too much of it."

We tied the horses to pines in the middle of the mesa, leashed up the dogs, took our rifles, and walked off through the pines to hunt bucks. We picked up shed antlers and examined them. Most were too dry, so we tossed them, but when we got two that weren't too weathered because they'd been cast under a bush or somewhere out of the sun, we sat down beneath the pines, and Sarge clattered them together.

The second time we rattled, I picked a spot on the sunny side of a big ponderosa trunk. This high up, nearly nine thousand feet, a guy would get too cold sitting in the shade too long; snow patches still clung to the shady north slopes of the little gullies. I had just started to doze off when I thought I saw movement. I figured I probably dreamt it, but when I came out of it, a big buck minced toward where we rattled. Sarge touched the antler tips together lightly, waited a moment, then clattered and rattled them a good ten seconds. The buck stood behind a big manzanita with just his antlers visible and stared hard in our direction. When he stepped out from behind the bush and took a step toward us, I let him have it.

"That there's a real macho," Sarge said, "jest look at them beams, an' he's so fat rain water pools on his back. What's fer dinner tonight, painter meat or buck tenderloins? Hot damn!"

Two days later, Sarge rattled in another buck. We shot two turkeys and we ran another lion, killing this one for the rancher. We found prehistoric Indian ruins on the south face of the big mesa, and old pots still with corn cobs in them. We found rotting sandals and parts of baskets in the caves and alcoves, paintings on the cave walls, and carvings on the cliff faces.

"Gotta git you back fer school," Sarge said one evening as he tossed a juniper branch onto the fire, "or yer old man the Major will kill us both." I hadn't thought about school since we'd left Sarge's pine-pole corral back in the Huachucas. I didn't want to think about it now.

But one dawn soon after, we packed up the wall tent and the small stove and the bedrolls and the mess gear on two pack mules, saddled the horses, and trailed off the meadow, down the cañon and across the mesquite and paloverde foothills toward the border and the Huachuca Mountains, hazy with distance to the north. I wasn't happy about going back, but this had been the best and longest trip Sarge and I ever took.

Sometimes Sarge and I rode abreast with the pack mules following as he told me stories of the old days and chasing "them pore Apaches 'til they hadn't no place to go." But when the trail got narrow, I fell behind and followed up the mules as we snaked up an arroyo or through a cactus flat. I was following a mule and daydreaming when I heard a *slap!* and saw a plume of dust jump from the canvas pack on the mule in front of me. A moment later, I heard the gunshot. Sarge pivoted in the saddle at the same time, yanking the '94 from the saddle boot, spurring his mount, and yelling "Let's git!" I whipped the rump of the last mule and dug the Mexican rowels into the flank of my pale gelding, following Sarge's

THE DANGEROUS GAME

lead as we galloped into the arroyo, keeping as low in the saddle as we could.

Once in the arroyo bottom, Sarge reined in. "See where that come from?" I didn't. "Seen tracks a while back—two horses with riders and two loaded-down mules trailing north just like we were. Wonder if they're some of them dope runners. Mebbe thought we was followin' 'em."

Sarge took the binocular and climbed up the bluff behind a mesquite. He glassed and glassed, then slid back into the arroyo. He slid the rifle back in the scabbard.

"Can't find 'em, but seen some dust a mile northwest. If that's them, they're movin' fast. Hope we seed the last of 'em. You can put that thing away now," he said, nodding at the .30-30 I held. "We ain't gonna have a shootout yet."

We trailed up the arroyo, Sarge riding his bay up the rim every few hundred yards. He stopped below the edge just far enough up so he could look over, then skidded the horse back into the bottoms. Finally we crossed the two-strand barbed-wire border fence and trailed on up Bear Creek. We made the rock house and the pine-pole corral as the low sun speared itself on a peak out toward Nogales.

When we had unpacked the gear, Sarge held up the soot-blackened coffeepot. A neat hole had been drilled right through the center of it, the edges silver where the porcelain had splintered off. We found the spent slug in the bottom of the pannier.

"Kinda fun, weren't it?" Sarge asked as he looked at the bullet hole in the coffeepot. "Minds me of the ol' days, only them wasn't no Apaches. We'd a been dead if they was."

As we lay in bunks that night and listened to the white oak roar in the potbelly stove, Sarge said, "Don't fergit, neither, it ain't the lions or the rattlesnakes or the jaguars or even those grizzlies yer gonna hunt that's dangerous." He paused for effect. "The most dangerous beast has two legs."

Just before I dozed off he said, "Best not to tell yer ol' man, the Major, neither."

MOST DANGEROUS HUNT?

"What's the most dangerous animal?" the university student asked, as he eyed the photos of slain polar bears, grizzlies, Cape buffalo, and African lions adorning my campus office wall. He was really there to talk me into a passing grade, but he'd momentarily forgotten.

I've fielded that question in one form or another from hunters who've read one of my hunting books, from scout troops touring the hundred-plus trophies in my house, and from little old ladies in sneakers. My answer invariably disappoints them—it's horses and mules.

Unfortunately, extended wilderness pack trips are largely a fond memory of old hunters. With today's penchant for comfort and busy schedules, it's hop a bush plane, fly in, blast 'em, and get out. The *kill* becomes the experience, not a part of a larger and more important event, and only a handful of us mourn the passing of the pack hunt. In most North American hunting, ATVs, snowmobiles, pickups, powerboats, and bush planes have replaced horses and mules.

Happily, saddle animals are still critical in dry-ground, mountain lion hunting in the desert Southwest and Mexico. Aside from polar bear hunting by dogsled on the polar ice pack, nothing is more dangerous than helling on horse- or muleback along rimrocks that drop far enough to let you say the Lord's Prayer before you hit, or through spear-sharp branches stout enough to skewer the heaviest hunter as you chase hounds baying lions.

Sarge Brown, an ex-cavalry trooper who taught me to ride and hunt, lived in a rock house at the base of the Huachuca Mountains in the borderlands of southern Arizona. Sarge had helped the famous Lee brothers chase and film lions, and he had seen the biggest cat they ever killed—a 212-pounder. Eventually, he gathered his own half-breed pack of lion dogs.

THE DANGEROUS GAME

I first hunted lions with Sarge and a couple of "slicks," as he called greenhorn clients, from Dallas. The first day, we'd run a big-footed lion into a tangled valley and over a divide leading to Old Mexico before we lost him in hopeless boulders. On the third day out, the hounds hit a hot track and let us know about it with no uncertainty. We couldn't keep up and within the hour were following their progress by upturned pine needle duff and tracks in sand. When we topped out, we heard distant baying, and we whipped the horses down the ridge before the cat could jump for it.

As we galloped through slide rock, one of the slicks banged his knee against a sandstone outcrop and catapulted off the downhill side of the horse. He fetched up against a piñon, bellowing like a treed bear. Sarge shook his head and clicked his tongue and looked wistfully toward the distant baying hounds. We got the slick to the hospital in Douglas after midnight—he'd fractured a kneecap—and drove back to the horses we'd left in a pine-pole corral. We hoped the lion was still treed. It was, and slick No. 2 killed it.

On another hunt, Sarge's horse steered too close to a ponderosa pine, and Sarge took a lance-sharp branch as thick as a cue stick in the thigh. He reined in the horse, an evil-tempered but surefooted Mexican cow *caballo*, yanked the bloody branch out of his leg, and continued the chase. That lion made it down a cliff and into a cave, and lived to eat more venison.

"Damned Mex cayuse did that on purpose," Sarge said, then jammed a thumb into the nag's eye to give it something to think about while he mounted. For two months, splinters the size of pencils worked out of Sarge's leg. Sarge limped and cussed the whole time.

Another time I was with Mexican vaqueros Jesús Campa Miranda and Armando Vacame Andrade in the Bacanora region of Sonora's Sierra Madre, and the ponies were blessedly mild-mannered and tractable. If they hadn't been, I wouldn't be writing this. Even more important, they were as surefooted as Himalayan ibex.

By that time, I'd been around saddle animals for three decades. Mexican cow ponies were easy to handle compared to most American saddle mounts for a good reason. Vaqueros wore vicious spiked rowels and used aggressive bits, and, if horses acted up, the vaqueros

MOST DANGEROUS HUNT?

could gut them with those spurs. American horses, on the other hand, were, as Armando told me, too spoiled for anything but rodeos.

We rode the *caballos* out of the mesquite corral that dawn, as *colas blancas*—Coues white-tailed deer—flushed into the foothills. Jesús and the outfitter, a city Mexican too fat to sit on a horse, skirted the peak and rode north with half the hounds. Armando and I continued up—straight up—the volcanic peak as the white-and-tan Walker hounds moiled about the horses' legs. The slope got steeper, and I got concerned. Sure, I'd ridden horses on too many mountain hunts to count, but this was as steep as I'd ever sat astride a saddle. Rocks were just at the angle of repose, and it didn't take much disturbance to send them leaping down the slope and over a precipice into space. We let the horses blow on a ledge, and Armando asked if I was willing to go on. He must have noticed my white knuckles. "*Sí*," I shrugged, hoping he meant afoot. But he spurred his horse upward, and I swallowed my heart and followed.

Partway up, the hounds opened, then raced around the shoulder of the volcano. We continued up and once on top glassed the country far below. From time to time, the yelp and bawl of a hound floated up in the warming air. Eventually, I found white flitting through the black-green of the oaks two thousand feet straight down. By careful glassing, I spotted the hounds and the tawny cat on a horizontal branch below. Armando swung onto his horse and turned it down the way we'd come up. If he could do it, so could I, I reasoned. I just wished he'd chosen to lead his horse so I could, too. Testosterone dementia has killed more than one horseman.

The skid down the peak was more harrowing than the climb up. At least climbing, a rider wasn't looking off a two hundred-foot drop. Skidding down, only the toes of my boots were in the stirrups, and I planted one hand firmly on the saddle horn for leverage in case I needed to vault free, which I expected to do at any moment. Boulders we disturbed bounded off ledges, free-falling until we heard them hit so many moments later, they made something catch in my groin. The horse was calm enough that it nipped mesquite shoots as we skidded by. This was all in a day's work for Armando.

Midway down, we met up with the corpulent outfitter, Homero Canedo Carballo. Sweat dripped from Homero's fleshy jowls and stained his flashy new camos, despite the chill. You could smell his fear. "Thees ees berry bad," he said.

Jesús winked at Armando and me and rolled his eyes and shook his head. Homero grasped the saddle horn with both hands, and his fat lips quivered.

We followed Jesús around the shoulder of the peak until we heard hounds baying "treed," and then, tying the horses to blackjacks, we stalked on foot to within twenty-five yards of the big male *leon*. As he bunched his muscles to jump, I shot him with the .30-30.

In hunting treed game, the shot is anticlimactic. The chase gives the danger, the rush. The simpler the chase—and the fewer mechanical and electronic gadgets used to swing the odds more surely toward the kill—the greater the thrill. We had no cell phones, two-way radios, or ATVs. I packed a Winchester Model '94 and Armando had a nondescript .22 six-shooter. Only Homero carried a watch.

* * * * *

Hunting desert lion is anything but sure. A Texas lawyer hunting Coues deer saw my lion and heard the story and got so excited he wanted to hunt lion, too. Jesús took him out the next dawn. They treed a cat that leapt over the dogs and escaped. They chased it until dark without catching up. Similar story the next day, and the next. But the lawyer returned each night sunburned, bloody, battered, and as happy as a *niño* in a sugarcane field.

I've caught lion on less than half my desert hunts. It's not nearly as sure as hunting lion in snow where hunters drive around, cut a track, turn the hounds loose, then follow on snowmobiles or head the chase off on another road. But it's three times as fun.

Cheri and I recently made back-to-back dry-ground lion hunts. We hunted first in southwest New Mexico's Gila River country, where that most famous of old lion hunters, Ben Lilly, had hunted and guided the likes of Teddy Roosevelt. That was my first hunt on mules, and they impressed me. They weren't as flighty or temperamental as horses, they were more surefooted, and they seldom kicked or bit. Still, Lou Probo, the outfitter, a transplanted Easterner, rode a horse.

MOST DANGEROUS HUNT?

We left the Bear Creek Outfit without a cat a week later. "We tried," Probo said, "and now you see why no honest outfitter guarantees dry-ground lion hunts. Those that do are offering you a canned hunt and a menagerie cat."

We drove directly to another hunt with Jared Nichols's outfit in Arizona. We barely made it into camp on the snowy, greasy roads. We rode out on mules the next dawn, up through cliffs to the border of the San Carlos Apache Reservation. We didn't cut a track, though we covered twenty-five miles in the saddle. In the snow, mud, and cliffs, the mules proved every bit as surefooted as the best Mexican cow ponies. Four days later, we still hadn't run a cat

Jon Kibler, another Arizona guide and outfitter (he'd guided for the largest Arizona lion listed in Safari Club International's latest record book), helped out. Jared ran his dogs one day, and Jon ran his the next while Jared's pack rested.

We moved west to the mountains outside of Phoenix. The first day, we found three sets of tracks, but none fresh enough to follow. That day, as Jon ate lunch with one leg crooked around the saddle horn and the reins loose on the mule's neck, a hound forgot itself and jumped against the mule's flank. The mule, also uncharacteristically, bolted down the arroyo while Jon hung on. Jon tried to grab the reins for a quarter of a mile, but finally bailed out before he got into serious trouble. A granite boulder broke his fall.

At lunch the next day, one hound nosing through mesquite found a fresh track. Neither the other hounds nor the hunters believed it. Jared finally looked, and the chase was on.

The dogs got confused three times. Jon straightened them out. They followed scent through three drainages and bayed the cat three times. Once we followed through a *chollal*, a thicket of jumping chollas (cacti), and the cactus burrs actually seemed to jump onto the mules. Four burrs fixed onto Pancho, Cheri's mule, a gargantuan and gentle animal with an IQ of two hundred. Pancho merely stood while we removed the burrs with a seven-foot stick, which we used to keep from getting kicked into Casa Grande. Most horses I've known would have launched into a rodeo then and there.

As the sun balanced atop a peak out toward Yuma, Jared called it off. No houndsman wants his dogs out after dark. The dogs had chased the cat for six hours in waterless desert and lay exhausted on the ridge. Cheri and I had hunted for twelve days in two states without luck, and now all of it was finished.

As Jared climbed up to catch the dogs, the big lion suddenly jumped from the rocks and flowed like quicksilver across boulders, golden-crimson in the late sun.

"Gawdamighty, I love lions," Jon said as we sat on our mules in the ravine and watched in a trance.

Finally remembering what we'd come for, I sprinted to head off the cat as the dogs trotted after it. They had no run left. They bayed the cat in a boulder cave, and as I pulled back and wondered how to get a shot, the cat streaked below—I mean twelve inches from my toes. I broke its spine with a lucky shot from the hip.

The excitement wasn't over. Jared's mule attacked the dead lion with both front hoofs, then kicked Jared in the ankle. In the end, we got the skin on my mule by wrapping it in a jacket. Then we tried valiantly to make the trailhead by dark. No luck. We fetched up in a vast *chollal* because it's suicide to try to snake saddle animals through one in the dark. We'd have had a vaquero rodeo had we tried.

We built a big mesquite fire in a ravine and wrapped up in wet saddle blankets and exhausted hounds for warmth, listening to Jon recite Robert Service poetry and trying not to remember we had no food or water.

* * * * *

"Yep," I told the student, "it's a horse or mule." He looked disappointed, then he remembered what he'd come for.

MORE HORSE STORIES

I suppose on the basis of close calls per hour in the saddle, I've had more of them running lion behind hounds in the desert Southwest and Mexico. I've written about some of these elsewhere in this tome. And while I've been seriously charged by grizzlies several times, been swept off in an avalanche hunting late-season mountain goat in British Columbia, hunted polar bears by dogsled in full winter on the Arctic Ocean ice pack, and lived through a handful of sweaty encounters with dangerous beasts in Africa, I still consider pack and saddle animals the most dangerous beasts hunters are likely to encounter on this continent. After man.

I've owned a couple of horses and have ridden half-broken Mexican *caballos* and green-broken, fifteen-hundred-pound "mastodons" up to Stone sheep pastures, so I know a little about pack and saddle animals and hunting. We had a temperamental quarter-horse mare when I was in high school. She always provided great excitement whenever I attempted to use her for hunting. Most of the time, she got her own way, too.

The first time I got into trouble with Delilah (my sister named her) was on a chukar hunt. I'd ridden her ten or twelve miles out from the house that morning before I got into birds. They scurried off into the stunted oak and boulders, so I dismounted, tied the mare to a stout oak with the lead rope, and started up after them. To shorten a long story and a longer climb, I caught the tail of the pod and managed to shoot down two or three. Later, I pushed the birds into the saddlebags, and as I slid the shotgun into the scabbard, the mare reared, snapped the halter, and lunged just out of reach. I made a jump after her, the shotgun in one hand. She folded back her ears and tried to bite, then whirled and galloped down the trail toward home. I thought very seriously about shooting at her with the 12-gauge, and I mean seriously. She showed up at home hours before I did. You can imagine what my parents thought.

Another time, I'd shot a big mule deer on the mountain across from the house. The buck was too big and bulky to work onto a horse, so I cut it up. When I rode Delilah close to the buck, downwind so she could scent it and know what was coming, she reared and plunged, but I was having none of it. I dug my heels into her ribs, switched her across the rump, and yanked on the bit. She plunged closer, to her own great fright. I was sitting on a rodeo champ by the time I'd worked her to within three yards. She got to plunging so badly on the steep and tangled slope that it was all I could do to keep my seat. She'd gone through a series of healthy bucks when her head came up just as mine came down. The back of her thick skull caught me in the mouth. I lost half an incisor when it went through my lip and shattered on her head. When I came to, I was lying on the ground, and I'd have shot her if I'd had a gun. I didn't quit seeing stars for half an hour. In the end, I carried the buck off the mountain piecemeal on my back. I wasn't unhappy when the family finally sold her.

As a freshman in college, I somehow managed to save enough from working that I could take a hunt in British Columbia for the unheard-of price of thirty-five dollars a day. After I'd killed two goats—in those days it was legal—in the snowy Cariboo Plateau country, we moved south to the timbered valleys for moose and deer.

The weather warmed, and the Chinook dumped two feet of wet snow on the old snow. The horses struggled as we packed into the high country south of Crooked Lake. We hunted out from a snow-laden wall tent on horses. Charley, a Shuswap mystic, guided me. While he guided, he taught me bushcraft and other things I would not understand until years later.

Charley had what today we call a "black" sense of humor. One morning, we rode horses up a steep slope and through a spruce forest. The snow wasn't as deep in the forest, but the horses still struggled. Mine slipped and slued sideways, and his legs went out from under so fast I couldn't vault free. I fell downslope, still in the saddle, and the horse rolled over me, shoving my head a full foot in the snow.

MORE HORSE STORIES

When my wind came back and I cleared the snow from nostrils and ears, I seemed OK. I could stand, then walk, and the only damage seemed a bloody nose. Charley laughed so hard after he found I wasn't seriously hurt that he could hardly stand.

Old-time mountain lion hunter Jon Kibler had a similar experience while chasing lion in Arizona, except there was no snow to cushion the wreck. A big mule rolled over him, and he was unconscious for an hour and a half. His client was a physician, luckily, and he watched over Jon and kept tabs on his pulse until he came to. It took another half hour for Jon to know where he was, who he was, and who the client was. Jon didn't get out of the wreck as well as I had. He broke five ribs, fractured a shoulder, reinjured his neck, and was laid up for months.

Another time, in British Columbia, a horse lost its footing and plunged off the trail, over a thirty foot cliff, and onto a ledge. We couldn't figure a way to get the nag off the ledge. If she stepped wrong, she'd soar a thousand feet straight down. Neither of us wanted to climb onto the ledge with the horse, even if we could get her off. Herbie, the guide, shot the horse. We reasoned it was more humane than to let her starve or fall.

We flipped a coin to see who would climb out and salvage what was left in the pack. I lost. I'm not fastidious, but I am more than a little giddy with heights. I made it to the ledge, cut loose anything I could, and left the rest. As I was climbing back up, shifting body fluids changed the carcass's center of gravity, and the mare rolled off the ledge. We didn't hear her hit for so long I thought hours had passed. I still get sweaty palms thinking about it.

On another trip to British Columbia, this time for Stone sheep with Folding Mountain Outfitters and guide Ralph Kitchen, we were the first hunt of the season. The horses hadn't been ridden since the previous hunting season, and most wouldn't stand a thing on their backs. Guides and wranglers threw horses flat or cinched them up close to a post. One horse threw its packsaddle with my duffel bag of sleeping bag and clothes into the creek. I fished out the gear and stood back to keep clear of the violence. Another big nag snapped its halter and galloped off into the forest. And yet another big mount reared over backward

THE DANGEROUS GAME

and nearly landed on a guide. If I'd had a movie camera, I could have made good money on reality TV.

By that point, I'd spent more time around horses and mules than I'd wanted to, but I'd never seen the collective violence I saw that day. And it wasn't just one or two of the horses, they *all* highly resented anything on their backs. So it was with some trepidation that I swung onto a pale mare while Ralph held the lead rope. When we trailed out of the ranch, I rode strung as taut as piano wire. I was fully prepared to free-form dismount if the horse got too feisty. After all, I'd paid for a sheep hunt, not to become a rodeo casualty. You can't stalk rams with a broken neck.

Whenever we came to a difficult part of the trail, I dismounted and led the horse. We trailed up into a high basin with no serious mishaps. I figured the horses had become resigned to work with the new weight on their backs and had remembered what their jobs were.

"Don't take the horses for granted," Ralph reminded me one morning. Ralph was also an excellent wrangler. "You can't trust 'em this early in the season."

Though I knew enough about horses, I lapsed one day. As we rode along a garrulous creek, I was watching the surrounding slopes for sheep grazing the still-green tundra. Suddenly, my nag jumped and kicked without warning, and the next thing I knew I was on hands and knees in a patch of shin-tangle.

"What ya looking for down there?" Ralph asked with a comical and perplexed look. He hadn't seen the horse buck.

"Rams," I replied and stood, then stretched a kink out of my back. I felt around, and nothing hurt too badly, so I climbed back on, but not before I broke a stick from a gnarled old spruce for a little discipline. The horse got it, and behaved nicely thereafter.

I've seen guides or clients skewered by pine branches while chasing lions, I've fought with downed horses on steep scree slopes where a misstep meant death, I've watched clients shatter kneecaps when their horse ran too close to a cliff, and I've witnessed guides and wranglers get kicked, bit, and rolled on. I've sat on horses and mules that tried to scrape me off on overhanging branches, and I've felt hoofs whiz by, inches from my skull. Once we came back from a hunt to find that a horse, hobbles and all, had pushed into the wall tent, knocked over the stove, the grub shelves, and the cots, and had crapped all over everything. It was after dark before we got the horse out and the mess cleaned up. I asked the guide how much it would cost to shoot the nag.

Given a choice, I'll walk.

TROUBLE

From the first time, my world rotated around hunting. The passion got me in a lot of trouble, too. I nearly didn't graduate from high school because I sloughed classes regularly during duck, dove, pheasant, and deer seasons, and that didn't leave too many fall days for attending classes. It nearly got me drafted because I insisted on taking autumns off from classes. My first wife decided enough was enough when she fully realized that hunting was my first love and that instead of investing in mutual funds, I insisted on spending every spare buck on hunting excursions and guns. It took me five years to graduate from college and eight to get my first master's degree, all because I refused to do anything else during hunting season. I don't know how many jobs I've quit because they wouldn't give me time off for deer hunting.

* * * * *

I drove the old Willys Jeep up the track along the creek that emptied into the south fork of the Ogden River, crossed it, and then switchbacked up a steep, scrub-oak-tangled ridge. I angled up along more ridges and snaked through aspen stands and into Douglas firs and spruce before finally coming out on top of a big plateau at eight thousand feet. I moved easterly across the boulder fields and brush flats, and then I turned the Willys along the trail into the conifers again and down the ridge, all the while thinking about the decision. It had seemed so important—the glory and the girls—to make the football team last summer. I had just quit because the coach wouldn't give me time off to scout for deer. I could arrange the time to get there for the games because most were evening games anyway, which meant they wouldn't interfere too much with deer season. But the after-school practices pretty

TROUBLE

well eliminated my hunting time. So I quit. I'd really wanted to play, too, but a guy's got to have priorities. Deer season was my Christmas, and most of the year was one, long, interminable Christmas Eve, where I waited and figuratively paced and watched, thinking summer would never end.

By the time I'd driven down the last ridge, I'd forgotten the practices and my old man's raised eyebrows. Raised, but from the twinkle in his eyes, I knew he understood the decision. He was no hunter, but he was a man's man and appreciated a person who followed his own mind. I looked forward to the hike down into the gorge to my camp in the willows, a haven on a little meadow beside a rushing creek, where the native cutthroat trout made darting shadows in the already dark waters. I looked back to be sure the fly rod was still there and the backpack hadn't unraveled in the bouncing Willys. I thought again about the trouble hunting had gotten me into, and I decided it was worth it.

Deer season opened in two weeks, and the early October, Indian summer days still hit eighty degrees. Up here, the nights would get cool, though it wasn't freezing yet. I slid down the steep, fir-needle duff slopes, down through the towering limestone cliffs and finally to the creek, then waded across and hiked up to my camp. Over the years, I'd built a fire ring and a kind of oven out of rocks, and I had dug a hole for a privy. I always left a night's worth of firewood stacked under the protective boughs of a big fir tree. I'd also left a cast iron skillet hanging from a nail driven into the tree and a hundred feet of manilla hemp, as well as a grill and a sooty coffeepot, a folding army shovel, a hand ax, a bow saw, and a heavy canvas tarp. A guy couldn't ask for more.

During the next days, I hiked up and down the creek and up the steep canyon walls into feeder canyons searching for a trophy buck. I found one, too, as he browsed out of a tangle of mountain mahogany and into the bitterbrush and sage tangles in the late dusk. He was there the next evening, and I knew where I'd hunt opening day. I didn't check up on him again because I didn't want to chance spooking him.

During the day, I drifted tiny dark, dry flies beneath the overhanging willows, hooking small, active cutthroat trout that fought, ounce for ounce, more than any fish I'd ever caught.

THE DANGEROUS GAME

The firm, light meat grilled with just salt and pepper always tasted better than anything I'd eaten before, too.

I hiked along the low taluses in the afternoon searching for rattlesnakes. I'd skinned and cooked one, and, yes, they do taste like chicken. Mostly I just caught them to see if I could, or teased them into striking. I was sixteen then, more kid than man, and I wasn't ready to change a thing. I wasn't in any hurry to grow up and become like my old man, driving off to work inside every day and coming home when it was already too late to catch the bucks coming out to browse. I liked to fish; I still caught snakes and lizards, still rode bikes, and still played sandlot baseball and football. And I still got into fistfights—and I liked them, too, when I won. I was happy enough with the old Willys Jeep Dad let me use. And at sixteen, I could hunt alone for the first time, legally.

One afternoon, I hiked up to find a big rattlesnake, which I'd seen slither under a rock a day earlier, sunning himself on a rock. I'd brought a burlap bag to put him in, and I hoped to pack him out of the gorge to join another rattler I kept in a terrarium.

The big snake lay torpid in the sun, curled half beneath an overhanging rock and half out in the open. I was afraid to reach over the overhanging rock with my hand, so I found a long stick and eased slowly down the rock slide. I slid the stick into position just behind the loop of his neck and then, with a flick of the wrist, tossed him out from the rocks. I jumped down and pinned his head gently with my foot and grasped him behind the neck. I'd done it dozens of times, so it was no big deal. He squirmed and twisted, half entwining my wrist with his coils as I held his neck firmly between thumb and forefinger. He was the biggest Great Basin rattler I'd ever caught, a good four feet. I had him in my left hand, but as I shifted him to my right for a better grip, a rock rolled beneath my feet. I stumbled to catch my balance and I loosened the grip just enough that the snake twisted and sunk both fangs into my index finger.

I dropped the rattler and backed off, staring at the two tiny blood droplets and a smear of something clear, and thought of the trouble I'd gotten myself into again. The snake disappeared in the rocks.

TROUBLE

I tried to remember what to do for snakebite. Cutting the crosshatches in the skin and sucking out the venom had lost favor because it introduced venom into more tissue and, as often as not, the guy ended up with gangrene. It would hurt too much, anyway. The tourniquet idea was out for a couple of reasons. If you didn't do it right, you could also cause gangrene, and if the venom dose was big the sudden release of the tourniquet caused a rush of hemotoxin to the heart, and that could kill you. I remembered reading in *Sports Afield* that keeping calm was good, and so were cold compresses. *If I can just soak my hand in the creek, that should work*, I told myself. Climbing out of the gorge and rushing to a hospital was out because I'd be working too hard and rushing venom to the heart on the climb out. I had one choice: Stay put until the venom had run its course.

I was sixteen, so I was pretty sure I was immortal. I believed nothing could harm me permanently, so I didn't panic. I walked slowly upstream to my camp and thought about the great story I'd have to tell in high school. In camp, I pulled on another shirt, rolled up the sleeves to the elbow, arranged spruce boughs and a bed on the stream bank where I could dangle my hand in the cold water, and made myself comfortable.

I felt the swelling and the elbow beginning to tingle, the discoloration appearing first in the index finger, then in the hand, and then moving up to wrist and forearm. "Keep calm," I told myself aloud. I did, and in the frigid water my hand seemed more numb. The forearm turned a bruised blue-green, with tiny red sunbursts under the skin, and the swelling moved all the way to the elbow. I began to feel queasy and splashed water on my face with the good hand.

I felt hot and sweaty, then chilled from the cold stream. My mind drifted to old memories I hadn't thought of in years—from my first Red Ryder BB gun at Christmas in upstate New York to the garter snakes I had caught and kept in a big screen cage. I must have been eight or nine. I remembered the fascination I had felt when I saw a big diamondback in a commercial menagerie on a highway out West when I was a kid, and I thought about how I had read everything I could find in the outdoor magazines about snakes.

THE DANGEROUS GAME

I rolled toward the stream and vomited, the current carrying away the mess. I stared beneath the creek's surface at my supersize hand, badly swollen even in the cold water. It didn't seem to belong to me. I rolled onto my back again, and the towering fir trees danced and waved and spun.

I came to when it was pitch black, shivering uncontrollably. I stood to get the sleeping bag to pull over me and felt the ground start to go, spinning away before I could get my head down. I awoke in the dawn shivering violently, dirt and vomit in my mouth, and lay there until thought came in some sort of coherent manner. I was so cold that I knew I would not warm up until the sun came out or I could build a fire. I seriously doubted my ability to get to the tree, find the matches, arrange the kindling and twigs, and get a fire going. I lay on my stomach for a long time shivering, in less violent bursts now, and hoping for the sun. I'd put the camp on that meadow because it got the sun earlier than anywhere else in the gorge. When the sun finally came up, I crawled to the spot on the grass where it was strongest and lay there, feeling the heat. But the pain in the right arm came again in rhythmic, throbbing pulses, then crashing, blinding waves. My wrist was swollen as big as my knee, and my forearm seemed as large as my thigh. The skin was shiny, tight, and transparent with the swelling, and it was yellow, brown, blue, and red, with red bursts under the skin.

I awoke again in the late morning and lay for a long time until I could make myself crawl back to the stream and put my hand in it to combat the swelling. My entire arm throbbed, and the swelling and discoloration had moved up past the elbow. Finally, I steeled myself against the pain and rolled onto hands and knees to crawl toward the water. The pain got so bad I think I blacked out, yet I somehow kept going until I looked at my reflection in the stream. I eased my hand and arm into it. I rolled again onto my back with my arm in the creek and stared up through the trees at the sky, fighting the nausea and dizziness.

The sun had set when I came to again, still staring at the darkening sky and listening to the evening sounds. They sounded unnaturally loud—the cricket from over by the campfire ring, the coyote yelping up the ridge, the small owl from upstream. I shivered. I had to get the sleeping bag and put it over my body for the night. If I didn't, I reasoned very clearly, I would die of hypothermia. I had to make myself do it, but I drifted off again. "Do it!" I shouted. I rolled to hands and knees and weaved in that position until the meadow quit spinning. Nausea slammed me like a tsunami, and the pain hit again. "Must do it," I said aloud in a weak voice. I crawled on.

After what seemed a journey through coals and brimstone and poisonous gases, I pulled the sleeping bag out of the tent and dragged it slowly back to the stream. Somehow, to this day I don't know how, I managed to get into the bedroll, drop my arm into the frigid stream again, and lie on my back. Before I drifted into unconsciousness, I rolled to the stream and vomited again.

I awoke in the dawn of the third day as stiff and sore as it is possible to be. I rolled very carefully onto my side and looked at the disembodied hand so unnaturally pale and yellow beneath the water. It didn't seem as swollen. The wrist, though still puffed so tight the skin reflected my image, seemed less painful. The swelling had all but disappeared above the elbow. Small movements didn't make my head spin so violently. I rolled slowly and pushed my face into the water and drank so deeply from the icy run that my head throbbed. Then I lay back, stared at the sky until the spinning quit, and tried to think. The venom had run its course, I told myself. But it would take time to recover.

For the first time in days, I thought briefly of food. I pushed my face into the stream again and drank until my head hurt. I drifted off to sleep with the hand in the water. The sun hung directly overhead when I awoke. I felt almost human. Almost. I looked again at my hand and I was sure the swelling had gone down. My forearm was less swollen, and the skin was no longer translucent. My elbow throbbed mildly and so did my shoulder, though that could have been from lying in unnatural positions for so long. *Probably that's what it was,* I told myself. I thought again of food long enough to catalog what I had that was bland enough to keep down and that required little preparation: a candy bar, a bit of hardtack soaked in the stream. "Best to wait," I told myself aloud. I drank again, lay back with the sun on my face, and slept.

THE DANGEROUS GAME

I awoke in the late afternoon and felt well enough to sit up and look around. I lay the still painful hand in my lap and examined it. The swelling and discoloration had lessened. I decided I'd live. I thought about trying for the candy bar in the tent. I thought about it awhile before I stood, slowly at first. I kept my head low so I could drop back to the ground if it started spinning too fast. I pulled myself up by an aspen sapling and stood until my head cleared, then walked cautiously and slowly to the tent. I pulled a Milky Way from the pack just inside the flap and peeled off the wrapper. I used my left hand, the good one, and my teeth to tear it open. I sat with my back against the spruce and my hand in my lap and stared at the last of the sun. The candy stayed down, but I didn't feel like eating again. I got to my feet again, pulled the canteen from the peg on the spruce and filled it, then walked back and put it inside the tent. I pulled the sleeping bag to the tent, I brought spruce boughs for the bed, and, when I'd got everything arranged, I crawled in and closed my eyes. I did not awake until the sun warmed the tent beyond comfort.

I was starved when I awoke, and though my arm and hand were very stiff and sore, I knew for certain I'd live. I thought about pushing up and out of the gorge and getting to the Jeep. I opened another candy bar and ate raisins and a chunk of hardtack. I felt good enough later in the morning to start a fire and heat water for tea. By evening, I'd made up my mind to start out the next day.

The climb out of the steep gorge the next morning took three times longer than usual. I had to shelter the sensitive hand against bumps and brush. I didn't have much energy, either. I drove home in the evening, taking it slowly along the rough road because the hand was too sensitive to do otherwise. I cushioned it in clothes on my lap and drove in one gear to avoid shifting.

At home, Mom and Dad didn't say much because they were used to my disappearing into the hills. For some reason I had developed a sore knee, and one morning when I climbed into the Willys, my sister noted me easing it in. I told her about the snakebite, and she swore to secrecy. She told—so much for a kid sister keeping a secret—and Mom hauled me to the doctor.

TROUBLE

By that time, however, the venom had worked through and there wasn't anything he could do.

My arm was too sore and touchy to hunt the big buck down in the gorge, though I did shoot a yearling above the orchard. Lesson learned? Probably not. That wasn't the last time my passion for hunting and the wilds got me into trouble.

THE APACHE PUMA

The skinny Mexican cow ponies struggled through the thick green of the arroyo and up the flanks of the mountain. I marveled at the green. "*Muy verde,*" I called to Armando just ahead. Very green.

"*Si, de la sangre,*" Armando said over his shoulder. The land was such a vivid green because the soil was rich "from the blood."

Deep within the mother mountains—the Sierra Madre—the vegetation is surprisingly lush. These heights have a violent past. Urged by Manifest Destiny, squatting ranchers, and border newspapers anxious to invent stories of Indian atrocities, the U.S. Army chased Apaches far into Mexico. Mexican forces charging from the south forced Yaquis, Mayos, and Apaches to submit or die. They slaughtered thousands of *Indios* to bring "peace" to the Sierra for the ranchers and miners. They sent Geronimo to Florida, then to Oklahoma, where he died in the dust. Chihuahua, one of Geronimo's chiefs, fled to a volcanic peak deep in Mexico, a mount later to be named Chihuahuilla. The ragged band of Apaches survived on the little desert pig and the odd cow. They harvested maguey to brew the potent mescal and planted frijoles and corn along broad arroyos between towering palms and mesquite thickets.

The Sierra is no less bloody today. In distant cañons, Mescaleros distil the fleshy maguey agave to produce the special mescal called *Bacanora*. They harvest the maguey on the steep slopes of the Sierra and pack it to a still on burros. Mescaleros build their stills from natural materials—palm trunks and fronds, stones, acacia wood, and soil. Since it's illegal, Mescaleros are likely to shoot first if someone unexpected gets too near their stills. On the *camino* just west, Mescaleros and *Federales* sometimes do shoot it out.

The surprising green of the desert mountain range comes from other sources, too. Two years earlier, a large male puma killed and partially ate an elderly Mescalero passed out under a blackjack. On rare occasions, small children of ranch hands disappear. "Eaten by *leons*," Jesús told me.

* * * * *

The big male puma stalked the flanks of Chihuahuilla in secrecy until one blistering afternoon in August. Cattle drifted to the water hole at the base of the mountain, and the big cat, perhaps because it was too hot to hunt the swift javelina, picked a large calf, lame from cactus needles. The puma pounced and crushed its windpipe, holding fast until the calf's struggles ceased.

Jesús Campa Miranda, the ranch foreman, and Armando Vacame Andrade, the head vaquero, found the partially eaten calf the next day. Jesús swung from his black gelding and measured the pug with his hand. He whistled softly. "*Grande*." They followed the big tracks into thick oak and slide rock on the flanks of Chihuahuilla until they lost them.

The wealthy absentee landowner wanted the cat trailed with hounds and killed immediately. After all, cattle were Sonora's gold. But Jesús and Armando didn't expect their first puma hunter until December. This was a big cat, one a trophy hunter would be proud of. Perhaps it would kill no more cattle. They kept tabs on the puma through the summer as they rode the *caballos* through desert and mountains. They always found pugs near the springs at the base of Chihuahuilla when they watered their horses. The cat killed another cow in November.

* * * * *

AeroMexico flight 2471 banked into Hermosillo late on a December evening. After customs and army formalities for the rifle and a few stops for supplies, we were off into the darkness, traveling east toward the Sierra Madre. Hours later, in the small hours after midnight, we rolled up in serapes on the concrete floor of a ranch building.

In the frosty dawn, we laced on chaps, swung onto horses, and rode through the foothills of acacia and mesquite toward

THE DANGEROUS GAME

Chihuahuilla, looming over the valley. A half-dozen brown and white Walkers milled at the horses' feet, and *colas blancas*—Coues white-tailed deer—bolted from thickets and raced off, waving white flags too big for their bodies. Jesús turned north at Chihuahuilla's base to skirt the peak and search for tracks.

Armando, the dogs, and I spurred up a ravine, climbing the side of the peak toward a saddle separating two lesser volcanic cones. We let the horses blow on a ledge where I could spit straight off into space, and Armando asked, with gestures and simple Spanish, if I were willing to go on. "*Sí*," I shrugged. I'd thought he'd meant afoot, but he spurred his horse up around cliffs and over volcanic slide rock.

The horses scrambled and lunged because if they stopped they would slide down. The peak was so steep that a simple disturbance sent rocks bounding down and into the air as if they had a life of their own. I maintained as little contact with my saddle as possible, the better to jump free if the horse slipped. My heart pounded in my throat.

Midway up the peak, the hounds gave voice and raced around the shoulder of the slope and out of sight. They'd scented the puma where it had sprawled in the early sun to rid itself of the night's chill. Armando continued up. I wasn't sure why he didn't follow the hounds, but he seemed to know what he was about. The horses, gasping and lathered from the climb, topped-out an hour later. We walked them through tumble-down stone ruins built by Apaches nearly a century earlier and tried not to step on pot shards littering the ground. If we listened, we heard the ghosts wail—or was it just the wind in piñon branches? And we heard distant, baying hounds. On the edge of a volcanic plug and a drop of two thousand feet, we listened and scanned for a flash of white hound in the dark forest of mesquite and blackjack below.

* * * * *

In the cool shade on the north slope of Chihuahuilla, at the top of a boulder slide and in a tangle of oak, the big tom lay along a horizontal branch and gazed at the hounds below. The hounds were too tired to give more than an occasional yelp as they looked up. The cat, who hours earlier had eaten most of a javelina, had caught his wind and was no longer worried by the hounds. He'd never encountered dogs before, but they seemed merely irritating, not dangerous. The puma was relaxed enough that his tail hung straight down, just out of the dogs' reach.

The tom couldn't see the men, tiny specs atop the cliff hundreds of feet up. Nor did he know that the gringos had spotted the white hounds in the deep shadows, then found the tawny cat in an oak tree. The *leon* didn't know that the men had climbed back on horses, or that two more men were at that moment riding up the slope of Chihuahuilla. The cat *did* know that the odd animals below him were making a racket, and he wasn't sure what to do about it.

* * * * *

If anything, the skid down the peak—"ride" is too moderate a word—was more harrowing than the scramble up. At least climbing, a rider wasn't looking continuously down into an abyss or a thousand-foot drop. Boulders bounded off the ledges and into silent free-fall until we heard them hit so many moments later that it gave me goose flesh. My horse nipped vegetation as it skidded by.

We met Jesús and the outfitter, Homero Carballo Canedo, halfway up the peak (or down, depending on perspective). Homero was a fat city Mexican and, in spite of the early morning chill, wiped the sweat beading on his upper lip. "Thees ees berry bad," he said and rolled his eyes. Both hands white-knuckled the saddle horn. Armando grinned and shook his head, and Jesús looked mildly disgusted.

Armando hadn't figured how to use my binocular, but through gestures and simple Spanish, I'd assured him the dogs had treed the puma. I did the same for Jesús and Homero. Halfway down Chihuahuilla, we sat on the horses at the same altitude as the cat and hounds. Jesús spurred his mount toward the distant yelping, and the rest of us followed. Then we dismounted and led the horses, tied them, and stalked the still-distant commotion on foot.

THE DANGEROUS GAME

The tension eased when I stepped off the horse and onto my own trusted feet, but it was replaced with another and more satisfying tension—that of the stalk. We scrambled as silently as possible over loose rock and through dense, spiny thickets, and hoped the commotion the hounds made would keep the cat from hearing us.

The big cat lay on a branch, staring at the hounds as they glared back and yelped. The tom looked big, with the blocky, angular head of a mature male. We circled for a clear shot.

I packed an old Model '94 saddle carbine with iron sights, but I couldn't with any certainty pick a path for the .30-30 slug through the brush. Anyway, I wanted to get in close for the kill, to hear the hysterical yelping of hounds when the cat fell, to be near for the last fight.

We climbed above the cat, then eased down through slide rock and brush. The *leon* had his wind back, if he had ever really lost it, and if he took off we might lose him or, at the least, have an all-day chase ahead of us.

Homero whispered that the cat was about to jump. "Shoot!" he hissed.

I still couldn't tell what part of the cat I'd be shooting at. I wanted to get closer, too, and if the cat ran for it, well, that was what I paid for. The tom stayed put.

The big puma paid no attention to the barking. Nor did he notice the rise in intensity in barking when he stood on the branch and looked toward the men up the slope. The cat had never encountered men in this remote wilderness, but instinctive fear made his muscles bunch and tail twitch. Instantly, he made the connection between men and dogs. He crouched and snarled. For the first time in his life, the cat understood danger.

The barking rose to a fevered crescendo, and the puma snarled loud enough for the men to hear it. One of them detached from the group and eased down the rocks to a tree ten yards away. Briefly, the cat thought of pouncing on the man, within easy range now, but he focused instead beyond the circle of yelping, hysterical dogs. As the puma bunched his muscles to jump, he felt the smashing shock of a hundred seventy grains of lead. He was barely aware of falling and the hounds

THE APACHE PUMA

mauling him, but in an instant he lunged to his feet and was down the slope, then leaping into a tree. A foolish hound followed the lion up the nearly horizontal branch, and the cat swatted him off in a graceless arc.

When I'd slid down to where the puma had treed again, he was losing strength. I couldn't shoot because of a dog in the tree, and as I circled to one side, the puma fell. I waded into the yelping hounds and kicked them away as they mauled the cat.

We loaded the big lion on a patient horse, then rode down through thick tangles of thorny acacia and blackjack. At a spring far below, we gutted the cat and fed the offal to the dogs "to give them desire," as Jesús said.

Homero, the outfitter, arranged his Cabela's safari hat just so for the photos then felt his billfold to be sure it was still chained to his belt. Armando grinned at Homero, and I watched as the cat's blood soaked into the thirsty volcanic soil.

HUNTING WITH THE MAYA

I heard a movement. I looked up from the smoking fire I had struggled to get going in the lowland rain forest jungle along the Usumacinta River. The man strode silently into the faint firelight, the single-bore shotgun held loosely in one hand.

"*Llamo Pedro, yo,*" he said. His Spanish was worse than mine. Straight black hair hung well down his back and down the front of the dirty, all-white shift that dropped to mid-calf. A bow and quiver hung across his back. I could faintly see two ghostly white figures floating at the edge of firelight against the black jungle.

He shouted at the ghosts, and they floated into the light. They talked a language I'd heard at the town of Ocosingo, two days' haul by donkey and another day by foot to the west. *And a millennium in the future*, I thought. They lay down their weapons—the shotgun, two bows, and two blowguns. Pedro squatted by the fire and stared at me, his eyes black like an animal's.

"*Mi llamo,* Walt," I said. He could not pronounce the name.

"*Ingles?*" he asked as he fumbled with something underneath the long tunic.

"*No. Soy de los Estados Unidos.*"

I kept an eye on what he was pulling free. He pulled out two leather bags and began to roll an enormous cigar. The contents were a mixture of dark and light objects—leaves and what looked like roots and dried flakes. He blew on the fire until it flared. One of the other men disappeared in the jungle, returning a few minutes later with dry under-bark, and suddenly my little flame was a real fire that lit the clearing and the giant ceiba trees. He put fire to the big cigar and pulled vigorously, then handed it to me. I do not smoke—anything. But to refuse seemed out of the question and the equivalent of refusing the peace pipe. I puffed, fought back a gagging reflex, and handed the cigar back. He handed the cigar to the Indians across the fire. They puffed energetically and handed it back to the chief—I'd already begun to think of him as "chief." *Chief Pedro*, I thought, then giggled. The chief's eyes glittered black.

The hunters were Lacandon Maya, the descendants of the creators of the spectacular ruined cities throughout the Yucatan Peninsula, south and west into the southernmost state of Mexico, and on into Central America. Just north a hundred miles, perhaps the most fantastic city climbed out of the jungles of Palenque. I'd seen the Lacandon in the streets and *mercado* of Ocosingo. I'd seen them wandering the streets of the city of Palenque, selling bows and arrows and ocelot skins to the Mexicans and the few European tourists who'd come to view the birds and ruins.

Chief Pedro handed me the cigar again. I puffed deeply and fought the urge to cough. The chief and his hunters grinned and laughed and said something in their Tzeltal Mayan. I fancied I could understand them. They must have been talking about food because one of the men pulled out a bundle wrapped in hide and spread it by the fire. They passed around a blackened monkey arm, the fingers curled and charred. Each carved a piece loose and chewed it. The chief cut a long strip free and handed it to me, then cut a piece for himself. I chewed, trying not to think of the tiny fingers or the fact that I was eating a phylogenetic cousin.

The men talked in Mayan, passing around the huge cigar again and more meat. The meat tasted salty. The fire leapt high and illuminated the jungle overstory. In the distance, deep roaring and hooting echoed through the trees. One of the Mayas pointed at the sound, then at the meat, indicating we were eating a howler monkey. The river pushed by in the black night, and I heard a splash and then another, heavier splash. The Indians grinned and said something about the noise. The chief pointed at his sandals made with caiman (New World crocodile) skin.

One of the Indians indicated the size of the caiman by pacing off a distance I judged to be twelve feet, and then pointed at the sandals. "*Comida hombre*," he said in his best Spanish. Eat men.

He pointed at the sandals again in case there was any confusion. I giggled at the thought that I was stranded in the jungle, miles and miles of foot travel away from even the outposts of civilization, smoking a huge cigar and eating a monkey arm with men dressed in white shifts, wearing long black hair, and armed with blowguns, bows, and a shotgun. The Indians watched me and laughed their deep, guttural laugh.

Chief Pedro pointed into the jungle and stood. They all picked up the weapons and disappeared, leaving behind the monkey arm. I wished they'd left another cigar.

"*Bueno,*" I said aloud to myself and the fire, "*muy bueno.*" I giggled again and tried to stand. My ankles felt rubbery, almost as if they had no bones. When I took a step, my knees wobbled and felt rubbery, too. The splashes in the river seemed deeply fascinating, and I walked over to look. Clear river rushed by and gurgled over the vines hanging in the current. Howler monkeys hooted and hollered in the distance. Insects screeched and tweaked in the night. I walked back to the fire, crawled into the tent, and slept heavily, though I dreamt weird and vivid dreams of giant walls hung with vines, of polychrome paintings on stones, of spotted cats big and small, and of the Lacandon with their black hair and white shifts.

Weeks earlier I'd visited the Bonampak ruins, renowned among archaeologists for the spectacular polychrome paintings within the stone structures. The place was too remote to be included on the "Gringo Trail," and only the most serious Mayan scholar ever visited the site. A government man in a mismatched uniform lived in a tin-roof, mud-and-wattle hut and guarded the place with an ancient, single-barrel shotgun for which he had no shells; he'd used up his allotment in hunting monkeys for meat.

After visiting Bonampak, I'd trekked a day down the track and caught a ride on the second-class bus running between Palenque and San Cristobal de las Casas up in the Sierra. I'd gotten off at Ocosingo and worked my way east toward the Guatemala border, where thousands of ruins reputedly lined the banks of the big Usumacinta River. Now I was camped by the river and staring at a monkey arm by the fire, wondering if I'd dreamt the night before. My mouth was dry and my head throbbed. The monkey arm lay by the fire, overblown with ash.

My stomach felt odd, but not too odd to brush the ash off the meat and pull strips from the bone for breakfast.

I'd planned to wander up and down the river and search for ruins. They'd appear as nothing but overgrown hillocks, and I'd have to look closely to realize they were even ruins. A thousand years of jungle growth would obliterate any edifice man could put together. Even the great pyramids at Palenque and Tikal in the Peten had been completely covered by growth until they were excavated.

I fought south through the tangle, moving downriver. I came across a hill set back from the bank that rose thirty feet. I pushed through the undergrowth, cleared off leaves and mold, and found big circular and carved stones. I found more stone cubes two feet across and more carvings. I found the lower part of a flight of stairs. When I climbed to the top of the temple—I like to think of it as such—I found a tree growing from a great rectangular trough. I found carvings of a deity I recognized—Yum Caax, the god of maize. I found another that looked like the Mayan Chac-Mool effigies I'd seen north in the Yucatan. I felt like Indiana Jones.

Very pleased with the day's explorations, I returned to camp with a pocketful of tiny effigies, some resembling faces, others full-breasted women without heads. I spread the artifacts out next to the tent, then I walked into the nearby jungle to find the tree bark the Lacandon had used to start the fire the evening before.

As I sat by the smoky fire in the deep evening dusk, the Mayas materialized out of the jungle like ghosts. Chief Pedro pointed at the smoky fire and grinned and said, "*No bueno!*" One of the men disappeared into the jungle again and returned with the dry, barky stuff, and suddenly the fire flared and illuminated the clearing.

The chief looked at the ancient effigies by the tent and said, "*No bueno.*" But this time he wasn't smiling. "*No bueno,*" he said again, and shook his head. The other Indians looked concerned.

I shared my pot of rice and cut a Hershey's bar into pieces and passed it around. But the men did not smile and seemed clearly preoccupied with the effigies. They stood and walked into the night. Pedro said "*Gracias*" from the dark.

When I awoke from a troubled sleep, the artifacts had disappeared. I didn't have to think too hard to figure where they'd gone.

I hiked off along the river in the opposite direction from the day before and found ruins within a half-mile of camp. The vegetation-covered ruins stretched on upriver as far as I could walk that day. Some climbed six stories above the jungle canopy. I found flights of stairs ascending partway to the top, great holes that had collapsed into what seemed a hollow interior, and, sometimes, a hidden passage that led into the interior of the big mound. In some places, I found square, heavily carved stelae still standing. On the sheer walls of the light-gray limestone structures, carved jaguar heads and human skulls lay covered with vines. I found more small effigies, but I did not disturb them. I took photos in the heavy cover when there was enough light.

Chief Pedro and pals returned in the evening. They paddled a dugout to the shore and hauled it out. Pedro shouted, "*Hola!*"

"*Hola,*" I said back and raised my hand in greeting. The Mayas seemed more cheerful. One pulled a spotted margay cat from the dugout and hauled it to the camp. In a moment they had the fire flaring high.

"*Cazador, yo,*" Chief Pedro said and slapped himself on the chest. Literally translated, "a hunter, I." He pointed at the margay. One of the Indians skinned the no-longer-stunning spotted cat.

"*Yo tambien,*" I said and slapped my chest. I, too, am a hunter.

"*Bueno,*" Pedro said, "*muy bueno.*" The Lacandon were in a better mood.

While one of the Indians quartered the margay, another hauled in dead branches of a reddish wood and heaped them on the fire. Pedro put together the fixings of one of the cigars. They'd brought a gourd from the dugout, too. I suspected it was *pox* (pronounced "posh"), a potent corn liquor.

One of the hunters excavated a hole a foot deep, and the other lay big leaves on the bottom. He lay the cat quarters in the hole, then covered the meat with moss and leaves and a thin layer of the red jungle soil. He scraped a heap of coals over the soil while the other man brought more wood for the fire.

The chief lit the cigar, took a puff, and handed it to me. I did the same. After all, refusing might have been an affront of some sort—plus they were armed, and I was not. I handed the cigar to the next Indian. Pedro's obsidian eyes glittered, and the other Maya grinned in the firelight.

"*Muy bueno*," I said and pointed at the cigar.

I kept my Spanish as simple as possible, but any words seemed superfluous. Pedro nodded and passed me the cigar. The jungle noises became more distinct, and I noticed the splashes in the river and the distant howler monkey hooting, and then farther away a deeper, guttural *owwrungh, owwrungh*.

One of the hunters pointed off at the sounds and simply said, "*Tigre!*" It was the jaguar, king of the jungle, the figure on the ruins and in my dream.

Pedro pointed at the gourd and said, "*Pox.*" He pulled the cob stopper and handed me the gourd. I'd tried the potent corn liquor at the *mercado* in San Cristobal de las Casas and knew it broadened your smile no matter the time of day.

We continued passing the big cigar with its mildly intoxicating mixture. Everyone grinned and laughed. The Indians lost much of their reticence as we waited for the meat to cook. One Lacandon walked to the dugout and brought back a bundle, then unwrapped it and passed the salted, dried fish around. Hors d'oeuvres, Mayan jungle style.

Finally, one of the men scraped the coals from off the soil, pushed the soil away, and lifted the steaming meat, laying it on broad leaves spread flat on the ground. It smelled like a back-home pot roast. The meat was so moist and tender you could pull it free with your fingers. We used a big green leaf for a plate and washed down the gods' meat with *pox*. I grinned.

Almost suddenly, I found myself squatting alone and staring into the fire. The Mayan hunters had gone. A margay leg lay on the leaves beside me, as did the nearly empty gourd.

The next morning, I sat on my heels by the fire in the mist, when the Mayas floated into the eddy and beached the dugout. "*Caza*," Pedro said and pointed at me.

THE DANGEROUS GAME

To hunt. I thought about it. My mouth was dry again and I felt a little light-headed. I felt more like crawling back into the tent, but a moment later I found myself gliding against the current as the hunters kept close watch on the banks. They discussed the hunting possibilities in Mayan since they weren't much good at Spanish.

When the sun hit the river vegetation, the hunters became quiet and watched more closely. Pedro slipped a shell into the shotgun, its forearm wired to the barrel. The Maya in the bow sat with a sharp, fire-blackened sapling spear across his lap. The Mayan hunters watched the bank and the overhanging vines and leaves. Hunters speak the same language, which isn't necessarily verbal. From the way one stiffened and moved the sharpened stick, I knew he'd spotted something. I saw the big gray iguana sunning on a branch above the current. Everyone had. The man imperceptibly raised and cocked his arm, holding the spear until the lizard was three feet from his face. He lunged just hard enough to put the spear into the thrashing lizard, but not so hard as to put it completely through. When he retrieved it, he smashed its head against the dugout. In an hour we collected another iguana and two four-foot caiman.

We passed a ruin partly cleared of vegetation on the opposite bank. The understory was trampled clean from the bank of the river to and around the single corbel arch that stood in the clearing. The inside of the arch was fire-blackened. An old man emerged from the arch and spoke. He was dressed like the men in the dugout, but his hair was white. Pedro answered something back in the Lacandon tongue and waved.

On the way back downriver to camp, the man in the bow pointed ahead to a big ripple moving downstream away from us. I felt the sudden tension. Pedro put the shotgun across his lap, and the man in the bow brought the spear up as we closed on the ripple. I saw the caiman's nostrils and eyes above the water; it was just like the croc on Lake Tanganyika I would hunt years later.

No one paddled now, or breathed. The bow man held his arm and spear fully cocked. Pedro had his thumb on the hammer of the 16-gauge but sat without moving. The current floated us nearer, and, infrequently, the hunter in the stern silently dipped the paddle into the current and pushed us ahead so we closed the distance. The crocodile was six feet in front when the hunter lunged and drove the heavy, hardwood ceiba sapling completely through the reptile and just behind its shoulders.

The hunter tried to hold the spear, but the big caiman thrashed too violently. The croc submerged, spear and all, and we paddled downstream a hundred yards and turned into the current. We kept our place by holding onto a vine while we all watched upriver.

After half an hour, Pedro pointed across and upriver. The man holding the vine grunted. When I searched the shore with the binocular, two signs helped me locate the big croc: The shaft of the spear was perpendicular to the water surface, and the croc had pushed his snout a foot up onto the bank. We paddled toward it in the blood drifting down the current, with the man watching closely and Pedro holding the shotgun up now. The man in the bow slipped a big, stone-sharpened machete from a green hide sheath.

"*Muerte*," Pedro said. Dead.

The hunter with the paddle eased the dugout onto the shore, and the man in the bow brought the gleaming machete up and down in a motion too fast to see, just between and behind the croc's eyes. The caiman shuddered violently, then began to slip into the current. The hunter pushed the spear into the mud to anchor it. Suddenly everyone laughed and grinned and chattered in the satisfaction of the kill. I'd seen this precise reaction on the tundra barrens of Nunavut and in the *bundu* of Tanzania.

We lashed the caiman to the dugout and floated down to the camp. While the three Mayas skinned the reptile on the bank, I wandered off into the rain forest to search for dry bark. I even found some. I also found more or less dry deadfall and dragged it to the fire. When the fire blazed nicely, I threw deadfall into it. As I picked up a branch, something dropped on my wrist. I glanced at the big, black scorpion, stinger poised, and shook it violently into the fire.

One of the men hacked the caiman's tail crossways with the machete into chops and wrapped them in the big green leaves before setting them on the coals. He scraped more coals on top, then mixed the fixing for another cigar. Fortunately, they were out of the *pox*. Both the cigar and the corn liquor at the same time was too much for me to handle.

After we'd passed the cigar around three or four times, Pedro fished the leaves out of the coals and spread them for us to help ourselves. We ate the caiman with our fingers, the meat white, firm, and delicate. Then the hunters left for the night.

The Mayas showed up again after sunup, and we ate more caiman and dried fish. Then we shoved off into the current again, moving downriver to the south as we hunted. The hunters killed an iguana and a small caiman, then they paddled to shore among big and numerous ruins and built a fire in a pit. We cooked the iguana over the fire as it was, the skin blackening and the tail curling. Finally, the skin split and the abdominal cavity expanded until it ruptured and sizzled its contents onto the coals. When it had broiled enough, we fished the lizard out of the coals and peeled off the blackened skin so we could pick at the white meat with our fingers. It tasted like iguana.

I walked around the ruin and found a hole tunneled into the midsection of a pyramid—pyramid is the only way to describe its shape. Pedro pointed at the hole and tunnel and said something in Mayan. I nodded, but had no idea what he was talking about. He's seen me look into the black hole.

Pedro then said something to one of the men, and the man disappeared in the jungle. He returned later with a pithy branch, clear sap oozing from the cut he'd made with the machete. Pedro pushed it into the fire so it caught and flared, then he led us into the tunnel. Thirty feet in, the wall became carefully fitted stone, corbelled into high, sharp-peaked ceilings. The torch lit fantastic murals in reds, blues, yellows, and whites depicting headless jaguars, headless warriors carrying spears and human skulls, human sacrifices, pregnant women, corn, and gods flighting across a starry sky. Pedro led us farther into a soot-blackened room with an altar of burned bones and scraps of charred hide and feathers. Pedro made another cigar, smaller than those at camp, but the Mayas did not offer any to me as they sat and smoked in silence.

After a while, the third hunter entered by feeling his way along the walls. He held a live rat trussed with vines. He laid it on the limestone altar and dragged heavily on the cigar. I sat back against the wall at the edge of the torchlight and watched. Pedro and the others sat near the altar and watched the rat thrash. They sat long, deep in meditation, when a movement in a seam of the fitted stones caught their attention. Pedro moved the torch and illuminated a big, velvety triangular head. The forked tongue flicked out and back, and the head glided toward the trussed rat.

We left then, and we all climbed silently into the dugout and rowed back to my camp. I stirred up the coals. One of the men approached, cocked his arm and the heavy spear suddenly, and hurled it at me. I shoved off and landed on my back. The spear vibrated next to the fire where I sat, pinning a thrashing snake to the ground. The Indian beheaded the snake with the machete.

"*No bueno*," Chief Pedro said and shook his head, and as with the figurines I found, he was not grinning. The creamy green and patterned snake had crawled next to the fire for the warmth.

I'm a biologist and have handled all venomous snakes in the United States, and many in Africa, but I'd never seen this one. I pried open the jaws of the bodiless head and noted the extremely large fangs. Venomous, no doubt. Probably the fer-de-lance, one of the most dangerous snakes in the western hemisphere.

My Mayan friends walked half a day out with me and then waved and turned back toward the river. The next day I caught a donkey cart ride to Ocosingo for two hundred pesos.

My visit to the jungle Maya along the Usumacinta River left me unsettled all winter, through the spring, and into the fall. I had to go back, and I couldn't pinpoint the reasons. Maybe it was simply Indiana Jones–type romanticism, or the thrill of stepping back into the last millennium, or the mysterious temples and cigars and the jaguar and caiman and snakes. Perhaps it was just a longing to feel again such unselfish, disinterested acceptance and generosity without expectation of payment.

I returned again in January, made the interminable bus ride south from Merida in the Yucatan to Campeche, and then south again to Palenque; caught the second-class bus to Ocosingo; and then spent three days hiking and riding a donkey to get back to the river. I waited at the campsite for days, but Chief Pedro and his pals didn't show. I wandered up and down the river exploring the ruins, hunting iguana and caiman with a heavy, fire-hardened,

THE DANGEROUS GAME

ceiba-sapling spear, and living off the land. I saw two or three Lacandons darting quickly out of sight among the big trees along the river. The old man was gone from his ruin.

On the way out in the village of Ocosingo, I searched two days for Pedro. More Lacandons wandered the *barrio* than the season before. I spent three more days in the city of Palenque, and by the previous year's standards, more Lacandons were there, too, peddling bows and arrows and ocelot skins to the Mexican tourists, but I still did not see Pedro.

That last season, the jungle seemed cold and gray and I did not feel at home. I felt as out of place as the Lacandon wandering the streets of Palenque—wary, unsure.

LEMON'S BEAR CHRONICLES

If Wade Lemon isn't the top professional houndsman in Utah, he's right up there. He's guided for the largest Utah black bear listed in Safari Club International's last record book, and he and his hounds have caught a handful of the bigger Utah lions and bobcats listed in the same record book, too. More important, he's the nicest guy you're likely to hunt with, though like any man who handles hounds, horses, or mules, he knows his way around a four-letter word—but, then, I wouldn't trust a wrangler or houndsman who didn't. Predictably, Wade has some good stories.

"This was in '98," Wade told me, "and the client was Thayne Alred. We were up in the Nine-Mile country. The dogs struck the bear scent from the truck, and we turned 'em loose.

"The hounds raced off and up through the sagebrush and spring quakies just starting to bud, darted over the ridge, then trailed down into Pole Canyon. We listened with big grins to the sweetest music a houndsman knows. The dogs bayed the bear in a big boulder pile, a kind of theatre maybe thirty, forty yards across. The bear charged through the dogs before my client could shoot, and we heard the chase race up and over a ridge half a mile away. The dogs caught the bear again, but the fight sounded oddly muffled. When we got up on the dogs, they'd bayed the bear in a den in a pile of rocks. We finally pulled the dogs off and let the dust settle.

"I have never been too worried about black bears," Wade said, "so I crawled into the entrance of the tunnel or den and stopped to let my eyes adjust to the dark. When my eyes adjusted to the dim light (the flashlight batteries were dead), I saw the bear—not down the eight-foot passage, but right next to me. I instinctively lunged back, and the frightened bear ran farther into the den. I saw faint light coming from the back somewhere, but I didn't know if the opening was large enough for the bear to escape. I stood and shoved my head out the entrance and told the client to crawl on in with his .44 Magnum. Alred edged past me and crawled down the passage toward the bear. The den was just tall enough for us to stand on our knees. Blaine Jensen, the ranch owner, waited outside with the hounds.

"I figured the bear would run over me as it tried to escape if Alred didn't kill it right off, so I flattened myself against the wall like a postage stamp. Back in the tunnel, Alred thumbed the hammer of the .44 and pulled off, but the bear didn't budge. Alred fired again, and this time the bear boiled down the tunnel and over me. When I rolled onto my hands and knees, I saw the light from the entrance blocked by the bear as it climbed out. The hounds went wild outside, and I heard Jensen shouting. Then the bear ran back into the den with the hounds on its tail.

"As they say, things transpired quickly, and once the fray quieted, we fished the dead bear out of the den."

* * * * *

In the spring of 2000, Wade Lemon and his client, Dan Brahman, struck a hot track, again up in the Nine-Mile country. The dogs ran a bear through broken sagebrush canyon country, and the bear fought all the way. The hounds finally bayed the bear in rocks, and the client took a quick shot with his 7mm-08 and broke the bruin's left foreleg. Little hampered by the injury, the bear charged through the hysterical hounds, and the chase raced up the canyon and through a big stand of conifers and aspens. Finally, the hounds ran the bear into an old den.

Not again, Wade thought. He pulled the dogs away and dug out the entrance to allow more light into the cave. When the dust settled, Wade crawled in, and when his eyes adjusted to the darkness, he found he was ". . . way too close," so he crawled back, fast. Brahman crawled in, shoving the gun in front, but when he tried to shoot, the bear swatted the rifle away.

Brahman backed out, dragging the rifle after him. After talking it over with his guide, he crawled back in very, very slowly. He pushed the rifle toward the bear until he felt the give of flesh and muscle, pulled the trigger by Braille, then shoved himself back out as fast as he could go.

The bear died trying to climb back out of the den entrance. No one cared at the time, but that bear's skull measured 21 3/16 inches, one of the largest bears killed in Utah.

* * * * *

Another time Wade Lemon was taking out client George Oliver, and his dogs ran a bear into a steep, rocky Utah canyon. Oliver sprained his ankle on the way down the steep, treacherous slope, so he hobbled slowly toward the bayed bear. Wade had gone on ahead, and when he got to the dogs, he found the bear sitting a few feet up a big Douglas fir. Wade had done it before, so he didn't think twice about breaking a heavy branch from a dead aspen, wading through the hysterical hounds, and poking the bear hard. Instead of climbing the tree as bears had always done before, this one charged down the tree and through the dogs. As the bear fought the dogs, Wade charged into the melee, screaming like a banshee, just as he'd done many times. He expected the bear to be so confused by the commotion that it would climb right back up the tree.

To Wade's great surprise, that bear charged straight at him.

He swapped ends and sprinted down the canyon as fast as his creaky knees would take him. He screamed all the way, hoping it would scare the bear off. It didn't. He felt the bear's claws flick his denim cuffs each time it swatted and tried to trip him up.

"This one was real determined," he told me. "I knew that if the dogs didn't tangle him up, he'd get me in a jump or two."

The hounds finally caught the bear and it turned its attention to battling them. They chased the bear up the slope, and as Lemon gathered the shreds of his dignity, Oliver hobbled up and asked what the problem was. Wade just looked at him.

The dogs chased the bear onto a sloping tree, and, when the hounds climbed the incline, the bear nonchalantly swatted them off. As Wade and Oliver maneuvered for a shot, the bear scented them and tore back through the dogs and up the canyon.

THE DANGEROUS GAME

The bear treed again, but it stayed low so it could make a run for it. Wade, reluctantly this time, ran up and swatted the bear with the club so it would climb higher. The higher a bear climbs a tree, the less likely it will run.

When Oliver finally hobbled up, they killed the bear. The bear had yellow ear tags, and, as it turned out, it was one of biologist Hal Black's study animals. "That bear got real mean," he told Wade, "from all the drugging and handling."

Wade said, "I'm still not too worried about black bears. They never scared me much, but after that ol' study bear, I swallow hard before I swat one in the butt."

REQUIEM FOR A BUSH PILOT

I tried to picture how it was from what they told me. The owner of the Yukon Trading Post in Circle, Alaska, had written me a brief description: "I know you and Joe were friends. I don't know if you heard that he was killed flying a moose survey a little while ago. . . ." *A little while ago* was winter on the Yukon Flats, the coldest place in Alaska.

Joe Firmin had told me about his death himself, though he didn't know it. He told it to me when he described flying low with a government biologist. He'd invited me along in his dark-blue Cessna 206 that time. I couldn't go. He'd described flying along the Sheenjek River in November, following a wolf pack by the gory moose kills in the snow. "They killed for fun," he told me as he described it. I didn't really believe it. As a wildlife biologist, I knew something else was going on.

He told me again when he described flying over the Yukon Flats taking moose counts with the biologist. "Fifty below," he said, "was too cold to fly safely. But it was good money and fun—flying low and banking and banking again and coming in to determine the sex of the animals because they'd lost their antlers by then. The air turned white, and without the instruments you couldn't tell which way was up. If for a moment you thought the instruments were wrong and tried to compensate according to your instincts, you were dead." He told me this as he sat across the table in my cabin on the Yukon River just outside of Circle. He paused and thought seriously about it for a long time. "That was too scary." It had affected him, and I'm glad I refused the invitation to fly along that time.

Maybe Joe had told me the first time I flew with him, on a trip into the Coleen River to hunt moose back in '81. He'd brought the mustard-colored Arctic Circle Air Service Cessna 185 down onto the beach too hard and had blown the tail wheel.

THE DANGEROUS GAME

We all felt the plane clank and shudder before rolling to a stop. I kept my fingers crossed when Joe shoved the throttle forward on takeoff. He made it.

Maybe he had hinted at it when I flew with another bush pilot, Roger Dowding, over Joe's wrecked bush plane on a mud flat on the lower Sheenjek. Joe had landed and hit soft mud on one side. The wheel dug in, and the Piper Cub looped and broke the landing gear. "Need a new wheel, tire, studs . . ." he'd radioed to Dowding. No one had been hurt, and in a few days Roger had flown the parts in, and Joe was up and off and back home in Fort Yukon.

He'd hinted at it another time, too. That time he was to fly some Fort Yukon Gwitchin natives up to Arctic Village on the Chandalar River. He'd wondered at the square, canvassed baggage that clinked when he moved it. The natives were smuggling booze into the dry village, so Joe angrily heaved it out onto the Fort Yukon airport gravel. The Indians were a little drunk and threatened him, but Joe was a big man, and even though he was soft-spoken, no one took him on without thinking seriously about it. "Later," he told me, "they got into the plane and tried to sabotage the controls. I knew they did it, but I couldn't prove anything."

Then there was the time he tried to fly out moose hunters on the Porcupine River. They were the in-a-hurry kind, and they just had to catch a flight and make it back to the big city "outside" for business that couldn't wait. Joe knew better, but he gave in. The wind had shrieked for days without sign of letting up. He radioed the sports to that effect, but they insisted. Joe didn't want to do it, but he thought "just maybe" it would be all right. He lifted the 206 off the airstrip and into the fifty-knot wind, banked, and flew up the Porcupine toward the Old Crow country. He landed on a long gravel bar—a very tricky landing in a quartering wind—and tied down the Cessna facing into the gale. Occasional gusts blew gravel across the beach, and small stones the size of golf balls pelted the wheels. But the sports had to get out. Not a minute longer.

Fully loaded and oriented into the wind as much as possible for a takeoff that would be tricky even without the maelstrom, he swallowed hard and shoved the throttle forward. A gust, maybe, caught the upwind wing and flipped the plane, totaling the 206. One client broke ribs, and another got a bloody nose. In typical Firmin fashion, Joe didn't mention his injuries, except to say that his insurance had gone through the roof. Maybe that wreck was more than a hint.

Perhaps Joe had told me about it all along. But I hadn't believed it because I remembered all those other flights that had ended safely: up to the dry lake bed on the upper Sheenjek River, pickups on the Porcupine River or on the beaches along the Yukon, just-for-fun flights over the Yukon Flats before the September willows lost their golden finery. I remembered the dark-blue 206 and the power dives on a pack of wolves on a Sheenjek island. I remembered the joy Joe took in flying over the bush, like a kid. He loved what he did. Just too much, maybe.

I tried to picture how it had been from what they told me: the winter (Was it the winter where the Flats never got above sixty-below for three weeks?), the perpetual deep twilight of the far north, the temperatures too cold to fly safely, the whiteout again, and Joe disciplining himself to watch only the instruments, to trust only the instruments and not let any instinct enter into it, and not trust his sense of balance or his hunches or his feelings. Who could tell what was up when everything looked and felt the frozen same? He'd made it back to Fort Yukon that first time, but even he knew he'd been lucky.

Probably that was why he'd flown into the ground and killed himself and the survey biologist.

INCIDENT IN THE HUACHUCAS

Huachuca Mountains, Arizona, December 2002: It was clear as we sidehilled in a circle through the juniper and piñon foothills on the south flank of the Huachuca Mountains that the wilderness was becoming crowded. Eight months earlier we'd hunted in the area, and I'd killed a javelina with a .44 Magnum revolver. Two months before that, we'd taken two good Coues whitetailed bucks. Now we found a well-worn trail where none had existed eight months earlier, a trail littered with Mexican chip packets, candy wrappers, and juice cans. Soiled tissue paper wads blossomed along the path.

We followed the trail in the direction of the camp. I felt thankful for the .44 Magnum in the shoulder holster. The trail slanted north and into Sunnyside Canyon, where another trail joined it. It continued north toward the boundary of the Fort Huachuca army base, where a lightly used trail dropped down onto the base, and another continued along the boundary westerly toward Sonoita.

"I wouldn't mind so much if they picked up their trash," I told Cheri as we sat by the campfire that night. "It spooks the game, too."

"There are more of them," she said. "They're getting bolder and using the main trails." I nodded and stirred the fire.

"We'll push up to Sunnyside in the morning and get up top. Maybe we'll call in the big lion."

We'd been hunting a long-toed, old tom lion for half a decade without catching a glimpse of him. Months earlier we'd called in everything but him—falcons, eagles, bobcats, foxes, deer, and bears.

The next day dawned gray and cold. "Feels like snow," I said as we sat by the fire and ate breakfast. "Dress warm."

We hiked up the road to the wilderness boundary, then up the trail and past the old corral at the spring. The trail, normally little-

INCIDENT IN THE HUACHUCAS

used and half grown over, had been packed down by Mexicans crossing illegally into the state. Their trash speckled the trail. Judging by the tracks, a group had come down the trail before dawn, their feet crushing the frozen mud. I wished for the rifle, but we'd planned to hunt in a twenty-mile circle, and carrying a revolver in a shoulder holster was a lot easier. Still, seeing the tracks, I'd have felt more comfortable with the long gun.

Twice we stopped along the trail to blow the rabbit distress call. Only Mexican jays swooped through the big ponderosa pines to investigate. The wind picked up, and the day got darker.

"It'll snow before night," I said, cinching up the camo parka. Cheri did the same with her jacket. We climbed on up the trail. Normally, we jumped the little Coues whitetails as we went, but this time we didn't see a one. We crossed a creek and pushed up a steep grade. I spotted them as they spotted me.

"I see them," I hissed and stopped.

I had the binocular up, and saw ten or twelve people. Two mustachioed men in camo jackets led the procession, and they stood rigid, staring. I watched. The men behind scattered and jumped behind rocks or trees as if they expected a shootout. They all carried identical brown canvas packs on wooden packframes. Another man unlimbered a long gun of some kind and slipped behind a big ponderosa. The two men in front carried no visible weapons.

I yanked the .44 free of the shoulder holster, watching them seventy yards up the trail. The two leaders approached, their hands well away from their sides. I could not see the man with the long gun—had it been an assault rifle?—and I wondered if he had one of us in his sights even then. I let the approaching Mexicans see the revolver. They looked like the bandits in *The Treasure of the Sierra Madre*, except for the military camo.

"Turn and walk back," I told Cheri. I took a last look and followed her, half expecting a slug between the shoulder blades. I'd seen the peons crossing before, but this group was different, more threatening, and I had no question about what was in those packs. I kept turning to check, and the two kept following. I noticed the man with the long gun in the trees, 150 yards up the stream.

THE DANGEROUS GAME

We walked fast and hurried still more when we got out of sight behind a turn in the canyon. When I looked again, the two men still followed, and they'd gained a few yards.

"Run when I tell you," I said to Cheri. When we'd rounded a bend, I said, "Go!"

We both run trails regularly, and this one was all downhill, so we outdistanced them. We didn't stop running until we got to the camp three miles downstream. Once in camp, I loaded the .30-30 and kept it handy. We stirred up the fire and waited. I did not really expect them to walk into camp.

Shortly after stirring up the fire, a storm roared out of the north and dumped half a foot of wet snow, not unusual in the Huachucas in December even though the Mexican border is a few miles south. We stayed the night so we wouldn't have to pack up the wet camp.

I awoke in the middle of the night to hear a distant vehicle engine, too distant to bother us. I heard it again between fits of sleep because I slept lightly, listening for anything out there in the dark and snow. The engine, if that was what it was, worked closer, and it silenced behind a bluff from time to time. It idled slowly up the road somewhere south, as if searching. I had just drifted off into real sleep again, when I sat up suddenly and heard it very near. Then the engine stopped.

I reached for the Model '94. I pulled on clothes and boots and slipped out of the tent. I moved from juniper to juniper, because I'd be obvious against the snow, even at night. I stalked in the direction of where I had last heard the engine, then sat under a piñon a hundred yards from the camp to watch. I heard nothing. I listened so hard and watched through the snowy trees so intently that my head hurt. Nothing. I waited until I began to shiver, then made a wide circle through the night and through the scrub forest back to the tent. Still nothing. I finally shivered myself asleep, then awoke to the sound of the engine again, this time far down the drainage.

We broke camp in the morning but kept both guns handy. Less than two hundred yards from the camp, we found where the truck had stopped in the snow, where the footprints had come out of the arroyo, and where the men had laid the packs in the snow. Two of the footprints in the snow went back into the ravine, and the truck had turned around and driven back down the road.

You put it together. My guess was the men carried drugs, and since only two returned to the ravine, they had been peons looking for a better life—you can't blame them for that—and had carried the drugs in return for getting guided into the promised land. We drove into Sierra Vista to the district ranger's office. The woman behind the desk offered little help.

"They haven't done much about it yet," she told Cheri. "They," I suppose, were the Coronado National Forest employees and the Border Patrol.

* * * * *

Three decades earlier, Sarge Brown and I had been shot at while returning from a pack trip in Mexico's Sierra Madre, only three miles from where Cheri and I camped. I learned an important lesson that day back in my early adolescence. It wasn't the bear, the cougar, or the rattler that would kill you. It was your own species. That lesson was reinforced when I saw the drug smuggler with the long gun slip behind the pine tree.

THE DANGEROUS GAME

EPILOGUE

I wrote both the district ranger in Sierra Vista and the Coronado National Forest supervisor in Tucson to report the incident. The following excerpts are from Forest Supervisor John M. McGee's written answer of 17 January 2003:

> I am sorry your recreational outing was disrupted in such a frightening manner. . . . It is clear you responded appropriately to prevent an escalation of the situation. Unfortunately, as you indicated, such border crossings are increasing.
> . . . One of my goals is to provide a safe and enjoyable recreational experience for visitors to the Coronado National Forest. To that end, I encourage you to publish an account of your experience in your upcoming book. Despite efforts of all federal agencies with responsibilities for public lands in southeastern Arizona, the problem of illegal border crossing will not be resolved in the short term. Your efforts to increase public awareness about this aspect of public land management will complement our efforts to make people aware of potential hazards near the border.

From the sheer volume of illegals crossing the border into the United States, as evidenced by the new, heavily trod and badly littered trails moving up the ravines and through the forests of southeastern Arizona, it would be a simple matter for an Al Qaeda brigade to infiltrate without a document of any kind.

KIBLER'S LION SCRAPES

On the last evening of the last day of the hunt, I killed my big tom mountain lion. Then we spurred the mules for the stock truck at the trail end with the misbegotten notion of making it there before dark. But we fetched up in a vast *chollal* of "jumping" cholla cacti that seemed to leap onto anything that walked through it. Snaking saddle animals through one in the dark was an invitation to a vaquero rodeo. We bivouacked in the ravine bottom.

I spread the wet lion skin on the brush to dry, while Cheri and Jon Kibler gathered mesquite and paloverde deadfall for a fire. The outfitter, Jared Nichols, staked out a sandy spot for his bed next to the fire ring. We built a fine fire in the sandy arroyo and wrapped up in wet saddle blankets and exhausted hounds for warmth. Frost was already settling.

Jon Kibler, a registered Arizona guide and outfitter who was helping out on this hunt, was an old-timer. He'd started running hounds when he was fourteen and, except for brief stints at ranch work, had only worked at hunting since. He was also a romantic, and he clung to the old ways with fierce loyalty. He recited Robert Service's poetry as flames leapt and flickered on the arroyo walls. Jared, the youngster in the group, still in his larval twenties, feigned sleep while we stared at the fire and realized this was one of those times we would never forget. We told stories, and Jon had some good ones.

"Only once in the forty years I've hunted mountain lions has one ever attacked me, a client, or anyone with me. Yeah, I sometimes almost got swatted in the face, but that was my fault. But in this one case, the lion attacked."

He stared off in the distance as he remembered. An owl hooted from deep within the bouldered, steep canyon we'd trailed out of. A staked mule chuckled from out in the dark.

THE DANGEROUS GAME

"When I got out of high school, I started to hunt lion a little. Lion dogs are smart, and if a fella knows what he's doing he can switch them from coons to lions without too much trouble. Mine knew they could hunt coons at night but only lions in the day."

I stood and wandered into the dark while Jon paused in the remembering. I hauled back a branch as big as my leg and dropped it on the fire. Kibler continued.

"A few years back, maybe in '95, I was back on the river of my youth, at night, trying to start some young hounds on coons." He pushed back the black Stetson and ran fingers through graying hair. "That night, I had three pups and three older dogs with me. I went to one of my favorite hunting spots, the thickets above Granite Reef Dam on the Salt River. The dam channeled into two canals and created a small lake and some sloughs. A salt cedar thicket runs two miles upriver from the dam, and it's a good place for coons and varmints. It's so thick you spend most of your time hunting on hands and knees. The old riverbed, dry now with the diversion, is still lined with big, two-hundred-year-old cottonwood trees.

"I unloaded the hounds and started down one of the trails I'd cut through to a small slough. I'd cut these trails over the years, but they'd got pretty overgrown. When following coons, it's necessary to go on foot. The hounds free-cast ahead, and Ed, a compadre, followed behind.

"We had crossed the slough and reached a sandy spot on the riverbank, when the older dogs opened. To my surprise, instead of a coon rack, we found the prints of a big tom lion traveling up the river."

Jon drifted into silence again. I broke a dead branch from a nearby paloverde and heaped it on the fire. Jon went on with his story.

"The hounds were all trailing and moving away. The highway runs parallel to the streambed, and I worried about having a hound killed on the road if the track crossed it. 'Ed,' I says, 'get back to the truck and drive along the highway, and if the hounds cross, flag down the traffic so they don't get hit.'

"While Ed went back for the truck, I tried my best to follow the hounds through the godforsaken thicket. Now, from where the track started to where the thicket ended was only a mile, but it was the longest mile in the world. It became a flat-out race, and the dogs left me far behind and crawling on hands and knees. But I kept moving toward them. Finally, they barked 'treed.' Half an hour later, I found the big tom twelve feet up a mesquite. Ed stood there smiling, and he wanted to know where I'd been."

Each time Jon drifted off into silence as he recalled that evening, I walked out into the night and hauled back more deadfall for the fire. The change of pace always brought Kibler back to the story. Jared snored on, oblivious to it all. Jon stroked Brownie's lion-torn ear and returned to the narrative.

"We both approached the tree together, Ed stopping in a clearing while I walked right in under the tree to encourage the hounds. After a minute, Ed said in a nervous voice, 'Jon, I don't care for the way that lion is looking at me.'

"'Good God, Ed, don't you know lions won't attack?'

"Ed said, 'That damn lion is watching me. Don't move or do anything. I'm gettin' outa here before he jumps me.'

"I turned just in time to see the lion leap and hit Ed on the back and knock him on his face. For a second, the lion just stood over Ed glaring down at him. Then all six hounds jumped the lion. Poor ol' Ed lay there with a lion and six hounds fighting on his back. In just moments, the lion broke free and the hounds took after him, but I'm sure it seemed forever to Ed."

Cheri and I sat up and stared at Jon across the fire. We barely noticed the coyote yelping out in the *chollal*.

"Except for his nerves, Ed wasn't hurt, thanks to his heavy coat. When the lion landed on him, the claws ripped through the coat and down the back from both shoulders, but it didn't draw blood. Why the lion jumped Ed instead of me I'll never know. I was closer, right under him, too.

"Soon the hounds had the lion up another tree. Ed was pretty excited and wouldn't get too close. When Ed pulled himself together again, I walked under the tree and leashed up the hounds. We left the tom for another time."

"Why?" Cheri asked.

"I always wondered if it was smart. He wasn't afraid of humans, and that part of the river was heavily used by recreationists. For years I half-expected to hear about a lion attack on the river, but it never happened. At least that we know of."

We three stared into the fire as Jared continued to snore. As the fire died to embers, Jon stood and wandered up the arroyo. I heard the breaking of dry wood and the low bray of a mule. Jon dropped wood on the fire and sat back against the saddle. Two shivering hounds pushed up against him.

"I remember one time, up in the Piñaleno Mountains. The hounds had bayed a lion in some bluffs. I'd left my mule and was on foot, and the wrangler was trying to work the client to me on mules. The hounds had climbed onto a ledge a foot wide that sloped another two feet to a hundred-foot drop. I couldn't think of a way to see the lion without getting out onto the ledge. The wrangler hadn't yet worked the client close, so I thought I'd edge out and get a look at the cat.

"The situation was real bad. The hounds could fall any time, and I wanted to get that cat killed as soon as possible. The ledge curved out of sight, so I eased along it, but I still couldn't see the lion. With my back to the cliff wall, I inched slowly along. Finally I could see a hound, so I inched closer, and that's when I saw the big lion not ten feet away."

Jon paused and stared into the fire. He panted a little with the fear of the ledge in his memory.

"The lion and I saw each other at the same time, and he leaped fifteen feet straight up and pulled himself over the top of the cliff. The dogs went nuts. They couldn't follow the lion, so they turned and ran right over the top of me. As they raced by, they knocked one of my legs out from under me, and I lost my balance. I teetered on one leg before I got my balance, and I almost went over the ledge. I wouldn't have survived the fall on those boulders, either. Too many thoughts raced through my mind on that ledge, and some weren't pleasant."

I took my turn to scrounge wood. When I got back and made myself comfortable again, Jon continued.

"One of the first things clients ask about is what kind of terrain they will hunt on. I say, 'See that mountain over there? Pick out the worst place on it, and that's where we'll hunt.' And that's about how it works out. Hunting rocky, steep bluff country is just part of dry-ground lion hunting. No getting around it.

"One time I caught a lion for a client in some nasty bluffs. The hounds had the lion bayed in a real bad place, with no way to it. The drop was a good two hundred feet. Straight down. We heard the lion growling, but couldn't see him without climbing down. My client took one look and said, 'No way!' We pulled the hounds and left the lion. The client was right."

Women on hunts have it made. No one expected Cheri to wander out and drag in firewood, so I took her turn. When I got back and tugged the soggy saddle blanket over my legs and pulled a hound across my belly for warmth, Jon spoke again.

"I guess the closest I've come to dying while hunting lions was over in the Superstition Mountains, scouting for an upcoming hunt. I was four miles from the truck. I was sidehilling a mountain, trying to drop into a steep canyon. A third of the way down, me and the mule ran into bluffs. I had just about worked around them when one of the hounds opened on top. I wasn't looking forward to taking the mule back up top because the slope was so steep, brushy, and rocky.

"I dropped the reins so the mule was ground tied and walked up through a gap in the bluff to where one of the younger hounds had opened. I found a bobcat track and scolded the pup thoroughly. When I turned, one of my spurs caught a root, and I stumbled off the bluff. I hit head first twenty feet below, and a big rock broke my fall. I came to facedown, with my arms above my head. When the fog cleared enough to get on hands and knees, something exploded in my head and I conked out again. When I came out of it, the sun was way lower. I lay still for a long time before I tried to move. My only hope was to make it to the mule and somehow get in the saddle. She was only twenty feet away, but that seemed like twenty miles.

"I slowly rose to my knees and stayed that way for a long time. Then I worked up to my feet. I was pretty wobbly. By holding on to brush, I gradually worked down to the mule. I finally got the reins and stood holding onto the saddle horn with both hands for an awful long time. Seemed like a year. I didn't have the strength for it, but my only chance was to somehow get up in that saddle. Holding onto the saddle horn with one hand, I slowly pulled the mule's head around until she faced downhill, and I clucked her downhill until we made it to the creek bottom. I half-stumbled, and she half-dragged me. She walked into the creek, and I followed on the bluff until I could slide into the saddle. She knew what to do. Once in the saddle, I dropped the reins over the horns and said, 'Maude, get us out of here.' That was the last I remember, but, true and faithful, she took me out.

"I do remember loading her into the horse trailer, but I don't remember anything about the hounds or the drive home. About noon the next day I awoke on the kitchen floor fully dressed. I still don't remember them missing parts.

"It looked like I was finished chasing hounds. It took a long, long time, but I eventually could hunt again. Once, one of my brothers asked, 'Don't you think about dying when you go helling after those hounds?' 'No,' I said, 'not at all.' To do so meant living in fear. I believed it when the Good Lord said that there is a time appointed for all men to die. My time just ain't come yet. No point laying around thinking about death until that day comes."

Jon stood and stretched. I didn't feel sleepy. Cheri wandered off to do whatever it is women do in the bush. I didn't see how she could, because we hadn't drunk a thing in nearly twelve hours. Jon hauled back a log for the fire. Jared slept through it all.

"Another time, up Bell Gulch in the Superstitions, I'd trailed this little female lion through boulders and in and out of caves, and I was sure she was close. I dismounted and walked around the rocks to see what was happening. I jumped onto a four-foot boulder, and it rolled. I fell in front of the boulder, and it rolled toward me. I landed on my back in front of another boulder, and my arm got wedged between two other big rocks. As a rock rolled toward me, it loosened the other big rocks. The biggest boulder rolled clear over my chest. Another scraped my head as it rolled by, and a third one landed on my arm wedged in the crack between the two rocks. No damage done. At least I didn't see blood all over and I felt no great pain. I pried my arm free and brushed myself off when I noticed my hat was missing. I looked high and low and finally found it back at the place where

KIBLER'S LION SCRAPES

I first fell. I dug it out from under a huge rock, all mushed flat. The big rock had crushed off the brim and mangled the rest of it pretty bad. If the timing had been off, my head would have been in that hat because it fell off right where I first hit. I got a little weak in the knees."

The owl up the canyon had quit hooting, and the coyote out in the cholla had quit, too. I tried not to think about water. No one had any pee left in them to walk out into the dark for. I threw a last branch on the fire and lay out as close to the coals as I could get. Cheri already bubbled as she does when she snores.

"I'm still hunting and I'm still guiding lion hunts, as you can see," Jon said, "and I will until my time comes. Sure, dry-ground lion hunting can be dangerous, but it's a way of life once it bites you deep."

LOST

On the weekends, Dad took me out tramping in the woods of upstate New York. When we'd gone far enough, he'd ask, "Which way home?" I'd point without a trace of doubt. He'd consult the compass and say, "Right." We'd walk farther. "Now which way?" I was always right. I don't think he was trying to teach me anything, rather he was reassuring himself that I wouldn't get lost because I was always "off somewhere." I never got lost—not in the eastern woods, or the Arizona mountains and deserts, or the Utah deer country. Not anywhere.

* * * * *

A wrangler, the guide, and I had packed up together from the British Columbia logging road, taking three pack horses and three saddle animals. I sat on a pale mare as we climbed in the November chill through two feet of snow in the heavy, dark, and gloomy spruce forest. I listened to a creek as it gabbled beneath the ice far below. When we rode into the wall-tent camp late in the afternoon, the Shuswap Indians unsaddled, started a fire in the oil-drum stove, then knocked the heavy new snow from the tent.

"Gonna take a turn around the meadow," I said to Charley, the guide, "to see if I can pick up tracks."

"Sure," Charley grunted, his breath a fog in the cold air. "See big moose, shoot 'im. Mebbe shoot caribou, too." Charley talked like Tonto.

The big meadow was overgrown with willows, and the tent was more or less the permanent moose camp during the season. After our hunt, we'd pack out the whole setup. I walked farther along the meadow, easterly, in the direction we'd ridden in. The clouds lowered and settled at treetop level and the chill dropped.

LOST

If I didn't keep moving I got cold. I found tracks—a cow and calf moose climbing out of the willows and into the forest. Later I found buck tracks, a day old at least, meandering away from the frozen creek. The late afternoon murkiness settled into dusk, and I crossed the creek ice and still-hunted through the willows. I found where a buck had battered a tree to kindling with his antlers, then I followed the tracks up and through the trees as they turned this way and that, as he looked for a bed. The tracks contoured across the slope in the direction of camp, and I followed, the light fading fast in the dense forest and deepening dusk. When it was too dark to follow, I dropped back into the bottoms and hiked along the southern side of the big willow flat toward camp.

I walked on through the dark along the trees. *Camp should be ahead a few hundred yards, on the other side of the meadow*, I thought. I pulled a scarf around my face against the cold and pushed the stocking cap farther down over my ears. I plunged my mittened hands deeper into the big pockets. It was dark now, black dark, the kind of dark you only get from heavy overcast in a conifer forest. But I could see the snow and figure out where to put my feet. I'd always had good night vision and I'd come back into deer camp long after dark many times.

I continued to trek down through the trees, pushing across the willow flat and over the frozen stream where I could pick up my trail and follow it back to camp. That way, I wouldn't have to break trail through the heavy snow. Man, I was hungry.

I didn't see the trail when I pushed out of the willows and into the open between them. I walked farther up toward the spruce, but I still couldn't find it. "I've passed it," I told myself aloud and circled back down toward the creek. It wouldn't have been difficult to walk across the trail in the dark. Still, I couldn't find it.

I stood a moment to figure it out. I wasn't worried, for I'd never been lost before and had no real reason to believe I was lost now. I must have followed the buck trail farther than I thought and passed the camp. I reasoned the camp had to be behind. I couldn't have passed the tracks any other way. I turned and walked along the dark edge of the willows, fifty yards from the black spruce forest. Snow began to sift out of the dark sky, and it had gotten colder, much colder. If I kept moving, I stayed warm enough. If I stopped to think, though, the chill sank its fangs in. Convinced that the camp lay ahead, I walked and walked, finally moving beyond the edge of the willows.

"Yo!" I shouted, and again. "Yo, yo, YO!" I listened for an answer. Only silence and boreas sighing through the black spruce trees answered. A snowflake hit me in the eye. I shivered, then walked on, looking ahead for the light of a fire against the low clouds or maybe a flashlight.

I walked another half a mile. *Surely*, I thought in sudden fright, *I'd have hit camp by now.*

I hadn't wanted to shoot the rifle earlier for fear of spooking game. Now, the concern seemed petty. I jacked a round into the chamber of the 7mm magnum, pointed the barrel into the sky in the direction of what I hoped was camp, and pulled the trigger. The shot seemed too loud in the silence. I listened for an answering shot. I listened so long I began to shiver from the cold. I fired another round and listened again. I'd never listened so hard for anything. I listened so hard I heard the snowflakes hitting the snow, but no answering gun shot.

Where now? I wondered. I had to walk to fend off the cold. I walked in the direction I'd been going, with hopes fading. I slid down a bank and across a frozen beaver pond and through willows with the idea of picking up my tracks on the other side where I'd followed the buck. Then, maybe, I could backtrack to camp. I wasn't surprised when I didn't find them.

I pushed harder, up the slope and into the black spruce forest. I had no idea which direction I lunged in, nor any goal. I felt my heart pumping blood to my legs and arms and head, and I felt the heat and the sweat start to trickle down my ribs. I stopped and put my hands on my knees, panting, and I tried to remember what I'd read about the Far North. Was it that people didn't freeze if they kept dry? If they didn't sweat? That mushers didn't wear much clothing when on the trail regardless of the temperature because sweat killed you when you stopped and the chill set in? Above all, I knew you didn't want wet clothes. I tried to think. *Don't sweat,* was all I came up with. Like an idiot kid, I hadn't brought matches. Matches would save me, but I didn't have any.

I leaned against a spruce and tried to remember the directions I'd taken after I left camp. First, east along the drainage for a mile or so, then south across the stream and through the willows, then west back toward camp on the buck's trail, then north again across the frozen stream and through the willows to where I thought I'd find camp. But it wasn't there. Now what? I tried to sort through my muddled thoughts: I had thought I needed to go west and then back east, but, when I went farther east, there was no sign of the camp. I then crossed the drainage again, and what should have been south, probably wasn't. Then I went farther in the same direction up into the forest. I should have hit the camp any way I figured.

I shot in the air again and listened. I waited five or ten minutes to give the guides, warm now beside the stove in the tent, time to come out and shoot in answer. I waited until I shivered. I fingered the cartridges in my pocket. Four. I had to save them. For what, signals or shots at something to eat? I wished I'd brought more.

I waded back down through the deep snow into the bottoms along the willows. I assumed it was the same willow flat, but it couldn't have been, because I hadn't found my old tracks or the camp. I could have gone farther than I thought on the first leg of the outward journey from camp. Maybe I'd wandered into a completely different drainage. I had no idea where camp was now, no idea which direction I was walking, and no idea why I was walking at all. *I'm walking to stay warm*, I reasoned with myself, *pure and simple. Just to keep warm.* I looked up and down the stream. I couldn't tell which way was up because the flat was just that—flat—and the water flowed beneath heavy ice. Even if I could tell which direction the water flowed, I wouldn't know how to interpret the information. And I couldn't just stand. It was too cold.

I started to walk back, or what I thought was back—I didn't care now—when I thought I heard a shot over my squeaking steps on the dry, cold snow. I stopped and listened hard. Another one from across the willow flat, and another from behind, then more from up the slope. The spruce trees popped like pistol shots in the plummeting temperature. I nearly cried when I figured it out.

Hallucinating, I saw my room at home, felt the warmth, savored the hot food. I envisioned the college classroom and one of the instructors I couldn't stand. His face seemed benevolent now, and I missed him and what he represented. I thought I saw a highway in the dark, the pavement as clear and real as anything, but, when I trotted onto it, it disappeared. I thought I heard a train whistle in the distance and started to sprint toward it but checked myself, and I was back in the black forest in the black November night panting again. For a moment I couldn't catch my breath, and I sat heavily in the snow.

When I calmed, I jacked another round into the chamber and pulled the trigger. I sat and listened so hard I thought I heard a shot—a distant, faint shot. But I didn't hear it again. *Probably another spruce popping in the cold*, I reasoned. It sounded different, though, even if I had imagined it.

I couldn't sit in the snow all night, so I walked toward the sound across the willow flat, with the willow branches slapping at my frozen nose. I crossed the frozen creek and walked up into the spruce trees and farther up toward the ridge line far above in the low clouds. I walked and walked and walked, having no idea where the ridge was. I walked through the woods in the heavy snow until I saw something in the snow at my feet. I bent and looked closer, and felt with my hands for confirmation. A track. My old track! I followed it a hundred yards before I realized I was following it backward. I turned and followed it the opposite direction, where the trail angled up through the spruce forest and seemed to circle then join another trail. I crouched and puzzled until I figured it out. I'd followed my own trail, the one I'd made just before I hit the back trail, in a circle.

I fell on my back in the snow and stared up through the trees at the gray clouds and gasped. I no longer felt hunger, only fatigue. Even the panic had pushed away. I no longer felt cold, only a heavy drowsiness. I closed my eyes and started to drift, but I heard myself shout "*No!*" I sat up, pulled myself to my feet, and leaned against the rifle. I walked, and I no longer had any idea where. "Just walk," I said aloud.

LOST

I walked and stumbled on through the black woods and blacker night. I came to a gentle ridge and an old burn, and I walked down a ravine into another drainage and stopped. Almost mechanically I jacked a cartridge into the chamber and pulled the trigger again. I had only two more cartridges. *Only two*, I told myself. While I stood, I thought about that time in the New York wood with my dad and his compass. "Right," he'd said with satisfaction.

I heard something. Was it a shot? I listened hard again, so hard I heard the blood coursing my veins. I heard the ideas forming slowly in my mind and felt the muscle spasm in my bowel. And I heard the shot, distant, below, and something else . . . a muffled shout?

I fired the rifle again and heard the distant shot. I trotted down through the old burn, into old growth forest again, and through the knee-deep snow. A branch struck me over the eye, and I felt a warm, wet flow down my cheek, but I paid it no attention. I heard something else again and stopped to listen, and then the shot, distinct, distant. I was almost certain it was a shot, not a spruce popping in the cold. I didn't shoot again in answer, but pushed, jogged almost, on through the night toward where I listened for the sound to come again.

When I hit the willow bottoms, I stopped to let my heart quiet and listen. I was too tired to run more. I heard only silence. The willow flat and the frozen stream looked exactly like the ones I'd just left over the ridge. I felt the panic push into my throat again, and I shouted in anguish.

"YO!" I thought I heard. I was no longer sure of anything. I croaked out a vocalization, then concentrated and yelled at the top of my lungs.

Kabloom! echoed from across the flat. I heard the shot again as I ran through the willows slapping at my face. I ran until I stumbled into the meadow and stopped when I saw the glow from inside the tent. A man stood in the night with a rifle.

"Where ya been?" the wrangler asked. "Yer late for supper."

A TROPHY WON AND LOST

Bull caribou perched along the high, blade-edge ridges in all directions—thousands as far as the eye could see. They had climbed to get into the wind that kept parasitic botflies and warble flies from laying eggs in their nostrils and in their flesh. As I watched, on this peak or that ridge, the wind would quiet momentarily, and half a dozen bulls would race in wild panic through cliffs and across treacherous slide rock until they outran the flies. Then they climbed back onto the ridges and waited.

They'd been that way for three weeks. I'd glassed thousands of good bulls, searching for one larger than I'd ever collected. I'd made stalks that failed because flies panicked the herd before I'd gotten close enough. Each time caribou sprinted off across the glass-sharp shale rock, they stood a good chance of slicing off a dewclaw or splitting a hoof. Hundred of cripples wandered the valleys, and scores of wolves had come for the easy pickings. And the grizzlies had moved in to clean up after the wolves. It had been a strange, warm summer in the Arctic mountains.

Weeks earlier, our friend Joe Firmin had flown Cheri and me hours north from our cabin on the Yukon River and dropped us at a tiny river bar, four hundred miles from the nearest pavement and hospital. We'd cached an inflatable raft and provisions in two steel drums for the three hundred-mile float trip "out" on one of the wildest rivers on the planet and through one of the most remote wildernesses. Then, we shouldered packs heavy enough to sink us knee-deep in the muskegs and trekked up into the barren, unnamed mountains.

A Gwitchin caribou hunter had told me that no hunters go that way. In a decade of wandering that part of the Arctic wilderness, I had yet to find an old campfire ring or a footprint. Forty miles

A TROPHY WON AND LOST

later, after three days of mosquitoes thick enough to turn a khaki parka black, we pitched camp in a high, nameless valley.

Wolves howled from nearby. Higher up, caribou avoided both the parasites and the predators. Bears and wolves wandered the bench within a long spit of the camp; they glanced at us and moved about on their own business.

I avoided the willow-lined bottoms when I hunted. Even though the scrub was only chest high, it could easily conceal a bear. Surprising a grizzly too close could provoke a charge. Instead, I glassed from high ridges and peaks. Grizzlies worked old wolf kills in nearly every drainage, and wolves chased caribou bands to test for cripples. When they found one, they ran it methodically until it could go no longer and turned to face them with lowered antlers. Within moments the wolves had torn through thin flank muscle, and the caribou would be down. Because the prey was so abundant and easy to kill, wolves ate only the choice muscled hindquarters, leaving the rest for the eagles, foxes, and grizzlies. Natural selection occurred at a furious pace: Crippled caribou, no longer of breeding value to the herd, were quickly culled.

One evening, I returned to find Cheri on a ledge behind camp. A sow grizzly with two yearling cubs had nosed around the tent, chewed a boot, pulled drying clothes from brush, and moved on. We were living in a country that hadn't changed in a hundred centuries, and we faced the same problems ancient man had. Fortunately, Cheri is an accomplished rock climber. She also knows to avoid grizzlies with cubs.

With the thousands of caribou, it was a matter of patience. Sooner or later, I'd get my chance at a behemoth bull. I spotted him one evening. Or them, rather. In the cooling dusk and lowering clouds, the flies became inactive, and three titanic bulls descended a thin, rocky spine onto a tundra slope to feed. Even without lifting the binocular, I knew the search was over.

I slid down the scree slope, hurried through the creek-bottom willows—my thumb on the safety in case I surprised a bear—then stalked up a shallow ravine. I slithered across a rise. The bulls grazed furiously on the still-green tundra, their

THE DANGEROUS GAME

antlers bobbing as if they had a life of their own. All three were bigger than any I'd ever collected. I thought briefly of taking them all, but though the limit was five, I could only handle one. The largest had a wide spread, long main beams, heavy and wide upper palms, and double shovels. Though I'd never list him, he'd score high in the Boone and Crockett record book of North American game.

The bulls were so completely occupied with feeding that they didn't notice me ease along the open slope, sixty yards above. Nor did they see me rest the 7mm-08 across a clump of dwarf willow. At the shot, the bull leapt straight up, swapped ends, and raced headlong down the slope, the huge antlers vibrating like tuning forks. He stumbled and skidded twenty yards to the base of the hill.

The velvet antlers staggered my imagination. I'd killed a dozen or so bull caribou of various varieties, and though they'd been excellent trophies, none even approached this one. The main beam had to push five feet, and the spread went nearly four. The antlers carried thirty-five points.

I cut free the backstraps from the carcass and draped them over my shoulder for a celebration feast later that night. We'd return and pack the trophy and meat into camp in the morning.

By late the next morning, we'd crossed a pass and dropped into the canyon where I'd killed the bull. We crossed the ridge, climbed down through the saddle, and worked down a slope. Suddenly, I tasted brass and felt a mule-kick in my gut. What remained of an antler, bone-white and stripped of velvet, lay on the slope. We descended cautiously. Bits of caribou were scattered across the tundra for thirty yards around—hoofs, stripped antlers, gut contents. Three ravens scolded from a boulder, and a golden eagle launched from the slope above. I stood in shock.

A movement below jolted me back to reality. We heard the rumbling, throaty growl of the huge sow before she charged. Without thinking, I raised the rifle as we backed away. A two-year-old cub, nearly as big, followed her. Both bears growled and bristled. I fired from the hip over their heads and jacked another round into the chamber, putting the

A TROPHY WON AND LOST

cross hairs as best I could on the sow's bouncing skull as she approached. The 7mm-08 wasn't the stuff for charging grizzlies. Even if I were lucky enough to drop the first bear, chances of killing the second were nil. The bears slowed with the warning shot but continued growling and trotting toward us. I made up my mind to aim carefully at the sow's spine and fire at twenty-five yards, then hope the second bear would run off. In the meantime, we kept backing.

The bears stopped at the carcass just as I started to press the trigger. They growled and slavered and paced. The big cub dragged the carcass toward the ravine. We kept backing until we got to the ridge, then hurried off and kept to the open country. We'd been lucky. Very lucky.

In another sense, though, I didn't consider myself so fortunate. I'd bagged the trophy of a lifetime and lost it. Yes, other big caribou wandered the valleys and the limit was five, but I didn't have the heart or energy to hunt another. Chances of finding another as big were slim at best.

When we were far enough away to sit and rest, we stared out over the wildest country on the continent. Though we could see fifty or sixty miles in all directions, there wasn't another human within that radius.

I'd always been drawn to wild places—the more remote, the better. So I kept coming back here. This was a huge, indifferent land where I could live as my primitive ancestors had. I had to rely only on myself, there could be no help, and I had only myself to blame if things went wrong.

We trekked back to the cache on the river and began the float trip out to Fort Yukon, nearly three hundred river miles away. We took our time, stretching the float trip out to nearly a month, fly-fishing for big grayling, hunting ptarmigan, and bagging good moose and decent caribou. We avoided the grizzlies that had congregated on the lower river to feed on spawned-out salmon, and we watched wolves fight over a bloody, not-quite-dead bull caribou on a river beach.

I've never forgotten the immense caribou on the treeless tundra mountain far north of the Arctic Circle, a place no man had walked before. Years later, there's still that sense of loss, of

THE DANGEROUS GAME

having the grail torn from your fist. But I now understand what the Gwitchin caribou hunter had told me: There, the country was so wild that I was only one more predator. Like Pleistocene man, I had to contend with predators larger than I, and killing game was no guarantee I could keep it.

SHOOT-UP ON THE YUKON

Winters are long in the very far north. Men retreat into themselves. They drink too much. They speak in short sentences. They anger too easily.

For months, the sun does not climb above the mountains just south of the village of Circle, not far from the Arctic Circle on the banks of the Yukon River. Fifty people, mostly Gwitchin Athabascans, live in the twilight and dark of one of the coldest places on the planet. When they leave twelve-by-fifteen-foot cabins, they hurry through sixty-below-zero air, cold enough to freeze and shatter spit before it hits the ground. At the Yukon Trading Post, they buy canned food and liquor, chat if there is anyone to chat with, then scurry back to lairs. They make bets on ice-out at the Trading Post Bar. They write dates and times on slips of papers and drop them into an empty pickled egg jar. The one that guesses closest wins the pot. "Breakup" is official only when the billion tons of ice surging down one of the biggest rivers in the world topple the crimson banner planted out on the river ice.

In the Far North, spring is not a matter of the calendar. It can read forty-five below zero on the March equinox. Instead, breakup signals the real beginning of spring. To men who have endured eight months of winter, breakup means twenty-four hours of daylight, fresh vegetables, and life again.

Dawn comes early in late April. A few ducks and geese have drifted down onto the Yukon Flats in anticipation of ice-out. They follow melting snow and ice north to the nesting grounds. In Circle, the ice can go out as early as late April or as late as mid-May.

The Cessna 206 flying mail twice a week downriver from Eagle village brings word. The ice is moving. The radio says the ice has passed the mining town of Eagle without flooding. Men are

THE DANGEROUS GAME

tense because the odds are even that the ice will dam at the bend below Circle and back up water and ice into the village. Cabins have been carried away in the ice, and most residents have been flooded at one time or another. Natives at the low end of town move valuables in with relatives at the high end. I tie a canoe to the porch and wait. Someone calculates the ice will arrive by sunup the next day.

Not long after the 3 A.M. dawn, shotguns thud from the village center. A hundred thousand snow geese, white-fronted geese, Canada geese, tundra swans, and sandhill cranes squadron down the Yukon River Valley and onto the Yukon Flats in anticipation of open water. Even more ducks of a dozen species whistle through the twilight in flights of thousands. The sheer number of birds alone is spectacle enough. But the ice is coming.

The sporadic thudding becomes a fusillade. Men who have endured eight months of winter must do something. Late arisers stumble from cabins with steaming cups and shotguns. Men dressed in old fur parkas and knee-high rubber "breakup boots" shoot from the muddy street. Ducks and geese plummet from the sky and bounce off roofs. A cartwheeling goose smashes a stovepipe off at the roofline. Staked sled dogs yelp at the smell of blood. Then a hundred half-wild village dogs howl like wolves. The shooting slows, not because the flights have tapered off, but because men are realizing shells are expensive. They choose their shots now, picking low birds or only shooting when the probability of a double or triple is high. Neal Roberts fires into a thick, flaring flock of geese. Four splatter in the muddy street.

The shoot-up at Circle has begun, as it will at Fort Yukon and Chalkyitsik and a dozen other Far North bush villages. For weeks, men will shoot at arriving birds. Most shoot in front of their cabins, but certain places provide the best gunning.

Waterfowl wing steadily up the slough in front of my cabin. I sit by the fireplace and watch out the big window. A dozen guns hide in the willows, and birds plummet from the sky. Birdshot rattles off the roof and stovepipe. A greenhead nosedives onto my porch, then a crane drops into the yard. The crane struggles, so I finish it with an ax handle.

SHOOT-UP ON THE YUKON

The clouds in the east over Canada flare with the rising sun. Upriver, ice fog accompanies the breakup grinding downriver. Men climb from the slough and stare at the growing mist, then shoulder shotguns and birds and walk to the village center. Everyone must see the banner go down.

People gather in the muddy village square. The red flag, the symbol of winter and night, flaps lazily a hundred yards out on the river ice. We feel it coming through the ground. Around the bend, low thundering, like distant artillery, echoes through the black spruce forest. The ice fog flows down the river and engulfs the village. The rising sun becomes neon-orange, and the mist has a rosy hue. Men, women, and children stand with steaming cups and stare in silence. The banner flaps. Neal looks at his watch, then upriver. Someone will win the thousand-dollar pot when the banner falls. At the bend upriver, immense cakes of ice climb three stories out of the river and crash over. The mile-wide channel of the river is a dancing, jostling white mass in slow motion. The flag flaps.

My cabin is on the slough at the low end of town. It will flood first, if it comes to that, and it's all I can do not to pace. The ice near shore groans, shatters, then, very, very slowly, moves. We sigh collectively. It's going now. The banner still flaps in the breeze, though. Groaning, cracking, rushing water, ducks and geese flighting by the thousands, the sun redder now than gore. An ice cake the size of a tennis court pushes slowly up onto the beach and into the village square. We step back to avoid getting crushed. The flag is still there. Neal looks at his watch.

"There," a woman says. The banner mast tilts, the banner touches the ice. We hold our breath. Then, as a cabin-size block of ice pushes up and smashes down, winter is gone. Fifty people cheer. Half a dozen fire shotguns in the air. A grinning old man passes around a jug of bourbon.

The water and ice in the slough in front of my cabin have risen eight feet. Since the ice flow slows the river, some rising is expected. But the water rises too fast. I pile bedding, tents, guns, and food on the roof. Murky water trickles across the road and climbs into the yard. It's up to the hood on Neal's pickup mired in the mud.

THE DANGEROUS GAME

Village sled dogs run free now, in packs and dangerous, so they can flee the rising water. Even old women carry guns against the dogs.

Waterfowl swirl and dip into the open water behind the ice flow upriver. Birds flight along the slough to open lakes beyond the village. The shooting has started again in the village. It is easier to shoot than to sit and wait to see how far the water will rise.

The water surges around my cabin, and immense ice cakes skid into the yard. The ice shoves the spruce-post fence against the house, and refrigerator-size blocks bump against the log walls. The water rises to my floorboards, and it's window-high on Neal's cabin. Lucy Roberts's outhouse floats by and drifts into the poplar forest.

Most have retreated to the high end of town. Perhaps foolishly, I stand in water to the top of my hip boots and fend off ice blocks with a two-by-four. Almost imperceptibly, the rising slows, then holds. Within moments, water and ice surge down the slough as if someone has pulled a behemoth plug. Uplifted ice cakes the size of a baseball infield and blocks bigger than a house litter the street, yard, and forest. The willow flat across the slough has disappeared beneath twelve feet of ice. It will not reappear until July. An ice block so large it will be a source of ice and water through the coming autumn leans against my cabin.

The flights of birds are slow in the midday, but the shooting continues in the village square. The winner of the breakup pot has bought three gallons of bourbon and set them on the square's single picnic table for all comers. Men shoot in the air in celebration. I return to the safety of my cabin. Neal tosses a yearling Canada goose onto my porch and waves through the window, then hurries off for the fun.

The shooting starts again in the twilight of the 3 A.M. dawn. Thousands of birds wing down the river, over the village, and up my slough. It sounds like a full brigade assaulting a hostile stronghold. I pour a thermos of tea and walk into the dawn. One family has a belly-high pile of ducks gathered in front of their cabin. Two cackling old women skin the birds and throw the offal to the snapping, snarling dogs.

SHOOT-UP ON THE YUKON

A man sits in a lawn chair with a coffee thermos beside him. He makes no effort at camouflage. When a flight approaches, he sets down the cup, picks up the shotgun, stands, and shoots. A four-year-old, chubby in a caribou hide parka, scurries after the birds that drop in the muddy street. A tipsy woman shouts encouragement each time a bird falls.

By full sunup, everyone is on the street, shooting, chatting, and gazing frequently beyond the immense ice blocks clogging the road to reassure themselves. The brown, surging river is free of ice for the first time in seven months. It's spring.

IN A TREELESS COUNTRY

It could not have been a better *or* a worse time for Wes Vining of The Trophy Connection, the hunt broker, to call. It had been a hard winter, and it wasn't over. El Niño had dumped six feet of snow outside my house in northern Utah. I was ready for any break. But I was in the middle of things, too, computing final grades for my English and zoology classes at Weber State University. And splitting cordwood and digging out the pickups took much of each day. If I went, I doubted Cheri could manage. After heated wrangling, two sleepless nights, and one red-eyed hangover, we mutually decided I wouldn't go. So that was that—a dream ending in a maze of practicality.

Originally, I'd inquired about a polar bear hunt in the distant and nebulous future, but Vining had a deal. And, so, the dilemma. Wes called again. He recognized in the delay the struggle we were having. He sweetened the pot.

* * * * *

"We have the flu here," Jaypatee Akeeagok said as he shifted his slight frame. "Most of the village has it." He stroked his skimpy goatee and looked concerned.

I stared out the window of the Grise Fiord Lodge at the jumbled ice pack that stretched into the sunset, and wondered what flu had to do with polar bear hunting.

"I hope you don't catch it," he said as if reading my mind. He was my guide, and by reputation the best bear hunter in Grise Fiord. He was checking me out.

"Hunting by dogsled is very slow," he said. "Don't expect the speed of a snow machine or a safari truck." That suited me fine. I hate hunting by machine.

IN A TREELESS COUNTRY

The quality of the setting sun in mid-March indicated moderate temperatures, but the thermometer outside the window registered -37 Centigrade. Readings on thermometers were just numbers, but I'd walked through that cold and wind when the cargo 737 had landed in Resolute Bay three days earlier, and I *felt* it. When I'd reached the airstrip shack fifty yards off, I was as cold as I'd ever been. The intensity frightened me.

I was stranded in Resolute Bay on Cornwallis Island for two days until the next flight in a Twin Otter to Grise Fiord 250 miles northeast. I tried walking through Resolute, population 130, when the temperature climbed to a balmy -28 degrees. I made it only two blocks before sprinting back to the High Arctic Inn. Early March is full winter in the High Arctic.

"We have to be careful of the cold." Jaypatee could look you in the eye, sense what you thought, and address it. "But we'll keep you warm. We have stoves for the tent, and you have your caribou clothes now."

Earlier, I'd been fitted out from the stockpile of handmade, half-cured, caribou-hide mukluks, mittens, pants, and parkas the Inuits kept in a big walk-in freezer. Fully dressed, I felt as awkward as a two-year-old in a first snowsuit.

"We stop twice each day to boil water for tea and eat something and move around," he continued, still sensing my anxiety, though I'd said nothing. "The tent is warm with two stoves going all night." He paused to see if his assurances had any effect.

"OK," I said, "I'm ready." I wondered.

"Pauloosie Attagootak will come for you in the morning," he said. "He's my helper and will follow with supplies." I could tell he had something else on his mind. Finally, he looked at my dark beard and said, "You're not with Greenpeace, are you?"

After Jaypatee left, I realized that other thing. *This is a treeless country.* I stared again out the window. I'd lived in wilderness and was comfortable with it. For much of my life, I'd spent two months each year north of the Arctic Circle, more than four hundred miles from the nearest blacktop—hunting, trekking, and floating in the wildest country on the continent, usually alone. If something happened, that was that. But there were always the trees, stunted as they were that far north. With a few twigs from

THE DANGEROUS GAME

a black spruce, I could start a fire anywhere. In the wilds, a man had to have a fire for warmth and for other reasons. *But here, what could you do?*

I'd felt that verge of panic before, once while hunting muskox, and another time Peary caribou on the High Arctic barrens. There, nothing grew taller than your thumb. The Inuits heated the tent with Coleman cookstoves. Without trees, I was at the mercy of technology, and technology fails. Then, I'd have to rely on the Inuits, and I wasn't even sure they could survive any longer out there without technology. Perhaps it wasn't the fear of the cold and the icy, treeless barrens so much as it was of having to depend upon someone else to survive. I hated even riding in a car with someone else driving. Unlike in other places, the wilderness didn't provide on the ice of the High Arctic. You had to bring survival with you.

The sun reddened the pack ice of Jones Sound at 4 A.M. I was tempted to scale the cliffs behind the village. They said you could see Greenland on a clear day. But that cold was out there, and I couldn't waddle up the bluffs in the clumsy caribou clothing.

Outside, the television satellite dishes looked out of place in the northernmost community in North America. Grise Fiord got its supplies six weeks each summer when the cargo ships idled in between the 'bergs. The rows of prefab houses looked even stranger in this isolated settlement. *What did you expect, igloos?*

Pauloosie arrived, and we snowmobiled to the pack ice, where Jaypatee was adjusting dog harnesses. Then we sledded off, Jaypatee shouting, "*Ay-Oook!*" and "*Ite!*" and lashing the green, twenty-six-foot, seal-hide whip over the dogs' heads. "We'll camp off that point." He gestured with his chin at an Arctic Diamond Head in the distance to the west. "It's twenty-four miles."

Sixteen Greenland huskies—bigger, meaner, and hairier than their Alaskan cousins—fanned out and lunged across the jumble of sea ice in a fog of their own body heat. The gentle jarring of the sixteen-foot sled lulled me as the naked, treeless cliffs of Ellesmere Island shrunk. From time to time I turned to see Grise Fiord, civilization, until by afternoon it had disappeared with the distance.

We stopped, and Jaypatee cracked the whip over the dogs until they lay down. Pauloosie fired up two gas stoves where we'd paused beside a four-story iceberg. After thousands of years, the salt leaches out of the ice and leaves only fresh water. He dropped chunks into the big kettles on the stoves. In a surprisingly short time, soup and tea steamed in the icy, dry air. I was too clumsy in the caribou parka and pants to be of any help. I trotted around and windmilled my arms to keep warm.

Warmed, we mushed off again toward the big point in the distance that seemed little closer than it had that morning. When I chilled, I ran behind the sled with my mittened hands holding firmly to the upstanders. We made the point shortly after sundown, and it took Jaypatee and Pauloosie three hours to settle and feed the dogs, pitch the wall tent, gather and melt ice, and arrange everything else. I was impatient with the time it took, but too clumsy to be helpful. By evening, my beard and mustache had frozen together in a one-pound ball, and not until the tent was warm would it thaw. The thermometer read -34 degrees.

The daily routine started with another three hours of breaking camp and loading gear. We'd mush until late morning and stop for tea, travel another three hours and eat lunch, then sled until after sundown before pitching the tent. The guides kept the wall tent warm enough so that we were comfortable in sweaters, while outside the canvas the temperature was 75 degrees colder.

"We're in real bear country now," Jaypatee said when we stopped the next day. I didn't need to be told because I'd spotted the first fresh set of tracks as I half-dozed on the sled. "Don't leave the tent without the gun. To *nanuq*, man is just meat."

If I ran afoul of a polar bear in the bulky parka, I'd have to shoot from the hip because I'd never get the gun to shoulder. The guides staked the dogs in a rectangle around the tent to warn of bears in the night.

"*Nanuq*," Pauloosie said, as if to clarify further the rectangle of dogs. "Come at night. Eat men."

I thought he was dramatizing for the greenhorn, but that night the Inuits slept semiupright and fully clothed, facing the flap, with the rifles just outside. We couldn't bring the guns inside because of condensation: They'd flash-freeze when we took them out again.

THE DANGEROUS GAME

I pulled the down sleeping bag over my head and went to sleep, but each time I awoke, the guides dozed on elbows, fully dressed as if *nanuq* might burst in at any moment. They were more ready for a sudden lead opening or a squall that way, too. I tried to resign myself to their care. I really had no choice.

In the morning, we spotted a sow and big cub from the iceberg where we'd camped. They showed nicotine-yellow against the blue-white ice and snow. Later, as the dogs followed a refrozen lead, we found another sow with two nearly grown cubs. Their tracks were as big as my mukluked feet. By midday, we'd passed the mouth of Muskox Fiord on the sea ice and mushed out beyond Cape Storm.

Jay climbed every iceberg now and glassed the pack ice carefully. Often, he'd spot bears four or five miles off. Mostly they were sows with cubs. I'd climb up to look when the terrain wasn't too steep or slick to negotiate in my caribou suit.

I hated the awkward clothing. Jaypatee and Pauloosie dressed in lighter clothes of polar bear, wolf, or dog hide stitched to synthetic fabric. They had warmth without the bulk and loss of agility. Still, each time Jay climbed a 'berg, I feared for his safety. I wasn't being altruistic, either, because if he fell, there'd be a good chance I wouldn't get out. I hated that feeling of dependence.

And I hated the cold. I work out regularly and haven't an ounce of fat, which means I have no natural insulation. I ran behind the sled three times as often as the Inuits, and even then didn't get fully warm. The hot tea and soup breaks helped, and those thermal packets you put in boots or mittens were a godsend, though I didn't use them until the sixth day out because the Inuits hadn't used them.

"I think eight-foot bear is out there, maybe eight and a half," Jaypatee said when he climbed down from an iceberg that afternoon. "Big enough?" He noticed my pause. "We go look anyway," Pauloosie put in.

Jaypatee and Pauloosie discussed something in Inuktitut since English was their second language and both felt more comfortable talking in the native tongue. If things got complicated or exciting, they lapsed into Inuktitut.

IN A TREELESS COUNTRY

We directed the dogs out to open ice and through a jumble of ice blocks the size of tanks. Within two miles, we spotted the bear standing on an ice ridge and staring back at us in disbelief. Jaypatee dropped the sled anchor and let the oblivious dogs slow to a stop. Through the binocular, the bear didn't look that big to me, but without trees to give it perspective, what could I know?

"Maybe eight, eight and a half feet," Jaypatee said as he stared through the binocular. He looked at me and I shook my head. "Your bear." He shrugged and turned the dogs westerly.

We didn't see another bear that day. Light clouds drifted from the northwest, so slight they would have no significance elsewhere in North America. The Inuits glanced at them with furrowed brows. "Storm tonight, I think," Pauloosie said. "Mebbe camp soon."

We camped to the east side, in what we hoped would be the lee, of a big iceberg. Jay staked the dogs, and Pauloosie hustled up the tent. Again, I was no help in the caribou suit. They hand-sawed blocks from the wind-packed snow layered over the sea ice. Jaypatee stacked the blocks into a wall around the tent and smoothed the seams. The clouds thickened and lowered. A ground blizzard raged four miles to the south. The thermometer read -39 degrees.

In the tent, Jaypatee warmed flashlight batteries on the stove and slipped them into a small, simple two-way radio. He radioed his brother in Grise Fiord, a hundred miles to the east, and we learned that winds were shrieking at fifty knots through the hamlet. The Inuit hunters who had been stranded by wind on the ice of Baffin Bay when we left were still stranded. You don't travel in wind and minus-thirty-degree temperatures.

We hunkered and waited for the squall. Jay built the semi-igloo around the tent to deflect the winds, but he was prepared for the tent to blow down. He'd brought in the emergency geodome tent to have it near, just in case. I slept poorly that night and awoke to hear the guides discussing something in Inuktitut over the popping tent canvas and humming anchor lines. Toward dawn, the wind quit suddenly.

In the brilliant cold morning, we mushed off southwest toward Grinnell Peninsula, closer to the magnetic pole. We found old

THE DANGEROUS GAME

tracks, but nothing fresh. At the morning tea break, Jaypatee spotted a sow and big cub to the north at the base of the cliffs of Ellesmere. Each time I glanced at the big island I was half-surprised not to see trees.

As we mushed, Jaypatee and Pauloosie hacked frozen slabs of raw caribou from a shoulder quarter and munched on them. "'Eskimo' means 'eaters of raw meat,'" Pauloosie said.

They offered me some, but I declined. It wasn't the rawness that bothered me, but the frozen cold. I needed every kilocalorie of heat, and I was concerned enough about it that I ate twice as much as I wanted at meals. I never understood how the dogs pulled a sled at a trot on a mouthful of frozen caribou and stayed warm enough at night curled on the sea ice in minus-forty-degree temperatures.

At the evening feeding, Jaypatee dumped a bag of frozen caribou chunks on the ice then jumped back as the big dogs lunged in a snarling, snapping frenzy. Pauloosie stood by with the whip in case Jay stumbled. If he did, he'd be mauled, or worse. (When we returned to Grise Fiord, we learned an Inuit girl had been killed by sled dogs in a village to the south.) Otherwise, Pauloosie stayed clear of the dogs. And the half-wild dogs, mostly males, fought continuously. Our trail was spattered with blood.

The days sifted by, like the snow on the day we stayed in camp because of a ground blizzard. Five feet above the ice there was no blowing snow, but you couldn't see your feet. We spotted a bear in the distance, but it was too dangerous to chase it.

As the days ran out, I became more sure we wouldn't kill a bear. But Jay was obsessed. He refused to quit. I'd already given up, and to my anger and anxiety, Jay mushed steadily southwest, in the opposite direction of Grise Fiord. By dogsled, we were four long days from the village. That left absolutely no leeway if a storm forced us to hole up for a day. If I missed the flight, I wouldn't get to Resolute Bay for another four days, minimum, and from there it was four days back to the States, depending on whether I met the complicated flight schedules. I'd be late for spring term. I was resigned to no bear. I now looked forward almost fiercely to getting out, to being warm, and to seeing trees. I'd relax again when I saw trees.

IN A TREELESS COUNTRY

We circled in a southerly direction until we sledded close beneath the cliffs of Devon Island, then swung back northeast toward the jumbled pack ice off Cape Storm. Late in the afternoon of a long day with no bears, we found immense tracks, the largest we'd seen.

"Big *nanuq*," Pauloosie grinned. "Eat men."

But the tracks, packed by the wind, were filled with drift-pocked snow. Later, we found the same giant tracks, but a day or two fresher. We sledded northerly toward Ellesmere's coast and a possible rendezvous with Jaypatee's brother and son. At least now we were mushing in the right direction. One step closer to getting out.

We met in the dusk. We'd been on the sea ice longer than planned and were running low on the food Iviq Adventures had packed. Jay's brother had volunteered to run supplies the hundred miles from Grise Fiord on his new snow machine. As they pitched tents, Jay climbed the iceberg and glassed. "*Nanuq*," he called. "I think it's big, too."

"Let's go," he called to me. "Are you cold?"

I was, but I reached for the .375 in the soft case. Jaypatee whipped the exhausted dogs into a trot, and then a gallop as we bounced over the jumbled and broken ice. I began to shiver in violent fits.

The bear was farther than we thought. Jay climbed an iceberg and glassed, then he shoved the sled around and mushed in a new direction. It was getting dark fast when the sled skidded down an ice ridge and we spotted the bear a quarter mile off. The dogs saw the bear at the same instant, and suddenly Jay didn't have to urge them with the whip. The dogs sprinted silently and intently after the bear with astonishing speed. I hung onto the rifle with one mittened hand and the lashing with the other. The sprinting pack hurtled around an ice block, but the sled slammed it, sailing twenty feet before it crashed down again, making my legs bounce off one side and Jay's the other.

The dogs closed, but the bear made time when he hit rough ice. If *nanuq* made the ice ridge in the distance, we'd lose him. But the dogs neared. To my complete surprise, Jay slashed the

THE DANGEROUS GAME

harness line with one swift stroke of his knife, and the dogs raced free. Within moments, they bayed the bear. They circled and feigned at the goliath male, and the bear lunged and swatted at the too-quick dogs. The action made it all seem comfortable and familiar. Jaypatee peeled the bulky parka over my head. I maneuvered for a shot, careful not to catch a lunging dog or have the bullet pass through the bear and kill a dog on the off side. I no longer felt the cold. I paid no attention when my bare thumb burned against the minus-forty-degree rifle barrel as it would against a hot poker. We all heard the bullet slap and saw the bear lunge into the dogs, swatting wildly. I threw the bolt of the .375, waited for the dogs to clear again, and pressed the trigger. The bear was down.

My hand had gone numb in the fingerless, light-wool shooting glove. Jaypatee slapped it against his thigh and put one of his warmed dog-skin mittens on it. It took half an hour for the feeling to return and another hour for my finger to blacken from the ice burn on the rifle barrel.

All five of us rolled more than half a ton of bear onto the sled. I felt no cold as we sledded toward camp. In the alpenglow, barren, treeless Ellesmere no longer looked obscene and unnatural. The hissing gas stoves in the tents sounded as welcome and natural as crackling spruce deadfall. Pauloosie tossed me a chunk of raw frozen caribou and grinned. I popped it in my mouth and grinned back, then bent to help with the skinning.

THE OLD WOMAN'S GIFT

"She died there seventy years ago," the old man told me.

In those days, the Gwitchin came from their winter village, sixty miles south, trekking with willow-frame packs and laden sled dogs through the mosquito swarms and across the tundra to spend the summer in the hills. There were caribou and moose, grayling and pike in the river and lakes, and, in August, plenty of blueberries. Then, late in August or early in September, the big migration would come.

"I remember," the old Gwitchin man said, "watching the caribou come for a week at a time. They came down the creek and stretched to the hills to the south. There were thousands."

He'd been a boy then, the year the old woman died. It was not unusual for people to die there; every summer it seemed one or two did. "Perhaps they died of old age or some sickness," he told me.

"It was really funny," he continued, "the caribou kind of slowed down after the old woman died. Fewer came the next year, and fewer still the year after that. After a few years, The People quit going out there. They changed the name of the creek and called it after the old woman." He leaned back against the log wall of the cabin and swatted a blood-gorged mosquito. "I think she was some kind of a witch, maybe a caribou witch."

He used the Gwitchin word for witch. I'd talked with the old Indian one spring, as he visited a relative, one of my neighbors, at Circle, a small village on the Yukon River.

* * * * *

I was sitting on the south slope of the cemetery hill, where the old woman was buried, in a hollow out of the wind and next to a fire of spruce branches, waiting for the caribou. I'd been to the

THE DANGEROUS GAME

hill before, had hunted moose and ptarmigan here, had gathered blueberries along the slopes, had wandered through the graves. Some were marked with four square, hand-hewn spruce posts bearing a curious cone on top. Others were marked with a blaze on a spruce tree, while still others were unmarked. It was a strange place. Not frightening, just strange. If you looked closely, you'd see human bones scattered about the tundra—a femur here, a humerus and some foot bones there, and, in one place, the shocking white of a toothless skull grinning up through the lichens. In a dry, cold climate, decay took centuries, and the bones were well preserved, except where they'd been gnawed. I didn't camp on the hill; it wouldn't have been right. I camped across the river, just above its confluence with Old Woman Creek.

Days earlier, I'd seen the first small band of caribou, far to the south. I couldn't have caught them even if there'd been good bulls in the herd, and there weren't. The mid-September air had turned cold. In spite of the calendar, I no longer felt the illusion of autumn—in that country, short and ephemeral at best—only the reality of winter. The wind had a January bite to it. I wasn't sure if the caribou had already left the country or were waiting for the first big storm to push them out of the mountains.

I'd already been in the Arctic bush for a month. Earlier, while I was trekking and hunting in the mountains to the north, caribou had been the farthest things from my mind. It wasn't until later, while floating down the glacial river to where I now camped, that I'd begun to think I'd like to get one. Now, for some reason, it had become important to hunt them, to hunt them in this place. But the season this far north was advanced, and I'd stayed dangerously late already. In less than two weeks, I was to rendezvous with the bush pilot on a gravel bar almost two hundred miles downriver . . . that was, if everything went right.

In the following days, I saw more bands of caribou on the distant dry-brown tundra south of the old woman's hill, but there'd been no trophy bulls. They may have been the last caribou in the country, and I was maybe just wasting time. And this late in the year, I knew, I could be wasting more than time.

As more tributaries froze in the mountains to the north, the river began to drop. It dropped slowly, inches a day, but if it

THE OLD WOMAN'S GIFT

turned much colder, which was not only possible but becoming *likely* this late in the season, the remaining feeder streams would freeze solid, locking up the waters that fed the river. Then the river itself would drop and freeze, making the hundred miles of rapids downriver impassable and thereby stranding me. I was gambling a lot for a caribou.

Snow squalls occasionally swept through, trailing curtains of wind-driven snow. At such times, the tundra plains looked wintry, the country hostile and desolate, and I felt like the last man on earth. Or the first. The snow didn't worry me since I was traveling by river, but the cold did. The ponds had already frozen. Still, I could find no caribou bulls.

One afternoon as I was huddled by my tiny fire in the hollow on the old woman's hill, I noticed a band of caribou loping easily across the plain. Perhaps two hundred yards behind was a very light wolf. The caribou weren't yet worried since they could easily outdistance a wolf in a chase. As the caribou trotted down a small hill and into a ravine, a second wolf broke from dwarf willows, forty yards away. The caribou panicked and sprinted for the river, but the wolf had the angle and closed. The big canine slammed a fleeing caribou and flattened it, its momentum carrying it past the prey. It then pivoted and sprang back on the cow as it struggled, tearing and finally pulling it down. It was joined by the first wolf, which licked the blood from the cow's wounds. The two lay near the dead caribou for some time, panting and resting, before one sat on its haunches and howled.

I watched through the binocular, and it was long moments before the rising then falling wail floated to where I huddled by the fire. It was oddly primeval and somehow familiar, as if I'd been here and watched it all before. A chill ran up my spine and I huddled closer to the fire, trying to rationalize it away, telling myself the chill had been only the wind.

The following day I didn't see a caribou, and none the next. The river continued to drop, and the ice moved out from the quiet water along the shore.

"Where are the bulls, old woman?" I found myself asking one day. After living alone for so long, it wasn't unusual to talk to imaginary beings or myself.

THE DANGEROUS GAME

They came that night. I lay asleep in my tent on the river beach, when I was awakened by a change. I came slowly up through sleep, remembering the fresh grizzly tracks on the bar. But then I heard the splashing and tinkling of breaking shore ice, and suddenly the river roared as if a rapid had started. My next thought was of a flash flood, but even before I burst from the tent I realized that was impossible—there'd been no rain, and it was too cold. Light humps ghosted about in the starlight and in the pale yellow and green shimmer of the aurora. Antlers clattered against each other. Caribou by the hundreds. I could have reached out and touched the nearest with the rifle barrel. They smelled musky-sweet.

The caribou trampled the embers of the fire, and I fired two shots into the air to clear the mass of bodies from around the tent. Once, a cow nearly shoved me into the stampede. And then they were gone as quickly as they'd come.

I walked up the beach in the daylight, almost wondering if it had all been a dream. The beach was three hundred yards long by seventy or so wide. Every square yard of it was caribou-trampled. I reflected that in spite of the crazy, sudden abundance of caribou only hours earlier, I still hadn't gotten one. Had it been an omen?

I felt optimistic as I climbed the old woman's hill later that morning and stood at her grave on the top. Two of the four hand-hewn posts had fallen over years earlier, and the entire top of the hill was riddled with parka squirrel burrows. Except for the collapsed posts, the old man had described her grave perfectly.

I saw no caribou that day, in spite of the optimism. It was colder, too. The next day was even colder, and the river had dropped noticeably. I'd give it one more day.

That day came and went, and I saw no caribou. The river dropped more, and previously submerged boulders showed above the surface. Ice formed in the quiet water and moved well out into the current. The lake behind camp had completely frozen across, and the last sea ducks down from the Arctic Ocean had flown south.

"One more day," I said aloud, this time meaning it, "and then it's finished."

THE OLD WOMAN'S GIFT

As it was, I'd have to hurry to make the rendezvous downriver with the bush pilot, Roger Dowding. I'd killed big caribou before; I couldn't quite figure out why getting another had become so important. It felt odd, this compulsion.

I climbed the old woman's hill in the dawn. The day was bleak and blustery, and a northwest wind knifed through the stunted spruce. Nothing stirred but a single raven flapping listlessly from tree to tree along the creek below. I felt content, knowing I'd leave the next day, caribou or no. I had no decisions left to make now. My decision was firm, and with it came a curious feeling of serenity. In the morning I'd be on the way out—ultimately to a hot shower and a bed with sheets and someone to talk to. I'd forgotten how those things felt.

I wasn't discouraged when I returned to camp that evening, even though I'd seen no game. I felt certain the caribou had left the country, and I didn't feel bad I hadn't gotten one. Seeing the wolves hunt and kill, and standing on the beach in the midst of the big stampede had made it all worthwhile. I loved this country, and though I hadn't even left it, I already missed it.

Breakfast was over by the time the sun climbed feebly above the southeastern hills. It offered no heat at this season and latitude, and it climbed only low in the sky, but I still welcomed it. I would travel in its direction.

I shoved the raft into the current and settled myself in, then looked up at the old woman's grave on the top of the hill. The two spruce posts were silhouetted against the southern sky. I was silently saying farewell when I saw it.

Something moved on the shoulder of the hill, halfway up. In that odd, ethereal northern light, I at first thought it was one of the pale, caribou-hunting wolves, but then I saw the antlers. The big bull's silver dewlap flowed in the wind that always seemed to come off the hill, and his mane glowed white in the low sun. His antlers were the stuff of visions and dreams. I nearly dropped the rifle as I fumbled with it in my heavily mittened hands. The big bull plodded toward where the old woman's hill sloped into the river. I floated toward where it intended to cross, sitting silently in the raft, letting the bull and the current close the distance. I tried to calm myself. I could scarcely believe the luck.

THE DANGEROUS GAME

When I had closed the distance and was out of sight behind the curve of the slope, I rowed quietly to the bank just across from the hill. The bull trotted down the slope as I eased into a sitting position and jacked a round into the chamber. I settled the cross hairs on his shoulder when he stepped out of willows. I pressed the trigger, and, at the blast, the bull pitched forward, struggled a moment, and lay still. I knew he was mine from the moment I'd seen him. I'd eat caribou heart for supper.

As I hurriedly skinned and quartered the fat-heavy bull, I couldn't help but think of the old woman, the caribou witch. I marveled at the strange, almost mystical outcome of the hunt: I'd given up on the caribou and had quit thinking of them when suddenly, just below her place on the hill, he came, like a gift, glowing in the early sun.

"You've been in the bush too long," I told myself aloud, "you're getting superstitious." (There's an old saw in the Far North about people who spend too much time in the bush: It's OK to talk to yourself, but when you answer yourself back, you'd better worry.) But I couldn't shake the feeling.

I hurriedly loaded the quarters into the inflatable boat. It was eight, nine days downriver; I had seven. They'd have to be long ones. But something was unfinished. It was only superstition, I knew, but I picked up the caribou heart and climbed up to the old woman's grave. I placed the heart on the weathered mound, just in case.

GRIZZLIES

I'd been solo in the Arctic bush for four weeks in one of the most remote places on the continent—three hundred miles from the nearest slab of what passes for Alaskan pavement. Four days earlier, I'd killed a one-ton, Boone & Crockett-class moose. I'd spent days backpacking my moose three miles up the Coleen River, then floating it across to the camp a chunk at a time. By the time I'd packed in the last of it that morning, it weighed two tons. Happy with the finished job, I crawled into the tent for a badly needed nap.

When I came slowly out of a dream about a steaming bath and an incredibly green chef's salad, a great golden head regarded me with curiosity. The grizzly could have drooled on my feet, and the .270 wasn't even loaded. Then it disappeared with a rustle of the tent flap. I lay there, convinced I'd dreamt it, but to be sure, I jacked a round in the chamber and looked outside. Big, long-clawed tracks cratered the mud. That was the closest I'd come to a live, wild bear of any kind, before or since.

The grizzly bear, *Ursus arctos*, is a brown bear, as are the Kodiak bear, the Kamchatka bear, the Eurasian bear, the Siberian bear, and so on. Contrary to Clinton Hart Merriam's 1918 publication describing seventy-eight species of grizzly, there's only one. If you transplanted a Yukon grizzly bear to Mongolia's Altai or Siberia's vast tundra barrens, it would breed happily with local bears and produce fertile offspring once it got past the language barrier.

Ursus arctos, subspecies *horribilis*, the common grizzly, ranges from the Yellowstone ecosystem to the Arctic Ocean, excluding southern and western coastal Alaska, where *Ursus arctos middendorffi* grows to enormous proportions feeding on salmon. The subspecies *middendorffi* includes the brown bears of Kodiak Island and the Alaskan Peninsula. *Ursus arctos*

THE DANGEROUS GAME

richardsoni is the barren-ground grizzly, ranging north of the treeline in Canada's Nunavut and Northwest Territories.

Grizz are hunted April through June, then again from late August or September through denning time, which varies with altitude, latitude, and weather. Grizzlies are eating machines and feed every waking moment, literally, to layer on the fat needed to survive hibernation. (While we're at it, grizzlies don't truly hibernate, they become torpid and can be roused with little difficulty.) Key in on what they're eating, and you'll see bears.

Salmon runs don't play an important part in most interior-grizzly populations. In some locales, though, bears do concentrate along rivers for late summer runs, especially after fish have spawned themselves out and littered the shoreline. The tributary rivers in the Yukon River system are good examples. There, float-hunting works well, as does still-hunting along the river. Hunt into the wind, since the grizzly has an exceptional sense of smell.

I'd guess 70 percent of interior grizzlies are killed when hunters return to pack out caribou, moose, or sheep meat and find a bear has appropriated it. Scott Ruttum of R&R Guide Service, the best outfit in the Far North, uses moose gut piles because, in all cases, a bear will find it in a few days. Most of his fall clients collect bears this way.

Though I haven't yet had to kill a bear over a carcass, I've had my share of close shaves. Grizzlies around Yellowstone National Park have learned to key in on gunshots. They know it means an elk kill and, at the least, a gut pile. I once killed an elk in Montana, just north of the park boundary. Before I'd gutted and skinned the six-by-six bull, a grizz showed up. Fortunately, it stayed downwind, so the mare didn't scent it. I tied her fast to a stout lodgepole pine and continued butchering the elk. The bear retreated into the forest. By dark, I'd packed what I could on the mare and led her to camp. When I returned the next morning, the bear had worked over the gut pile, eaten an entire hindquarter, and left enough scent to scare the mare into Canada. Luckily, I had a good hold on the lead rope, and, when she had finished dragging me through every deadfall in southern Montana, I loaded her up with what was left.

GRIZZLIES

In true wilderness, such as Nunavut, the Yukon, and the Northwest Territories, bears haven't learned this trick. Just the same, they have uncanny scenting abilities and can follow scent for miles. Pack out the meat and trophy pronto.

Grizzlies focus on berries in the Far North interior. There, grizz is king and knows it; except for a bigger bear, he has nothing to fear and is easier to stalk than prey animals like caribou. Just the same, watch wind direction.

My more pleasant memories involve sitting atop "pingos"—conical frost-heaves sometimes a hundred feet high—glassing vast tundra berry flats for caribou, moose, or grizzlies. The best weather in the Arctic is in late August and September, and glassing amidst the polychrome riot of crimson, gold, burgundy, orange, and bronze is so agreeable that spotting game almost becomes secondary. Almost. You nearly always see game, be it migrating caribou, a lone wolf, a moose browsing dwarf willows, or a grizz. Then, you circle into the wind, while noting a distant peak or large willow for guidance, and close to thirty yards. If you can quiet your thumping heart, the shot is anticlimactic.

Nearly twenty years ago while I was hunting caribou, however, the shot definitely was *not* an anticlimax. Normally, caribou flooded the drainage by early September, but that season, I couldn't buy one. Instead, I found a grizz. Though I had a tag just in case, I didn't really want to shoot a bear and had planned on "shooting" him with my camera. After spotting the bear, I picked a quick coffee can of blueberries to mix with flapjack batter and walked back to camp for the Nikon SLR.

Still looking for caribou, I eventually stalked to just across the ravine from the bear, but, when I peeked over, the bear had fed to my side and was busily stripping berry bushes twenty yards below. I eased below the bushline and, as silently as possible, jacked a round in the chamber, thinking it best to be ready this close. Possibly the bear heard or scented me. He rose to his hind legs like those bears in "B" movies, his massive head rocking from side to side. In one motion, he grunted, dropped to all fours, and rushed like a steam engine in a silent movie. The .270's bullet broke his neck as I shot down at him—he was that close.

THE DANGEROUS GAME

As a biologist, I performed my usual gut analysis. The bruin had eaten blueberries, of course, as well as cranberries, soapberries, crowberries, ground squirrel (I found the feet), part of a shed moose antler (for calcium), grass, moss, poplar bark, dead willow leaves, and a stone the size of a golf ball. Whether he'd ingested the stone accidentally is anyone's guess.

While I was hunting bear along the west coast of Russia's Sea of Okhotsk in 2001, they were still emerging from dens in mid-May. In the spring, hunters track or glass for bears on snow just after they've left dens. Normally, bears leave dens in April, though in the very far north, they may not leave until May. Fur is dense and long, but bears start rubbing soon after leaving their dens, so if a perfect hide is the objective, hunt very early in the spring. Early in the season, bears may rely more heavily on old vegetation, but they quickly shift to winterkilled big-game carcasses or old salmon. Bears may also specialize, hunting newly dropped caribou and moose calves.

I killed one such bear in the spring of 2003 with R&R Guide Service partner Rob Jones and guide Scott Ruttum. Even though the bear was a fish-fed coastal brownie, he reacted the same as any interior brown bear. We'd hunted twelve days without luck and had finally moved camp into the midst of more than two thousand caribou. They'd begun to calve, and the predators—eagles, wolves, wolverines, foxes, and, finally, bears—had concentrated in the area. That morning, we watched cows giving birth and new calves trying to follow their mothers. We must have seen hundreds of newborns, and we'd already seen three bears working through the caribou.

Late in the afternoon, Cheri found the first good bear we'd seen on the hunt. It had crossed from one drainage to another over a high saddle and was in sight for only moments. Cheri got me on the bear for only a moment, but in that glimpse I knew it was a taker: It lumbered and didn't have the teddy bear look of smaller bears. Its neck was long, its head seemed small in proportion to its body, and its movements were purposeful. We discussed the chances of collecting the bear; after all, it was three miles away and moving. We decided we had little or no chance. Then we decided to go for it.

GRIZZLIES

We hurried down the slope. Rob, Scott, and I loaded up our backpacks for staying overnight, and we took off at a near run. When we'd climbed to the top of a ridge more than an hour later, Scott found with his binocular the monster bruin on a distant ridge, tossing a calf caribou in the air. We plunged down the slope, through the bottoms, and up the intervening ridge, then glassed long and hard. Nothing. We had decided to move toward a hundred caribou below when I looked down the slope just in time to see the big bear walk away from the spruce.

We circled back to get out of the wind, then went down the benches to head off the bear. Fortunately the bear killed another caribou calf and was busy eating while we stalked. We approached to a hundred yards and watched for fifteen minutes while the bear lay with its rump toward us. When it stood, it turned suddenly toward us, and I hit it in the chest with a 300-grain A-frame softpoint from the .375. The bear galloped off, and I spined it. That nine-foot-plus bruin survived on caribou calves for that part of the spring. Within just thirty minutes, it had killed and eaten two of them.

To most, the grizzly bear is synonymous with ferocity and horror (hence the subspecies name, *horribilis*). I lived a decade in Circle, a Gwitchin Athabascan village on the Yukon River. Each year I spent a month trekking and photographing in grizzly-infested Denali National Park, and two months trekking, hunting, and river-running in the Arctic wilderness. I've had close encounters with more than four hundred grizzlies. Bears have walked into my camps; I've chased them off caribou, moose, and sheep kills (though just often enough to keep things interesting, it's been the other way around); and I've surprised them at close quarters. Yet I've had only three near misses.

The last one streaked my beard with gray. Cheri and I had been hunting in the Arctic bush for eight weeks. Mush ice had started showing in the Sheenjek River, and the September chill sank its fangs into us and hung on like a wolverine. We felt the impending winter as we floated out toward Fort Yukon, two hundred river miles south. If the river froze before we got there, we'd get stranded.

THE DANGEROUS GAME

We rowed into an eddy one evening, and I climbed ashore to look for a campsite. I wandered through the close-growing spruce, searching for a spot big enough for the tent. Behind me I suddenly heard brush splinter, so I pivoted to see what was happening. There in the dusk, its fangs flashing ivory, a bristling grizzly was smashing through deadfall straight at me and faster than I could have imagined.

I had no doubt whatsoever I was about to be mauled. "Get the gun!" I shouted at Cheri, invisible below the bluff and waiting at the oars of the inflatable boat.

She immediately yelled back, and the bear, momentarily confused, skidded to a stop behind a soapberry bush five yards off. Without thinking I hurled blowdown timber and then dived off the bluff, shouting, "Row!" in midair. I hit the boat and nearly bounced out again, and Cheri leaned into the oars. Half a second later, we'd caught the current, while the bear searched the shoreline for us. A person gets giddy when he finds himself surprisingly alive and healthy just moments after he realizes he is dead meat. I was giddy. I guess the bear was protecting a carcass, but I didn't check.

Grizzlies have mauled several acquaintances. Barrie Gilbert was a postdoctoral fellow at Utah State University when I was studying elk ecology there. Shortly after I left USU, Gilbert was seriously mauled by a grizzly in Yellowstone. It rearranged his face, among other things. Faye, the postmistress at Circle, Alaska, got mauled while camping along the Yukon River. Sammie, a Shuswap guide in British Columbia, had his face and scalp altered by a grizz. It affected his mind, too. He jumped at any noise, be it chipmunk or chickadee, and he continually flicked the safety of his Springfield off and on while hunting. I made sure he kept in front.

Brown bears aren't tough to kill. Of those I've collected in Asia and North America, all but one took only one shot, and that one, a big coastal brown bear, was dead on the first shot— he just didn't realize it. Experienced bear slayers of my acquaintance say the same thing, though Alaskan guide Scott Ruttum has been charged half a dozen times by bears that clients wounded. In my opinion, though, it's the bears that you surprise, crowd, or push off a carcass that pose a threat. And sows with cubs are especially dangerous.

GRIZZLIES

I've been asked more than once about the best places to hunt grizzly. Too many factors enter into the equation to make everyone happy with any recommendation I could give. Some hunters are concerned only with trophy size and others with odds of success, while still others prefer to hunt as near civilization as possible. Qualities important to me include isolation, pristine country, and bear size, more or less in that order. I won't hunt in country with another camp just beyond the ridge.

Given my biases, my first choice is a barren-ground grizzly hunt in the Bathurst Inlet region of Nunavut. I hunted muskox and central-Canada barren-ground caribou near White Owl Lake with Inuit Sam Kapolak of the Bathurst Hunting and Trapping Association (who works with Boyd Warner of Tundra Camps out of Yellowknife). Sam was an exceedingly competent and modest guide, never prone to exaggeration, and I believed him when he said they usually collect eight-foot bears on spring hunts. That's a huge grizzly anywhere. Bears weren't plentiful, but the country was as isolated, barren, and haunting as you could get in continental North America.

My next grizzly hunt choice might be along one of British Columbia's coastal rivers. I hunted goats there years ago, and, at the time, bears roamed river shorelines searching for spawned-out salmon. Politics are confusing British Columbia's bear hunting these days, so check the latest regulations. Many bears I saw had to square eight feet. The gloomy, brooding, old-growth coniferous forests and rushing broad rivers seem like something out of a Bierstadt oil painting.

Next, I'd hunt in the Wernecke or Ogilvie Mountains in the Yukon Territory, or in the Mackenzie Mountains in the Northwest Territories, simply because I love the wild and isolated country. Grizzlies won't be huge, but you can combo with Dall sheep, moose, caribou, wolf, and black bear. Packing in, rather than flying, is half the fun.

Sure, you'll hunt moose, deer, and other species by hunting where they feed. But grizz is always eating, and if he's not he's looking for food. Find that food, be it spawned-out salmon or blueberries, and you'll find him. And, yes, grizz *is* dangerous, especially if you surprise him, flush him off a carcass, or get too

THE DANGEROUS GAME

near a sow with cubs. But hunting in his country keeps you glancing over your shoulder. Your senses sharpen, and you become as alert as you'll ever get. Without grizz's presence, the Far North would just be more real estate.

This is a typical ruin in the jungle. The steps lead up the face of a small temple. (Book III "Hunting with the Maya")

A pleasant camp on an island on the Yukon River, near my cabin at Circle. (Book III "Shoot-up on the Yukon")

Peccary, a bonus when hunting deer or lion in the Sierra Madre of Mexico, back in the old days. (Book III "Deadly Lesson")

I killed this nice caribou only to lose it to a family of grizzlies. (Book III "A Trophy Won and Lost")

This is my cabin after the spring ice breakup on the Yukon River. The flood has just uncorked, leaving this river ice in the yard. Sometimes it's worse! (Book III "Shoot-up on the Yukon")

The Old Woman's grave on top of the ancient Gwitchin cemetery hill (Book III "The Old Woman's Gift")

I'm posing with the fruit of one of my first solo expeditions into the remote Arctic. (Book III "The Old Woman's Gift")

Old-timer Jon Kibler with an Arizona tom lion. (Book III "Kibler's Lion Scrapes")
(Photo by Jon Kibler)

Yours truly and a very nice bear I collected with top Alaskan guide Scott Ruttum. (Book III "Grizzlies")

This hunting camp in Nunavut was as remote as you could get on mainland North America; it took five hours from Yellowknife by Twin Otter to get there. (Book III "Grizzlies")

This is the dog team that got us out onto the pack ice. Ellesmere Island is in the distance. (Book III "In a Treeless Country")

This is one of our polar bear hunting camps. We moved camp everyday. It may look sunny and pleasant, but the temperature is thirty-seven degrees below zero! The south coast of Ellesmere Island is in the distance. (Book III "In a Treeless Country")

R&R Guide Service guide Scott Ruttum and outfitter Rob Jones with my nine-foot-plus brow

ska. (Book III "Grizzlies")

Arizona outfitter Jared Nichols and I are hauling a big tom out of the rocks. Can you imagine trailing mules through this? We did it, though. (Book III "Most Dangerous Hunt?") (Photo by Cheri Flory)

The author, the Apache puma, and Jesús in the Sierra Madre of Old Mexico. (Book III "The Apache Puma")

One of our camps far out on the pack ice. We're cutting snow blocks to protect the tent from an impending gale. (Book III "In a Treeless Country")

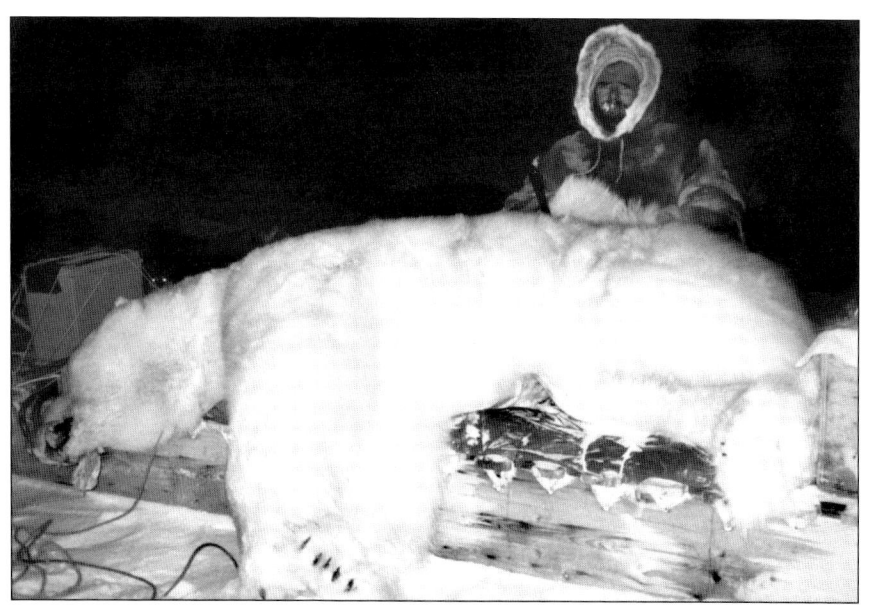

The temperature is minus thirty-nine degrees (note the ice on my beard), and we've just dog-sledded the 10'4"-polar bear into camp. (Book III "In a Treeless Country")

The second guide, Pauloosie Attagootak, eating raw, frozen caribou on a break while hunting polar bear. On that hunt, the temperature didn't get above minus thirty degrees! (Book III "In a Treeless Country")

My friend Jannie Thompson and pal. If you're not sneaky about it, it's easy to approach sheep from below, even this close. (Book IV "The Happy Hunting Grounds")

Dall ram. (Book IV "Solitude")

This big bull moose is shedding his velvet and is very cranky. (Book IV "Home to a Place I've Never Been")

Bull caribou silhouetted against the north slope of the Brooks Range. (Book IV "Solitude")

I'm posing with the fruits of my first solo expedition into the remote Arctic. (Book IV "Home to a Place I've Never Been")

Now the work begins. (Book IV "Journey to the Dog Salmon")

Cheri with trophies, meat, and raft on one of our annual expeditions in the Arctic. (Book IV "Call of the Sheenjek")

One of my sheep camps. (Book IV "More Solitude")

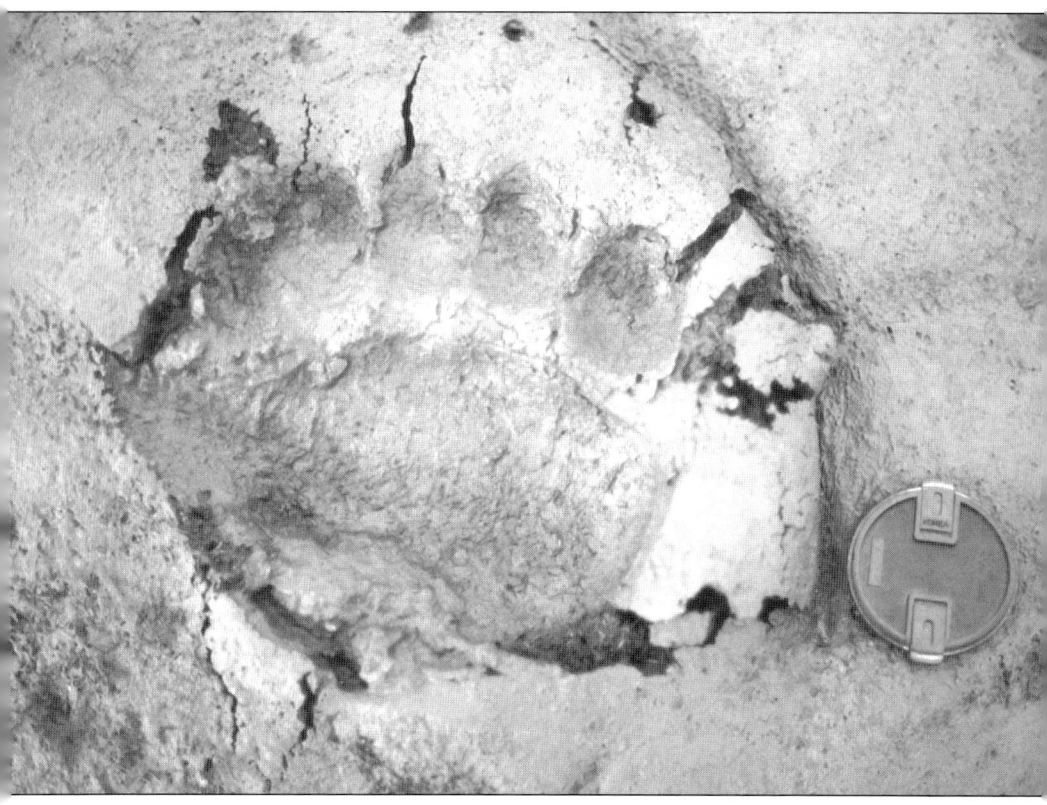

This gets your heart going, especially if it's just outside your tent! (Book IV "Home to a Place I've Never Been")

I'm building a supply cache on my property at Circle, Alaska, on the Yukon River. It keeps curious bears from getting to your gear or meat. (Book IV "Home to a Place I've Never Been")

Caribou steaks for supper! (Book IV "Solitude")

On my first solo expedition, I used this dime-store inflatable to ferry a bull moose and a caribou across the Coleen River, believe it or not. (Book IV "Home to a Place I've Never Been")

A very fine ram head, skinned out and ready to pack into camp. (Book IV "Leaning Out")

The bears helped themselves to my moose meat. Note the track next to the moose wrist. (Book IV "Home to a Place I've Never Been")

A sheep hunter's fantasy in the Brooks Range. (Book IV "Solitude")

The rewards of a good hunt—a bush feast. (Book IV "More Solitude")

A morning's shoot worth of tasty ptarmigan. (Book IV "Call of the Sheenjek")

Maybe the best part of hunting: caribou chops and the dinner fire. (Book IV "Call of the Sheenjek")

THE LAST BUSH PILOT

From the first time any small boy takes a bush flight, be it in a big Twin Otter with floats or a small Piper Cub, he wants to become a bush pilot when he grows up. Roger Dowding, in his gleaming, blue-and-white Cessna 185 Supercargo, made big boys want it even more.

Not that Roger fit the romantic stereotype of the bush pilot—a Steve Canyon type with carefully trimmed mustache, slicked-back hair, and leather bomber jacket. On the contrary, Roger looked his antithesis. His thinning, curly hair set far back on his forehead, his grimy jeans and white T-shirt, his slight paunch, and his short legs didn't give him heroic proportions or pretensions. Just the same, each time I climbed into or out of the Cessna—and I did it many times—I vowed to get a 185 and fly just like Roger. I went so far as to price planes, new and used, and I seriously considered buying one.

What really stopped me from buying that Cessna 185 was that I couldn't do what Roger did and I didn't know how I'd learn. I'd either become a bush pilot wannabe or I'd wind up dead. So I didn't follow through, and I continued to charter Roger and his Cessna at least twice a year to fly into the remote parts of the eastern Alaskan Arctic.

Much of how Roger flew was designed to enforce that heroic image of the devil-may-care, seat-of-the-pants pilot, the kind of hero who rescued women and children with a shrug of the shoulders. I remember flying north with Roger from my cabin on the Yukon River toward the upper Sheenjek. Once north of the Porcupine River, he climbed, adjusted the trim-tab controls—a sort of autopilot—and spread a *Playboy* on his lap, seeming to study it with great interest, though he wasn't reading the articles. As a licensed pilot, I kept an eye on the altitude and horizon indicators, just in case.

THE DANGEROUS GAME

Once, I looked over and Roger's eyes were closed. I wasn't quite sure if he was doing it for effect or if it was for real—he'd been flying twenty hours a day in the nightless Arctic summer, ferrying tourists to the North Slope or supplies to the Inuits on the Arctic Ocean. The 185 seemed to fly itself up the Sheenjek, and we weren't noticeably losing or gaining altitude. Knowing Roger, he could just as well be feigning sleep, and I still suspected that was the case. As a precaution, I kept my eye on the plane. Finally, Roger opened his eyes and shook his head slightly. He glanced my way to see if I'd noticed, then went back to reading the *Playboy*, leaving me no wiser.

Roger wasn't a reckless, barnstorming type of pilot—he just wanted his passengers to leave with that impression. In many ways, he was meticulous; he walked through a routine before he cranked the engine for any flight. He'd carefully buff the exterior Plexiglas wind screen and do the same for his aviator glasses, double-check the big balloon tires, and so on through the rest of the plane.

I'd flown with Roger for two years before I learned he had a wife and child in Fairbanks. Given his busy summer flying schedule out of Fort Yukon in northeastern Alaska, he probably didn't see them all summer and well into the autumn. But I suspect I didn't find out because being a family man didn't fit the image. I wouldn't have found out at all, except his wife was on the Fort Yukon airstrip one day when Roger was flying me and some friends into the Brooks Range.

Roger propagated the Steve Canyon image with his stories. Once he flew supermodel Cheryl Tiegs and her photographer husband onto the north slope of the Brooks Range. Cheryl sat up front next to Roger, of course. One of the controls was on the floor between the two front seats, and Roger told me, "I kept altering it. Each time I did, my arm brushed Cheryl's leg. I didn't mind that." Finally, as Roger told it, Cheryl caught on and asked, "Roger, are you feeling my leg?"

Another of Roger's stories involves a white man and his Gwitchin wife, who had homesteaded on the middle Sheenjek River many years ago when it was still possible, and they lived in the wilderness full time. They ran a trapline along the river in winter and then trekked up to the fishing camp on a lake in the high country for the summer. Their name was Hansen, if I recall right, and I met them several times on my floats down the river, usually in September. They were friendly, articulate, and intelligent people, not the kind you'd expect to live such reclusive lives. So much for stereotypes.

One winter, the Yukon Flats were hammered with a steel-hard cold snap—temperatures all along the Flats hovered colder than sixty degrees below. No one flew in that kind of cold because it was just too dangerous. Gas lines and carburetors froze, and if someone went down, rescue was out of the question.

"Anyway," Roger said, "the Hansens radioed Fort Yukon. The wife was in labor and having problems, and they had to get to a hospital. The state troopers wouldn't consider a rescue flight in that temperature. So I thought, 'What the heck,' and started prepping."

Roger took off from the Fort Yukon ice, which raised the eyebrows of the state troopers and more than a few bush pilots, and swung northeast toward the Sheenjek River. He landed on river ice without much trouble, loaded up the family, all dressed in shedding caribou hide clothing, and taxied as far down the river as he could for a straightaway takeoff shot. As he pivoted the plane for the takeoff, the tail skid broke through overflow ice, then one ski. When Roger felt the give, he gunned the throttle and just barely horsed the plane free. "Too close for any kind of comfort," he said as he remembered.

Certainly Roger exaggerated some details for effect. He knew I liked his stories. But from what I heard later from others, including the Hansens, he hadn't exaggerated much that time. Roger wanted you to walk away with that Steve Canyon image, but he was truly courageous—a hero in the dictionary sense of the word, larger than life.

I remember Roger most for his flamboyant flying. He knew just what his abilities were and had no qualms about showing them off. I remember a time on the Sheenjek, just across from Lobo Lake. He'd flown a couple of pals in (I'd already been hunting, trekking, and floating in the mountains upriver for a month) for a three-week float hunt. He banked and lined up on the long beach, came in low, and then touched one wheel down

THE DANGEROUS GAME

to test the surface give. He flew four hundred yards down the beach with one wheel on the sand and the other wheel two feet in the air, only lifting off when it seemed he had already run out of beach. He then banked low and came back and did it again. Neither of my pals was familiar with bush flying, especially with pilots like Roger. I'm sure Roger did it for the effect.

My camp was at the end of the beach. After Roger had dropped the guys off, he taxied to the far end of the beach and wheeled the 185 around. He gave it full power but held the plane on the ground until the very end (he could have lifted off a hundred yards sooner), roaring by with one wing only feet above our heads as we watched. By then, I was a veteran of Roger's flights, but even I was impressed. My pal, Bud Hendrickson, a Colorado buckaroo and ranch owner, said, "Jeez, that's real rodeo."

Roger, Cheri, and I became fast friends beyond just the plane charters. Whenever he flew in the vicinity of Circle, Alaska, he'd drop in for a salmon steak and a beer and talk as we sat at the table and watched the brown Yukon River surge by.

Roger really pushed it in the summer. He seldom slept more than three or four hours a day, and he often did that in the plane when he landed on a tundra ridge or a river bar. If he wasn't flying in river runners and sightseers, he ferried fuel in big blue plastic drums for his fuel caches scattered throughout the Brooks Range. Many of his flights went far beyond the fuel capacity of the 185, and the closest source was Fort Yukon at the confluence of the Porcupine and Yukon Rivers.

Once, Cheri and I hunted sheep and caribou in the high country of the upper Sheenjek River. We'd floated down to a prearranged rocky beach rendezvous halfway down the river. Roger had cached fuel on the big beach for just such a meeting. All had gone well: The hunting had been good, and the country as usual was lonely, haunting, and comfortable.

As we were floating, the headwaters in the mountains to the north had been socked in with black, angry cloud banks. That meant the river would rise, but I didn't know how much or how long it would take for the flooding to hit where we were. As we camped at the rendezvous beach the first night, I heard a change in the sound of the water. I crawled out of the tent. The river had come up, but not

THE LAST BUSH PILOT

enough to cause problems. Still, I was concerned. *From the looks of those clouds upriver, the river might well flood*, I thought.

And it did. Before dawn we were loading gear into the raft, and then I rolled the fuel drums onto the highest place I could find to keep them from getting carried off. From the looks of the angry torrent, I wasn't at all sure the place was high enough. The "airstrip" was under two feet of murky water.

We pushed off into the torrent and floated down, dodging the logs surging downriver while watching for new "sweepers" that would flip the raft if we hit one. Ten miles downriver, we found a place high enough above the river that I felt sure wouldn't flood. The big river bar was badly grown in with willows, and immense spruce and cottonwood logs had been heaved across the flats by spring breakup flooding.

By afternoon, the river had begun to drop slowly. We put together a camp on the beach, and I paced it off. I felt sure Roger could land once we cleared away the debris. I spent two days swinging a double-bit ax, cutting the spruce and poplar logs into small enough pieces so that Cheri could roll them out of the way. Then we hauled rocks and filled in the depressions. By the third day, we had a respectable runway.

The river continued to drop to the level it had been before the flood. I knew Roger would look for us upriver, and I hoped he'd then search downriver when he found we weren't there. He did, banking low to fly along the "airstrip," and then again, and finally touching down without a problem. Roger paced up and down the airstrip, looking at it from this angle and then that. I couldn't figure the problem because we'd flown into and out of hairier places. Knowing him, I suspected it was all for the dramatic effect, but with Roger sometimes you just don't know.

We loaded up the Cessna, then Roger taxied to the far end of the beach. "I'm gonna try it," he shouted over the revving engine, "but if I think I can't make it I'll shut 'er down." Roger gave us that worried look. "Here we go!" he shouted over the headphones. I grabbed the sissy bar.

The Cessna lurched and bounced down the beach. Roger held it on the ground long after I thought necessary, until we ate up the final yards to the end of the bar and the drop down to the

THE DANGEROUS GAME

river. He held it until we sailed through the willows and out over the river, the leaves and twigs slapping the struts. My hand hurt when I let go of the sissy bar. If he was doing it for the impression, he succeeded.

In later years, I saw Roger on a TV documentary, flying notables into the Arctic National Wildlife Refuge. And I read about him in some general interest magazine. Yes, at least half of the fun of bush flying for Roger was the thrill he could give passengers. Even though I understood he did many things just for show, it didn't change my image of him. He was the Steve Canyon of fantasy, and I was always startled when he walked up the dirt road to my cabin on the slough south of Circle—short, balding, a bit paunchy, in oil-grimy jeans and T-shirt. For that moment, I was surprised to see he was just a man. He was among the most competent pilots I had ever flown with.

That's why I didn't believe it when the U.S. Fish & Wildlife investigator attributed Roger's final flight to carelessness and pilot error. "He flew into the mountain at full throttle," the agent had said. "Both Dowding and the passenger were killed instantly."

I tried to picture him flying up the canyon in the Brooks Range, scouting for caribou or merely flying to a landing spot he knew of in the next drainage. Perhaps he had searched so intently for game he hadn't noticed the lowering clouds at the head of the canyon and the obscured ridge he had to clear until it was too late to climb and bank. I like to think the impact came as a total surprise.

BOREAS'S STARE

In the heavy dusk of early afternoon, the thermometer duct-taped to the plane's strut read twenty-three degrees below zero, a safe enough temperature if a man is careful. Stars glared from behind the aurora shimmering in black outer space.

"Gotta go," bush pilot Joe Firmin shouted over the idling Cessna, his breath a fog in the gray air. "And you're crazy." He made a circular gesture with a mittened hand at the side of his head and shrugged.

As the Cessna taxied slowly over the ice-covered rocks of the river bar, Joe gave a thumbs-up for luck through the frosted window and shoved the throttle forward. The engine bucked through the heavy frozen air in the shadowed river bottoms, and the skis clattered until the plane leapt, disappearing suddenly in the ice fog.

I'd kept two LP canisters in pockets next to my body so they would stay warm enough to start. Even LP gas won't start without warming at those temps. Then I gathered driftwood from spring flooding jams, shoved birch bark and caribou moss—better than paper for fire-starting—underneath, then covered it with a tarp in case of an emergency. A man couldn't be too careful in the Arctic in winter. A quick fire has saved more than one life.

On a trek months earlier, I'd discovered a mountain littered with Dall sheep bones and horns. As a professor of zoology, I was predictably curious, though I thought I knew the answer. As a last outing before the interminable northern winter, I'd come for confirmation. But the puzzle was only an excuse; civilized man required justification in tangible terms for any endeavor too far out of the ordinary.

What little that wasn't frozen beneath the paltry headwaters of the Sheenjek River trickled beneath three feet of ice. I swung the double-bit ax into the ice until I'd hacked a hole two feet

THE DANGEROUS GAME

wide by two feet deep, then fired the .270 into the bottom. Water welled up and filled the hole. I dipped a bucket and put it in the tent vestibule. I couldn't use the stove gas to thaw water. Of course, bathing wasn't an option.

Late the next morning, the thermometer propped against a rock in the thick twilight read thirty-six below. Still a safe enough temperature if a man was careful and didn't get wet feet. The only way here to get wet feet was to step through overflow ice, which formed over a spring or where a river had frozen to the bottom, dammed, and then pushed to the surface, forming a skim of ice. A man would break through if he didn't recognize it, and without a fire, he'd freeze from the wetting. The big danger was that snow would drift over and camouflage the overflow ice.

I stuffed lunch, birch bark, paper, matches, and dry socks into my pack, shouldered my rifle, and started upriver. The hiking was easiest on river ice, but when a patch looked suspicious, I climbed the bluff and sweated across the tussocks.

By early afternoon—the brightest time of day, though still only twilight—I'd climbed to the slope where I'd found the sheep graveyard. Forty-four dirty-white Dall sheep grazed and bedded along the half-mile ridge. An oddity of geology and climate caused the wind to blow the snow from the ridge in big ghostly plumes in the twilight, exposing the dead grasses and lichens on which the mountain sheep fed. Since old, weak, and sick animals die during winter extremes, these had predictably died where they spent the most time—on winter grazing range. Puzzle solved.

It was too dim and cold for photos. Neither the shutter nor the flash would operate. I sat across the ravine and watched with the binocular, then quickly took notes. I could only write for minutes at a time before my fingers numbed in their light-wool gloves. Then I'd strip off the gloves and jam my hands in my crotch to warm them. Even in heavy underwear, three layers of clothing, and caribou hide outerwear, I'd begun to shiver after forty minutes.

Twilight deepened to darkness. I put the two LP canisters under my arms so they'd start the stove when I got back to camp, and I kept the flashlight batteries next to my body, too; frozen batteries provided no power. *Take it slow,* I told myself, *no mistakes here.* That—not the visual poetry of ice, snow, and aurora—was the real beauty of Arctic camping in winter. The inherent danger kept you as alert and alive as you'd ever be because the stakes were extreme. One small mistake could kill.

The temperature had dropped to fifty below zero. I crawled into the tent, fired up the stove with the warmed canister, and cooked in the vestibule to avoid condensation in the main part of the tent. After eating, I moved the stove to the main tent and closed off the vestibule.

The temperature had dropped another six degrees by 11 A.M. the next morning. Old Lucy Roberts, my Gwitchin neighbor down on the Yukon, warned that only fools or cheechakos traveled at fifty below, especially alone. She shook her head at me through the window of her tiny log cabin as I hauled gear to Joe's Cessna. She knew, because her daughter had left the cabin one morning to check ptarmigan snares across the slough and never returned. Forty-five-year-old Bertha broke through overflow ice, wetted herself to the knees, became chilled, then wandered a quarter mile down the frozen Yukon River, finally freezing beneath a bluff only yards from the village center of Circle.

But the slope I camped on was only two miles upriver, and I was prepared. I double-checked the matches and birch bark in a pocket, the gas canisters and flashlight in a fanny pack next to my shirt, and the lunch in an inside pocket to keep it from freezing. I shoved extra socks and Power Bars in my shirt and shouldered the rifle.

I thought about a story repeated so often that you couldn't help but wonder if it was a myth, like the crocodiles in New York sewers. A trapper on the Old Crow, lost in a blizzard, killed a moose, gutted it, then crawled into the carcass for warmth. He survived and staggered back to the tiny trapline cabin the next day with only frostbitten toes.

By the time I'd reached the ridge, condensation had frozen my beard and mustache together into a ball of ice. I broke a small hole and fed lunch through it a bit at a time. More sheep had migrated onto the ridge. I counted seventy and tried to write notes. In the wool gloves, my fingers numbed so fast it frightened

THE DANGEROUS GAME

me. I hurried them back into the double-dog-skin mittens and banged them against my knees until the feeling returned. I left the pencil where it lay in the frozen shadows.

I hiked clear of the river ice and kept to the tussocks as I hurried back to camp. *Don't take chances*, I told myself. The aurora lighted the way, and the exertion pumped blood to the extremities, warming them.

When the stove hissed evenly in the tent, I hacked another hole in the river ice and fired the rifle into the bottom again. Only three inches welled up, steaming and turning immediately to slush. Before long, the entire river would freeze to the bottom. I scooped the slush into the bucket and hurried it into the tent. The mercury had dropped to fifty-nine degrees below zero. I spat, and it crackled in the air.

In the warmed tent, the thermometer read forty *above* zero. I stripped to thermals and cooked, then sipped tea and ate a rice concoction with pudding for dessert. On the other side of the centimeter of tent fabric, it was ninety-nine degrees colder, fifty-nine below freezing. Out there, the river ice groaned and wailed like odd notes from a pipe organ. The stove hissed at full blast to keep the tent warm. I hadn't expected it to be this cold, and I couldn't afford to run the stove continuously. The fuel would give out if I did.

The temperature stood at sixty-four below zero in the gloom the next morning. Spruce trees a quarter mile away popped like rifle shots in the cold. Without thinking, I walked over to contribute to the growing stalactite of gold. The stream vaporized and crackled as it hit the ice, and the pain was immediate. Next time, I'd use the jug in the tent.

Gas was going too fast. And the temperature continued to drop. I'd never been out in anything like this cold. When I turned off the stove inside the tent, the temperature dropped to that of the outside within minutes. Even in two goose-down sleeping bags, I couldn't stay warm. I'd have to spend more time outside next to the fire to avoid using the stove.

Outside, the birch bark and driftwood caught on the third reluctant match, sputtered, then flared. I dragged driftwood into camp and stood next to the fire. Wood became tougher to find because I'd scrounged everything nearby. I hiked half a mile across the tundra to a stand of stunted spruce. Near the northern tree line, a seven-foot tree was three hundred years old. They didn't get bigger. I lugged deadfall across the flat and arranged another pile of branches and twigs for a quick start. The thermometer read sixty-six below zero.

A metal bucket of river ice on coals at the edge of the blaze steamed, and the vapor turned to snow when it drifted away from the heat. I stood close to the blaze and hurriedly drank a cup of cocoa before it turned to slush. My nose and cheeks, the only exposed flesh, had frosted, and they throbbed now in the heat from the flames.

After one last run for wood in the full darkness of late afternoon, I crawled into the tent. I fashioned a strip of cloth to tie across my nose and upper cheeks to keep them from more severe frostbite. The temperature hung frozen at sixty-six below.

Joe couldn't fly in that kind of cold. No one could. Fuel lines froze and carburetors iced up long before the mercury dipped that low. He would have no chance if he went down, either; the state wouldn't even consider a search. My pickup flight wasn't due for another day, but in this cold, Joe wouldn't come. I'd heard stories about the throbbing extremities, the uncontrollable shivering, the final, merciful numbing, and the last sleep. *Don't think,* I told myself as I lay in the bedroll in the soft blue glow of the stove turned to low.

I further rationed gas and spent the next day hauling spruce deadfall to camp. When the wood gave out in the nearest stand of trees, I ranged farther afield, up- and downriver, and kept warm with the exertion. If I rested, my fingers and toes pulsed, and if I stood long enough, they numbed. Then the shivering would set in. So I stood by the fire or hauled wood. I wasn't using the canisters during the day, now, because they were critical at night. If they ran out, I'd freeze even in two bedrolls.

With a full day of hauling wood for the fire, I was using too much energy and eating even more just to maintain core body temperature. The food was going too quickly. Nothing could survive this cold without sufficient food calories to maintain body heat. I couldn't ration what little was left of the food, or I'd freeze that much sooner. Catch 22.

No one could have expected extreme temperatures this early in the winter. Firmin had radioed Kaktovik on the Arctic Ocean before starting out, and the temperature then was a balmy twenty below. I'd expected the pickup flight to be on time; with this cold, it wouldn't be. If the cold held—and it had before—Joe might not fly for a month. Panic pushed into my throat. I started to sprint down the beach, but checked myself.

The mercury held at sixty-six below. It could get colder. The record at Fort Yukon, a hundred fifty miles south, was seventy-eight below. At my cabin on the Yukon, it had once plummeted to seventy below.

As I hauled another load of deadfall across the frozen tundra, I mentally inventoried food: I had one Power Bar, a quarter pound of rice, two ounces of jerky, and half a pound of raisins. Two days' worth, maximum—less, at the rate I was burning calories. Without sufficient food, irreversible hypothermia was only hours off.

While I was concentrating on the food problems and plodding upriver, the ice groaned and sagged suddenly. Without missing a step, I shied toward the near bank. Snow had drifted over the overflow ice of a spring, and in the twilight it could not be seen from the elevation of a man's eyes. I veered away from the frozen river and labored across the tundra.

My thoughts riveted on food. I thought of one last blowout and fantasized about gorging on everything in camp. I'd planned to spend the holidays with family. Hallucinating, I beheld the steaming yams, hot ears of corn, and baked turkey we'd eat. I stumbled to a stop and dropped the wood. The mountain sheep! Yes! Shoot a ram, and sort it out with the wildlife authorities later. What's a two-grand fine next to the loss of your life?

I hiked quickly upriver in the 10 A.M. dawn, crossed the frozen river while watching carefully for overflow ice, and climbed the ridge. I stood there dumbly, then swept the ridge again with the binocular. Not an animal in sight. I stood a moment in shock, then shouldered the rifle and climbed the ridge in case they'd crossed to the other side. Droppings and tracks crisscrossed the wind-scoured snow and tundra, but they'd left. I glassed distant ridges in the twilight, but still nothing. Numb, I slid down the slope to the river, then hiked to camp without thought of overflow ice. With the exertion of the fruitless hunt, there was only enough food for one more day.

With the hunting, I hadn't replenished the wood supply. I stumbled through the near darkness, across the tussock flats, and over an esker to a distant spruce stand. While breaking off deadwood from the spindly trees, I tripped over something rigid beneath the snow. I brushed the dry snow away with a mitten. Frosted fur. I swept away more snow and uncovered a dead wolf, frozen hard as quartz. Other wolves had partly disemboweled it, probably in a territorial battle, and it had gotten away and died. A bulge of intestine protruded from a tear in the belly.

I shouted at the top of my lungs. In the heavy, frozen air, the echo bounced slowly back from a bluff. I fought a compulsion to race across the tussocks for the ax and sprint back again. *Think it out*, I told myself. Running in the extreme cold would frost my trachea and lungs. I gathered an armful of spruce deadfall and walked back to camp. Back with the ax, I hacked the carcass into quarters, shattering a dollar-size chunk out of the frozen ax bit.

In camp, I chopped frozen slabs into a skillet on the coals and fried it to a kind of wolf bacon. I split the bones with the ax and lay them on the coals until the marrow thawed, then I dug the marrow out with a knife. Marrow fat was best. I hacked out frozen roast-size chunks and lay them on the coals at the edge of the blaze. They broiled to charred lumps, and I wrapped them in wolf hide and placed them near the fire. I thawed the blue coils of intestine, slit them open, emptied them of the bone and hair contents, and then lay them on the coals to cook.

What was left of the carcass back in the spruce was as safe as if it were in the tent. Grizzlies hibernated now, no wolf could tear into the granite-hard frozen meat, and polar bears didn't wander this far inland.

I scoured up- and downriver for wood, and by evening, had accumulated an eight-foot pile. I hadn't used gas all day, keeping warm with the exertion and meat. With the activity, I'd forgotten

THE DANGEROUS GAME

the temperature. The thermometer read seventy-two below zero in the flashlight beam.

You lose track in the Arctic wilderness. Dates are for calendars. With the wood cache, the wolf meat, and the remaining gas, I'd survive, for now. Later was later. I paid no attention to the frozen twilight beauty, the otherworldly polychrome aurora, or the palpable silence—all inspirations for a poet. Instead, I bit into a charred hunk of wolf heart, hot blood dribbling into the ice of my beard.

BOOK IV

THE HAPPY HUNTING GROUNDS

HOME TO A PLACE I'VE NEVER BEEN

It was time. Time to satisfy a craving that started when I first read Jack London's *The Call of the Wild*, intensified with Robert Service's north-country poetry, and became focused when I came across Russell Annabel's stories in the old *Sports Afield*. The time was right, too. Many things had ended—a marriage, a dozen years in universities and four degrees that left me as stupid as before, and a saloon and grill I'd sold.

For a time, I sailed solo around the Caribbean on a twenty-eight-foot cutter-rigged sailing yacht. Eventually, I got shipwrecked in a "norther" off Cay Gordo, in the Bahamas. When the insurance company paid off, I spent winters among the Mayan ruins along the Usumacinta River in Chiapas, Mexico, hunting caiman and howler monkeys with the Lacandon Maya. But I really longed for the Far North.

Wild country has always attracted me, be it the uninhabited islands of the Caribbean or the rain forests of southern Mexico. And I love solitude. So when I finally stepped off the little Arctic Circle Air Cessna 185 and unloaded a small pile of duffel—intended to last a month—onto the tiny rock beach on the upper Coleen River in Arctic Alaska, I wasn't worried. Nor was I worried when the plane taxied down the beach, turned, and roared off into the wind and disappeared. Truth was, I felt as elated as when I'd dropped anchor in a secluded, leeward cove on a deserted, white-sand Bahama island and rowed the inflatable to shore. Truth was, I felt even more elated. I felt like I'd come home to a place I'd never been before.

The feeling of homecoming stayed with me the whole month. I have never quite felt the same anywhere else. I would learn that whenever I flew into that country and the bush plane ejected me and my gear onto a river bar or lakeshore or tundra flat, I would always get that homecoming feeling. That feeling was a lot stronger than when I actually returned to my house in the mountains of Utah or my log cabin on the banks of the Yukon River.

I'd spent the summer trekking and photographing in Denali National Park to get my Alaska legs. I'd gotten very good slides of caribou, moose, and Dall sheep, but I wasn't comfortable getting close enough for really good photos of grizzly without a rifle slung over one shoulder. Yet I couldn't get all there was out of the country because the gravel road was no more than a few hours' walk down the drainage, and yellow buses full of tourists had to take me out. Somehow, people spoiled the full feel of the wilderness, the full experience and understanding of it. Still, it beat the ivory towers of academe and living too low to the ground earning a salary, or trying to justify why you didn't.

I didn't need to justify anything to myself or anyone; however, to me, unless I could become an integral part of the wilds, it was only half-living. I wanted to hunt for meat as man was intended to do. One doesn't have to travel to the caves of Lascaux in France or Altamira and gaze at the prehistoric yet most moving art man ever created to understand that.

I hauled the gear into the willows in the late-August evening sun to get out of the cold breeze drifting downriver. I pitched the tent, started a driftwood fire, and arranged my gear just so. I tried for over an hour not to do it; there might be caribou or moose nearby, and I had tags for both. I tried so long I nearly burst. So I gave in, first to quiet humming mixed with bad whistling, then in final indulgence to full-fledged song. I never felt uninhibited enough to sing around others, but out in the bush, I couldn't help but sing. First I attempted the old Johnny Horton song "North to Alaska," then I tried to put Service's "The Call of the Yukon" poem to tune. It didn't bother the caribou.

Within twenty minutes after the plane had flown off, a band of them clattered down the rocky beach, splashed into the river, and swam across on their way into the Yukon Territory a few miles east. They were all young bulls, cows, and calves. Legally, I couldn't have shot one anyway since in Alaska you

THE DANGEROUS GAME

can't shoot game the same day you've flown in. It is a good rule, even though regulations seem centuries away up there—more than a hundred miles from the nearest fly-in bush village of Old Crow, over in the Yukon. But I wouldn't have wanted to shoot a trophy bull had there been one. I'd just arrived, the mere beginning of my four weeks out. Better to let the country soak into you before you start blasting away.

Caribou clattered up and down the beach two or three times an hour until dark, or what passed for dark that far north. Even in August night only lasted an hour. I sat by the fire and worked on a pot of noodles and hot cocoa, trying to control the swelling ecstasy in my chest. I'd felt it before along the jungle rivers among the overgrown Mayan ruins, with howler monkeys booming their weird roars through the jungle night, and big caiman splashing in the water. I'd felt it, too, on deserted, sandy mangrove islands in the Caribbean and out on the Wyoming high plains. A wolf howled across the river—a deep, wavering, sad call. I fancied it was an acknowledgment of some sort, and I felt it was as much a part of my new home as the creaking hardwood floors in my old.

As I sat by the fire next morning, squinting against the willow smoke while I cooked flapjacks speckled with lowbush cranberries and blueberries I'd picked near the tent, more caribou crossed the river. Still no trophy bulls. I didn't really care . . . to a point. That point was hunger. As a philosophical exercise, I had brought little food so I'd be forced to live off the land. A few packets of Ramen noodles, two pounds of sugar for tea, twenty pounds of salt for the capes I hoped to collect, one small box of pancake flour, and two candy bars were shoved into a corner of the one-man tent. I could live on that for two or three days. After that, I'd have to kill something and eat the crowberries, cranberries, and blueberries that grew in the tundra flats set back from the river. I wasn't worried because it should only be a matter of time before a big caribou bull trotted up the beach, and I could fill my tag. I had a fly rod, a leader, and dry flies, too. I'd never been anyplace that wouldn't feed me.

After the flapjacks, I rigged the fly rod, grunted into hip boots, and walked down the rocky bar to an eddy in the current and a deep hole. I flicked the small, smoke-colored dry fly into the swirling eddy and let it float in toward the beach. The fly disappeared in a swirl, and, minutes later, I'd landed my first grayling. I caught two more between two and three pounds, the biggest grayling I'd ever caught in North America or Siberia. I had no doubts that the country would feed me. I'd just have to ration the noodles and goodies for variety.

As I cleaned the fish, a very light, bloody-faced wolf trotted up the gravelly bluff on the other side. He'd been eating caribou for breakfast, and, as a hunter, I thought briefly of collecting his rippling fur. But somehow a shot would interfere with the solitude, the silence. I didn't want him badly enough, and another hide wasn't justification enough. I know plenty of hunters that hate wolves because wolves kill game, and that means fewer game animals for human hunters. Wolves came across the Bering Land Bridge with the first game, long before man. I had a tough time bringing myself to kill one, partly because man doesn't eat them (though to survive I had once eaten a wolf), and partly because wolves generally kill what is easiest—the old, sick, and lame. If anything, I was doing more harm to the caribou population than the wolf. I was hunting for a prime, healthy bull.

The days drifted by, and I wandered the river looking for a big caribou bull. I was also searching for a bull moose—moose season opened soon. Meanwhile, I fished for tasty grayling, picked berries for dessert (the chocolate bars had been eaten), rowed the department-store raft across the river, and hiked toward Canada to watch Arctic loons on the small lakes. I couldn't have been more content, except that I hadn't seen a mature bull caribou. Plenty of younger bulls crossed the river with the cows and calves, but I was in the wrong place for the big ones.

As I sat by the evening fire, I worried for the first time. Aside from the lack of mature bull caribou, I hadn't seen a single bull moose, and the season opened in a week. There'd been cows and calves, but not one palmated antler. My dinner of a big grayling, the last of the noodles, and berries sweetened with the last of the sugar was over when I heard splashing. I

THE DANGEROUS GAME

walked out with the rifle, but more cows and calves crossed. I'd scarcely gotten back to the fire's warmth—the evening downriver breeze was strong and frigid, and the quiet water along the bank had a skim of ice—when I heard more splashing.

The sun had set when I pushed through the willows. Two big bulls trotted through the shallows on the other side of the river and onto the bar. I sprinted in the hip boots to a rise and threw myself prone like Audie Murphy in those old war movies; picked out what looked like the best bull, one with the heavy double shovels and the very black velvet; held on the shoulder; and touched off the .270. He dropped with scarcely a twitch. Still, I held the cross hairs on his neck for minutes. When I was convinced he was done for, I hooted so loud an osprey flapped from a snag upriver. I ran back to camp, hauled out the inflatable raft, and rowed across to admire the bull. I'd killed not only my first caribou, but my first head of Alaskan game. I didn't know it at the time, but I'd started a bad habit of hunting in the Far North that has lasted, to date, a quarter century, and promises to last until I draw my final breath.

Both bulls had been in velvet, and the one I shot wore his so dark that it looked black. He carried big double paddles, twenty-nine points, and a forty-inch spread. I hooted again before I bent to gut, skin, and then quarter the carcass. It was fully dark before I'd floated the last of it across the river and hung the quarters in the willows by camp.

I set the tea kettle on the coals and threw driftwood onto flames and propped the bull's head just back from the fire. I mixed a dollop or two of Scotch whiskey in the hot tea and watched the firelight dance in the bull's glazed eyes. I couldn't have been happier. After another cup of tea and Scotch, I cut a slab of bull lard into the skillet and added two loin chops, set the skillet on coals raked off to one side, and watched them sizzle. Nothing ever tasted better.

* * * * *

I still-hunted up- and downriver for a big moose. The season opened in two days and I hadn't seen a mature bull. The caribou migration to the southeast into the Ogilvie Mountains in the Yukon Territory had slowed. Only the occasional band crossed, until one day they quit altogether. When they'd gone, the wolves quit howling; they followed the herd.

I eventually found a concentration of moose three miles downriver. That's a fair piece for one man to haul an animal that might weigh close to a ton. I found cows and calves browsing the willows; I watched one walk up an old willow, pushing it down with its breast until it could browse the tender new shoots at its top. I found big tracks, longer by a full two inches than those the cows made. And I found where a big bull had battered a stout willow branchless with his antlers. One evening I spooked the bull in a jackspruce tangle and heard him smash saplings to kindling as he raced off toward the Old Crow River.

I'd picked up some kind of a bug in the jungle that past winter, and once a month the chills and fever came on. I crawled into the tent and drifted off, sleeping the better part of a day. Late in the afternoon, I saw a big, golden head gazing through the tent flaps in what I hoped was curiosity. Then, without sound, it disappeared. For a moment I was certain I'd dreamt it, but I jacked a round into the .270 and looked out. Long-clawed tracks cratered the mud. That was the closest I'd ever come to a wild grizzly.

One evening I was still-hunting my way upriver to camp in the dusk when I heard the *OO-ooo-ughk-OO-ooo-unngh* of a rutting bull moose. I'd never heard the sound before, but somehow I knew what it was, and then I heard *ungh-kkk, ungh-kkk*, followed by a lapping sound. I climbed a high spot on the low bluff where three flood channels come together and waited. The noise of splintering branches came nearer as the bull smashed his way toward me. I had a good chance of seeing the bull if he crossed one of the channels. More branches broke, and I saw the tops of several trees sway violently. He moved closer.

When he pushed into the open twenty-five yards away, with fire in his eyes, I settled the cross hairs on the leading edge of his shoulder as he stood quartering-on and squeezed off. He

THE DANGEROUS GAME

rocked with the impact, but stood glaring. I fired again, with the same result. I moved the sight picture from the shoulder to the base of the neck where it swelled into the chest, and I touched off again. The bull staggered sideways and collapsed with a groan in a foot of water.

Four days into packing the meat upriver to camp, an ambitious black bear found the meat. Not content to worry the gut pile and the rib cage, he thieved the boned-out meat hanging in cheesecloth bags. I stepped up the meat hauling so I could get as much of it as possible. I sweated bags of moose meat from dawn to dark. From the tracks, I knew it was a black bear, and a big one. I didn't figure I needed the rifle, and I certainly didn't want to haul extra weight, but once I came face-to-face with the bear. He carried a bag of meat in his jaws. Instead of dropping it and running, he merely stepped off the trail and disappeared, still clutching the meat.

In heavy dusk one evening, I hefted a load of meat onto my back and started up the dry slough that led to the river. I had taken four or five steps when my progress was arrested by a deep growl, rumbling from the black shadows of spruce a few yards off. I knew it wasn't the black bear. I backed off, heard the bear growl again, then circled well out through the spruce forest toward the river and the trail to camp. I carried the rifle with me to the meat the next morning and, after making sure the bear wasn't around, looked for the tracks. They were seven inches across the front pad, long-clawed, and definitely grizzly.

It had taken the better part of a week to skin, cape, bone, and pack the meat and antlers three miles upriver and then float them across to camp. The antlers spread sixty-five inches and had a total of twenty-six long, heavy points. Later, out of curiosity, I scored the bull two points above the Boone & Crockett minimum, for whatever that is worth.

I loafed the last week and ate a sinful tonnage of moose steaks; it stayed with you and satisfied more than caribou. I drank Scotch-laced tea in the evening, fly-fished for grayling in the day, picked berries, and hiked out toward the Yukon to watch loons again. I even wrote a poem about ravens.

HOME TO A PLACE I'VE NEVER BEEN

One classic Arctic Indian summer day when the sapphire skies gleamed and crimson and gold tundra leaves danced and the air had a bite like chilled gin, the mustard-colored Cessna winged up the canyon. I tossed an armful of green willow branches on the fire for the smoke to indicate the wind direction and the location where I'd camped—the tent was hidden in willows. The plane drifted in and clattered to a stop.

While I was happy to beat the Arctic winter—I felt it more each day in the bite of the wind and saw it in the leafless birch and willows—I was leaving home. I was already pretty lonesome for it before the plane landed in Fort Yukon.

YOU *CAN* GO HOME AGAIN

    Thomas Wolfe, the novelist, was wrong: You *can* go home again. I did it in 1983 when I went back to the Coleen River, in the wildest chunk of wilderness in the United States, the Arctic National Wildlife Refuge (ANWR). Yes, this is the same place King Bush and his oil-pumping pals want to ravish. (By the time you read this, the deed may well have been done!)

    When I stepped off that same mustard-colored Cessna 185 onto another gravel beach, I knew it without a doubt. When I waved off Joe Firmin, the bush pilot, and my lady friend, Jannie Thompson (she'd flown in for the adventure), I suddenly felt more relaxed than I had since I'd flown in back in 1981.

    The previous season I'd built a log cabin in the Gwitchin Athabascan village of Circle, population fifty-two, on the banks of the Yukon River. At the end of the summer, short on both time and money for the bush flight into the real wilderness, I hitched a ride up the oil haul road to the mess the oil companies made on the north slope of the Brooks Range, got off in the vicinity of the Gates of the Arctic National Park, and hoofed it west. Since the haul road was just east, the place was too accessible to adventurers who didn't spend the kind of money hunters did on bush flights and licenses and whatnot. I trekked west along the divide between the north and south slopes, camping and photographing and trying to recapture just a little of that sense of contentment I had felt on the Coleen the year before.

    I never really did recapture that sense of well-being. Part of it was because the country was more traveled. Every other day or so I came across a Vibram-sole boot-print in mud, or an old campfire circle, or a granola wrapper. The knowledge that the haul road was only about three days east didn't help me achieve any sense of isolation, either. And the stakes weren't as high as they had been the season before on the Coleen when I had to live off the land. But it was a relief to get back into fine, pristine country and away from writing and teaching.

The only thing of real note that season occurred one morning as I heated water for oatmeal and tea. I heard a rustle in the bush ten or fifteen feet off, so I eased to the tent and lifted the Ruger Super Blackhawk .44 Magnum off the sleeping bag. I returned to the fire, and the rustling in the chest-high willow came closer. A bear eventually stepped into the little opening where I'd pitched the tent. He'd stalked me into the wind and knew I was there.

I thumbed back the hammer of the .44 and held it on his head at four yards as he growled, low and menacing, then popped his jaws. He took another step forward and growled again, the hair along his back rucked up, either with bluff or fear. I sat staring down the barrel from across the coals, with the bead fine on a line with where I figured his brain was. The grizzly grunted, turning his head first one way and then the other. I was winning the staring match. I kept the sights fine between the bruin's eyes, and he growled again. I took a step back but kept the gun on him until he turned and looked first one way and then the other, again. Then I stepped sideways to take another look. He stepped back into the willows, and once out of sight, crashed off upstream.

*****

Now I was back on the Coleen. Given the difficulty of collecting a big bull moose two years earlier and the battle I had had with the bears, this time I'd concentrate on caribou. They were smaller and easier to pack, and, if I didn't hunt too far from camp, it wouldn't take long to haul them in.

I hunted a week without seeing anything worth shooting. Moose browsed in the bogs behind camp, but I couldn't buy a caribou bull. Either they'd already migrated through to the Ogilvies in the Yukon, or they hadn't gotten this far yet. I was hoping for the latter. I did catch big grayling, which supplemented my diet of rice, flapjacks, and the rare ptarmigan. It didn't matter so much if the caribou didn't come, but I did want a good trophy, and I'd promised old Lucy Roberts, my Gwitchin neighbor in

THE DANGEROUS GAME

Circle, some "Indian meat," as she called any kind of venison. I wanted some fat bull for my freezer, too, and I'd envisioned heroic caribou antlers so often in the preceding year that I'd be heartily disappointed if I didn't collect a set or two.

They came one dusk of a gray and blustery day, with snow flakes sifting ahead of a brittle-cold north wind. The wind and snow worried me. I had no intention of getting stranded in the tiny backpack tent for the winter, and I worried that if it snowed too much, the Cessna wouldn't be able to land. I hadn't yet learned how resourceful Alaskan bush pilots were. I sat by the fire, back in the willows, off the beach, and out of the wind. From time to time I stood and wandered out on the beach to look around.

As I stepped into Boreas's teeth, a big, silver-mane bull caribou climbed from the river on the other side. Three or four other sets of antlers were disappearing above the poplar scrub. The last bull lunged up the gravel bluff and shook two gallons of water from his coat, but I couldn't take a shot because of the poplars. The bull trotted off toward his disappearing pals, but as he veered out along the open bluff for a moment I got a quick shot. The bull staggered, then wobbled into the scrub. I shot through the brush and saw him falter, regain his footing, and keep going.

I rushed back to the tent, untied the cheap, inflatable boat, which I'd fastened to the willows to keep it from blowing off in the gusts, and hauled it across the beach. I rowed across the river and tied it off again; then I set out to find the bull's tracks. I'd hit him on both shots, and the blood trail was easy to follow. I followed at a trot and was so intent that I literally stumbled over the dead bull. I thought there might be a chance of catching up with the other mammoth bulls, so I sprinted off through the poplars and up onto the tundra—but they'd gone.

The bull's antlers were massive, the main beams as long and heavy as any I'd ever seen. Though short and spiky, the antlers had twenty-seven points, but the sweep of the main beam back over his hips made a hunter smile. I had good meat, too. I caped the bull, skinned the rest of the carcass, then quartered it.

It was nearly dark when I finished, and the gray skies continued to spit snow. The raft wasn't big—I think I bought it in Fairbanks, at Sears—so I'd need to make two or three trips to get everything across safely. I slid down the steep gravel bluff to the river and piled the bull's head in the boat. I brought a shoulder quarter next, then lay the rifle on top of the load. I climbed back up the sliding gravel slope to untie the line, then slid back down, holding tight to the rope.

As I stepped into the raft, I let the slack out of the line holding the boat close to shore. The current caught the raft and pulled it away from the bank. I had one foot in the raft and one on shore, with the current pulling the boat farther out—you get the picture, just like Laurel and Hardy. I couldn't hold the boat in toward shoreline with one leg, so I plunged into the river. The bluff dropped straight off, and there were no shallows, and I was instantly in over my head in the numbing current. I wore hip boots, and yes, I knew they held air and could be used as floatation devices *if* you could keep them above your head or chest. I couldn't, and I went straight down, the boots filling with water and acting as anchors.

In the boots and bulky clothes, I couldn't get up from the bottom. I remember trying to pull off the bottom and up the line to the boat, and I was making progress . . . but I was also running out of air. As I neared the surface, I gasped too soon and inhaled half a gallon of frozen Arctic river water. I coughed in reflex and breathed in more water, instantly seeming to lose strength. I couldn't hold onto the line, but it tangled around one arm, and the boat towed me downriver. I'd begun to relax and see distorted images and flashings when my knees ground onto gravel. Then, somehow, I was sitting on a gravel bar and coughing and spluttering and trying to relax the gagging responses enough to get a little air. The loaded raft had ground onto the shallow, and the line was still tangled around my arm.

When I'd finally coughed up enough water to leave room for air in my lungs and recovered some strength, I hauled the raft and its load onto the gravel and staggered off toward the tent. I didn't retrieve anything else until the next day, and I was plenty careful climbing into and out of the raft.

More caribou drifted into the country on their way to the rutting grounds in the Ogilvies. Bulls and cows crossed the river, mostly in the evenings before dark. They'd bed and feed on the higher tundra barrens between the river drainages, then time their migrations to hit the river valleys late in the day. That way they could climb onto the next high bench before going on the next day. But I didn't see bulls as big as those in that first bunch.

As I walked back from fishing late one afternoon, something clattered in a dry slough behind me in the willows. Of course, with all the bear and caribou, I'd slung the .270 over one shoulder. I lay the mess of grayling I'd caught on the gravel and waited. Fifty yards upstream, two cows broke from the brush and waded into the rapids. Migrating caribou key in on the sound of rapids and riffles because it indicates shallows and good places to cross. Four more cows then a dozen more and several young bulls waded into the rapids and crossed the river. Two nice bulls brought up the rear. One had so many points I couldn't count them. He also had two big shovels. I shot just behind the shoulder so as not to spoil much meat. The bull very cooperatively backed up into the shallows and collapsed.

I sweated him ashore. The bull's antlers carried thirty-eight points and dramatic bez tines, though his main beam was shorter than the first bull's. I decided to work on the bull in the morning. The only reason to gut an animal immediately is if it's warm or the animal has been running. Since neither was the case, I opted to keep the innards inside where they belong. That way, I'd be spreading less bear-attracting scent along the bottoms. I didn't want to fight a bear for the meat.

Two bald eagles and at least twenty ravens had found the carcass before I got down to it the next morning. But other than covering the hide with white streaks, they'd only had time enough to enlarge the bullet hole. Had I'd gutted the carcass, they'd have fouled a lot of good meat.

I relaxed. I had enough meat for old Lucy, her clan, and me, though another bull wouldn't hurt. So I sat around the fire, picked blueberries, and read. The feeling of contentment came on again, stronger than ever. I never feel the same contentment at home because of the responsibility of paying bills or the obligation to get out and earn a wage. There, I lived too earthbound. In the Far North I had only to worry about collecting driftwood for the fire. Since it lay all about, "worry" isn't the right word.

I shot one more bull as it trotted up the beach in front of camp, simply because of the meat situation. I didn't look forward to the pickup flight.

JOURNEY TO THE DOG SALMON

I'd spent two seasons on the Coleen River. In spite of an honest feeling of belonging there, a thing tough to find these days, I wanted to see new country. One river drainage west might do it. The country had all the game the Coleen had as well as Dall sheep in its upper reaches.

"Ain't nothin' but small sheep up in the Brooks," the Tok hunting guide told me on a visit to Fairbanks that summer. Another outfitter echoed his sentiments. But I bought a small, quality, Achilles inflatable raft; a better tent; a capacious, but light, Lowe internal frame backpack; and other gear. I took it all on shakedown treks in Denali and float trips on the Yukon River between Circle and Fort Yukon. By August, I was ready for the new country.

I chartered a Cessna 206 with floats and flew up the Sheenjek to Last Lake, so named because it was the last lake where you could land a float plane, and it was the last thing officially named in the drainage. In fact, except for the river itself and two lakes, nothing on the upper Sheenjek was named; it was that remote. The white man hadn't tried to label it all yet, and that left me space to come up with my own monikers.

I camped two days at Last Lake to wait out the storms rolling through the country, fishing for grayling and listening to the loons and their youngsters that called the place home. Caribou wandered the opposite shore, and once I spotted a blond grizzly nosing the lowbush blueberries two hundred yards from the tent. I did not see the telltale white specs on the surrounding peaks that would indicate sheep. So I shoved gear into two steel drums to protect it from grizzlies, shouldered a seventy-pound pack and the .270, and trekked out to the river. I somehow managed to ford and swim across without getting my gear, camera, or gun wet. I then trekked west through bogs, and then up a big, nameless valley that I later named "Caribou Walk."

JOURNEY TO THE DOG SALMON

As I slogged through the bogs in the bottoms, I disturbed clouds of mosquitoes so thick they changed the color of my khaki pants to a black-gray. The sweat washed off the bug dope I'd smeared liberally over my face and hands, and by afternoon I was one big welt. I pushed up the rocky creek bottom, found a level, open bench above the creek where the breeze kept the mosquitoes down, pitched the tent, and had a scrub spruce fire going as evening set in. Last Lake lay across the valley far below, and with my binocular, I made out the steel drums that protected my food, gear, and raft. (Leaving gear unprotected is foolish. A hunter had once left his Piper Cub airplane on a gravel bar while he hunted, and a grizzly had chewed it up. The pilot duct-taped the fuselage and damaged frame and somehow managed to fly back to Fairbanks.)

After I'd pitched the tent and boiled water for tea and rice, I heard a commotion in the spruce tangle a few yards off. I picked up the .270 and jacked a round in the chamber. I found a bare spruce with claw marks higher than I could reach and golden underfur stuck to the sap dripping down the trunk from the claw marks. I caught a glimpse of the grizzly as he crashed off. I slept lightly that night and kept the rifle handy; I was thankful it didn't yet get fully dark this far north, too.

I trekked farther up the valley and through the mosquito fogs, with occasional biting gnats thrown in, then followed a southerly drainage that branched off of Caribou Walk Canyon. According to the topo, Caribou Walk ended above the headwaters of the Chandalar River, twenty-five miles northwest. I'd planned to keep to the Sheenjek drainage because that's where I'd cached my gear. I intended to float out in a month or so along the Sheenjek all the way to Fort Yukon, about three hundred river miles.

I camped the night beside a soft coal outcropping on an open creek bar, in a breeze that promised to keep the mosquitoes down. I walked upstream for a look-see and found a hot spring. The water was too hot to stick my hand in, and it smelled like a rutting moose. Grizzly tracks crisscrossed the wet sand of the creek bottom, and caribou wandered the higher hills browsing the lichens, arctic birch, and dwarf willows. These caribou were not migrating. A bull moose, its small antlers black with velvet, browsed on creekside willows. A wolf howled from a side canyon, and another answered farther up. Small grayling darted into the deeper pools of the tiny stream.

Rain kept me locked in my tent the next day, so I spent the time reading material I never had time to read in civilization, but should—Chaucer, Chekhov—all in compact paperback, of course. The wind picked up the following day and gradually tore away the clouds and mists, so I tucked away the gear and the still-wet tent, hiking higher and arcing westerly.

I jumped a grizzly with two yearling cubs, and they churned through the stream and straight up the ridge until they disappeared. Caribou grazed the tundra slopes. I camped on a high, barren flat overlooking a divide that, according to the topo, dropped off into the Chandalar. Two wolves, one light and the other black, sat across the stream and watched me pitch the tent and arrange the camp. They occasionally yipped like frustrated pets from less than sixty yards.

By evening, the air had turned cold enough to put skim ice on a pot of water. I was at least a hundred miles north of the Arctic Circle and at an elevation of more than five thousand feet—it probably froze every night of the year. Dinner was a grayling I trapped with my hands, rice, pudding, and tea. I couldn't have been more content if I'd dined in the finest Parisian restaurant.

The following day, I trekked to the ridge above the Chandalar then turned south. Rain started late in the morning, again, and the peaks were quickly covered by the scud. But when the clouds tore apart for a moment, I spotted distant, dirty-white specs against the wet black scree, and I knew they were Dall sheep. Rain kept me in the tent for the next two days, but on the third, the clouds tore from the black peaks, and the Arctic sun shone brightly in the sapphire sky. I trekked southerly, over a col and down into the headwaters of Old Woman Creek, one of the few places named in that blessedly anonymous country. Somehow, I resented the name, though the Gwitchin had tagged it long ago. I'd been naming the features as I hiked: Arctic Hot Springs, Coal Strike, Wolf Ridge,

JOURNEY TO THE DOG SALMON

Black Mountain, Dark Canyon, Grizzly Creek, Ram Basin. The unnamed country gave me a sense of pioneering.

Though I found at least a hundred sheep at Old Woman Creek, I didn't find one exceptional enough to kill that far from the Sheenjek. The packing would be tough that far. So I hiked through the high drainages of the waterway, then up and out to the east. Over a high, windy divide, I hid in rocks to get out of the wind and ate a lunch of raisins, watching big caribou bulls trudge slowly through the pass in their eastward trek. By sundown, I'd hiked down and into an emerald-and-ruby basin that held sheep grazing the higher slopes on two sides of the camp.

I found no big rams there. After all, the outfitters had said the Brooks Range had no big sheep. The bears ignored me or ran, and the caribou wandered the country in small bands. Even when they scented me, they weren't unduly alarmed. Two wolves tested a band of grazing sheep for old or sick animals, but they gave up the chase within fifty yards because the sheep were hale and made it to the scree where the wolves had no chance. A grizzly grazed on blueberries a quarter mile down the creek. I was in no hurry to leave this Shangrila.

I finally killed a full-curl ram, and though it was no trophy, it was legal. I shot him late in the afternoon, and after skinning the carcass, I hefted the head, the cape, and a hindquarter and made for camp. I collected the rest the following morning, then lay around the camp eating sheep meat—the absolute best of wild meats—watching the game, and studying Chaucer.

The same grizzly visited my camp twice, but I wasn't overly worried even though he had the wind on both occasions. He didn't threaten and he didn't retreat; he merely wandered off and went about whatever business he had in mind in the first place.

One day I hiked up to glass for rams for the fun of it, and on the way back I heard something in the creek-bottom willows. Tawny fur and a growling noise rushed straight at me. I hadn't carried my rifle, so I backed rapidly up the slope, shouting and waving my arms. The growling, rushing beast continued at me until a big cow moose burst from the willows, her back fur rucked up. She was as angry as she looked. She slowed when she saw or scented me, then still more when a calf stepped out of the brush.

THE DANGEROUS GAME

When I reswallowed my heart, I made a big circle up the slope. I had no spit. Mad cow moose have killed men before.

In that remote country, any injury can be fatal, especially if the hunter is alone. No one knew when I would return or where I had gone. But then, that was the point. The moose notwithstanding, there's a lot of freedom in that kind of realization. That is, that you are completely on your own, and survival depends solely on yourself. You have no one else to blame if things go bad. In a powerful sense, that makes you free. You become no more omnipotent than the ram you just killed, the caribou you might shoot next week, or the grayling you will eat tomorrow. You understand your own mortality, that any day can be the last, and this knowledge pushes you to make the most of each day, to take things as they come.

I trekked down the canyon for two days and hit the Sheenjek River, fifteen miles below my cache at Last Lake. I set up camp and dashed upriver through the bogs and mosquitoes, then swam the river—it had risen with the rains at the headwaters—and jogged to the cache to keep warm. I had dry clothes in the steel drums, and when I packed the gear and the raft to the river, I was more than warm again. I hurriedly inflated the raft and floated downriver in the lingering dusk—it was dark for only a few hours at this time of year—and watched the banks for caribou or wolves. I spotted a bull moose with a deformed antler and saw a wolf kill a caribou on a gravel beach and a grizzly grazing along the stream. I felt as though I were floating through Eden, that cliché again, but the animals were unalarmed and unafraid. You wouldn't see more game in Denali or Yellowstone, and, even better, there wasn't a human within a hundred miles.

I'd eaten what was left of the sheep meat, so I pitched the tent on a gravel bar where I could watch up and down the river for crossing caribou. I still had plenty of the basics—rice, oatmeal, cocoa, flour—but there's something satisfying about red meat in the bush. A hunter craves it.

No good bulls crossed the river, so I floated down to Lobo Lake. The lake was named by naturalists—the Muries, and perhaps George Shaller—probably back in the '60s. I camped on a beach near the lake and hiked over to see their old camp. Nails in spruce trees, tin cans, and a skillet indicated the site. I didn't collect a bull caribou at Lobo Lake, either, but I clipped the heads off of ptarmigan with the .270, and while I lusted after red meat, I wasn't worried. A hunter can survive on rice if he has to, but a rare steak would work better.

The nights got colder and longer. Occasionally, snow spat out of the north, and the quiet water along the river edge stayed frozen all day. I pushed off into the current again and floated out toward Fort Yukon, down on the Porcupine River. Of course, I saw game, but no bull caribou.

One morning, I killed a Canada goose with the .270 as it flew overhead. Very unhappily, I had no one to witness the event. Then I killed another as the flock flew back down the river. I've given up telling the story—I've had too many skeptical stares over the years—but it happened. Mostly, I lived on rice and grayling, though at one time I ran two wolves off what was left of a caribou kill on a riverside beach. I cut off most of a hind leg, and I ate it all in two days.

I floated through the fast water of the upper Sheenjek and hit the flats where the river slowed and meandered. In places, the wind was so strong I rowed with the current to make any headway at all. One day, the Sheenjek spat me into the bigger and clearer Porcupine River that flows out of Old Crow country in the Canadian Yukon. I camped at the confluence, then floated a long day to Fort Yukon. From there, I chartered a flight to my cabin at Circle, sixty-five miles up the Yukon River.

Trekking through the Sheenjek drainage and then floating out was to become an annual event. The rest of the year existed only so I could go home again.

SOLITUDE

Solitude is a fine thing. Today, too many of us have lost the desire for it because it forces us to confront things we'd just as soon not. But some of us would rather spend at least some of our allotted time on the planet alone, so we do confront things about ourselves, our existence, and the world around us we would not otherwise face. For me, this is even more true in the bush or wilderness.

First, we have the noise factor: Two people make three times as much noise as one. That noise drowns out other sounds we might otherwise hear, and it frightens off wildlife. Just as important, wandering around the wilds alone allows us to see just how petty the concerns of other places are, especially when a misstep or a bad guess can determine whether you see the sun rise again. Another human along in the bush reinforces the awareness of those petty, civilized concerns—things like HMOs, taxes, and politics. A few weeks alone in the bush makes all these things seem less important than gathering a handful of fresh-picked blueberries, landing a fat grayling for dinner, or stashing a pile of spruce deadfall for the morning fire.

Still, *Homo sapiens* is a social animal, and most can stand only so much solitude before they have to hie it back to the masses running the Skinnerian mazes. So, friend, it's natural to invite a good companion along to share the best wild country you know.

Flo Krall was one of my professors while I attended graduate school at the University of Utah. Though I only took one class from her, we became lifelong friends. I'm not sure how it all came about, but the short of it was she decided to fly into the upper Sheenjek for at least part of what had become my annual expedition.

We flew into the country in Roger Dowding's Cessna 185 and landed on a winter ice overflow plain called Dry Lake, very near Last Lake. We grabbed the two small rafts and all the gear and packed them a mile to the river. There we inflated the rafts and floated downriver to where a big, nameless creek dumped into the Sheenjek River from the west. It was the same place to which I'd trekked out of the sheep heights the season before. We camped on the river bar, then hiked up the next day. Flo was in her fifties then and was fairly sedentary as her career as a professor might dictate, but we made it to a bench I'd picked out as a good camp spot the season before. It overlooked a stream and had a view a mile upstream and two down, and there were mountains on both sides of the stream. The ground was level and the tundra well drained and dry. A spring bubbled out of the slope a hundred yards away, and willow deadfall lined the stream two hundred yards down the slope. If anything moved in open country, we'd see it from the camp.

As I hauled the dead willow wood out of the bottoms for a fire and Flo crawled into her bivvy-sack tent for a rest, I noted a single white sheep, high on a green tundra basin on the mountain across the creek. I grabbed the rifle, forded the creek, and started up, first through the shale scree, then up into limestone cliffs and into the heavy clouds dropping down the peak.

I climbed up into the lowering clouds. It felt just fine getting off by myself again. The rain turned to big, wet glops of snow, and the wind picked up. An hour later, I climbed into what I figured was the lower end of the big green basin, though I wasn't sure in the fog and snow. Visibility was less than thirty yards, though occasionally wind whipped apart the scud and I could see two hundred. I didn't see the ram.

The wind eventually ripped off the top of the fog above, and I spotted him. He was better than the one I'd collected the season before. The wind tore in from the right and whipped my scent away from the sheep, but he made me out anyway. He stood in the cliffs, and though he had me pegged, he wasn't worried. No wolf could catch him in those rocks and cliffs, and he'd never seen man before. The clouds closed in again.

I worked up toward where I'd seen the ram, careful not to roll rocks and give myself away. When the wind thrashed the clouds apart again, the ram still stood in the same spot, less than

THE DANGEROUS GAME

a hundred yards above me. He was definitely bigger than the one I'd seen the year before. Still, he wasn't as good as those big rams I'd photographed in Denali, but I knew the Brooks Range rams weren't as large.

I settled the cross hairs low on the shoulder and touched off. He collapsed at the blast and started to slide, almost imperceptibly at first, then more rapidly, going over a ledge and bouncing and flying and cartwheeling through the air with an escort of rocks the size of big pumpkins.

I had two problems: first, how to stop him before he broke his horns; and second, how to keep clear of the avalanche. As the free-fall rocks caromed right at me, I decided to address the latter. I ducked, and, as it turned out, just in time. The slide and ram crashed by, running themselves out in the tundra below.

I packed the head and backstraps to camp. Bad weather hit the next day, and we were snowed in. The following day, though, we hiked up and retrieved the rest of the boned-out meat.

* * * * *

Flo had this thing about grizzlies. At first I thought she was dramatizing, but I found later she is truly afraid of them. It's wise to respect grizz and give him plenty of room, but to fear him to the extent that it ruins your appreciation of both him and the bush is foolish. Still, it's easier to say that than really understand someone else's problem. And I wanted to trek around by myself. It was exhilarating getting off by myself again, though Flo had been as good a wilderness companion as anyone could ask.

I suggested Flo hike up the drainage and take her binoc and bird book. She was a serious birder, and it would be a good way for her to relax and simply enjoy the country. "Stay to the bare country and out of the creek bottoms, and you won't surprise a bear," I told her, adding, "Relax."

I knew she wouldn't, at least not for the moment, but with a bit of solo walking and perhaps spotting caribou or wolves or merlins or ptarmigan, she'd get her mind off grizzlies.

I climbed a steep canyon that I'd trekked into the season before. Beyond the base of the peak I called Black Mountain because of its black shale, I'd spotted some sheepy-looking country. I'd climb into that basin and over a ridge, and then I'd come back down into the canyon where I'd sent Flo. If she had problems, I'd hook up with her.

We hiked our separate ways the next day, too. Flo became more at ease alone, but she preferred company. I offered to let her haul the .270 to give her peace of mind, but she wasn't comfortable carrying a rifle. I didn't haul it, either, and I was certain she was in no danger from the bears.

She was more relaxed the next day when we hiked out together. I carried a rifle that day because I intended to work down a small canyon thick with creek-bottom willows, and I remembered too well the encounter with an angry mother moose the season before.

We took the left fork, crested the ridge, and hiked into a high basin below Dark Mountain. We sat on the springy tundra in the sun and wind and glassed for sheep. I found a band on the north shoulder of the mountain across the basin, and another band of six rams—I could just see the horns with the 10X binocular—up the stream.

Flo sat in the sun and watched while I stalked the rams just for fun. I climbed the rocky creekbed, getting below and out of sight of the sheep, and then I climbed the tundra toward where they were when I last saw them. I eventually worked close and eased around the boulders. There stood a ram on the tundra with wide-flaring horns, dwarfing both of the sheep I'd collected so far. So much for "no big rams there"!

This one was a good ram anywhere, even in Denali. Other rams stood up from their beds, and, finally, there before me was a vision I can still see if I close my eyes twenty years later. It was the biggest Dall sheep I'd ever seen, or would ever see, rising from his bed to stare at me from twenty-five yards. His right horn was broken six inches back, but the other pinched in close to the cheek and flared out before starting downward again for at least four inches, like the horn of a Marco Polo argali. The bases seemed as big around as Mike Tyson's biceps, and I was certain they'd measure well over fifteen inches in circumference. The horn had to measure forty-six inches around the curl. This was a ram for dreams and quests, and that vision largely made me into the avid sheep hunter I am today.

I stood dumb. The rams weren't in the least afraid. The big ram stared at me as I stared at him in some kind of acknowledgment. He then grazed the tundra, but he grazed slowly away. The other rams followed. I stared for at least an hour, following slowly until they crossed the ridge. I walked down the tundra slope and then across the bottom of the basin in a trance. I found myself fervently wishing I had not already killed a sheep. What a trophy he would have been, the trophy of a lifetime. Though the phrase has become a cliché, in this case it was very true.

We stayed more days at the sheep camp, hiking and watching game, reading and identifying strange birds, and eating up as much of the wild mutton as possible so I would not have to carry it down to the river.

Let me tell you about wild sheep meat. It's the best of wild red meats. Moose is exceptional, and elk very good. I love Coues whitetail and mule deer. One of the finer venisons is pronghorn, though most hunters don't care for it, and it gets turned into jerkies and sausages and hamburgers that taste like nothing at all (it's naturally seasoned with sage). If the animal hasn't been badly run and if the kill has been rapidly gutted, skinned, and cooled, few wild meats taste better. But wild mountain sheep is consistently the best of meats, be it a Dall ram or a Stone sheep or a Siberian snow sheep. They're all exceptional.

It took us the better part of a day to hike back down to my cache on the Sheenjek River. We camped on the river bar where the stream emptied into the river. That first night back down on the river, I built a fire of spruce coals—a big extravagant fire after the skimpy fires of the high country where firewood was scarce. We sat on the bar as the river surged by, listening to red-throated loons wailing around the bend, drinking bourbon in hot tea, and eating the last of the ram meat—the last of the best.

While photographing in Denali during the summer, I'd met Rick Lowe, who would meet us on the Sheenjek in time for a moose float-hunt. Flo would fly out later. The next day was sunny, and early that day Dowding's blue-and-white 185 roared overhead and up the Sheenjek toward the landing site at the dry lake bed. An hour later he flew back over and waggled the plane's wings on the way downriver. The next afternoon, Rick Lowe floated around the bend.

We stayed at the camp another day, then pushed off into the river current and floated half a day farther downriver. We had plenty of time to kill before Flo had to fly out and the moose hunt started. We set up camp on a black-sand beach below Brushman Mountain. In the morning, I hiked up toward the lower slopes to get away from all the company, picked blueberries, and wished the caribou would come into the country on their migration southeast.

When I stood from picking, I saw something light on the slopes above, and I thought immediately of caribou. When I looked through the binocular, however, I saw it was a grizzly bear. I had a grizzly tag, just in case, but I really didn't want to shoot one. All the same, I decided to stalk close enough for a photo, if possible.

When I had eased across the rise with the camera at the ready, the bear had stalked to my side of the ravine and was rapidly stripping blueberries from the low shrubs. I eased back behind the rise and jacked a round into the chamber, thinking it best to be ready this close. I checked the camera, cranked the zoom to 150mm, and then crawled through the arctic birch and dwarf willow, pushing the rifle ahead as I closed.

The bear somehow sensed me. He stood suddenly on hind legs, weaving to keep his balance. I stood, too, ready to face a charge. (Facing a charge on hands and knees is like diving into four inches of water.) The bear dropped to all fours and rushed like a locomotive in silent movies. He crumpled at the blast, a yard or two from my toes. He was so close I shot down at him, and the muzzle blast singed the platinum fur on his neck.

The next day we all skinned and butchered the bear. I boned off the backstraps and one hind leg for meat to see what it tasted like. I'd never eaten grizzly and wanted to try it. The bear had been feeding on berries and I thought he would taste good, not fishy like bears eating salmon. The bear meat *was* good, albeit a bit tough. It tasted a little like beef, and even more like the tortoise I'd eaten off the coast of Belize.

THE DANGEROUS GAME

We floated downriver the following day. Rick was in his department store raft, while Flo and I were in the Achilles. Late in the afternoon, we landed on a beach at Lobo Lake where Roger would eventually pick up Flo, and Rick and I would begin our moose float-hunt downriver. We watched the waterfowl massing on Lobo Lake before the big migration, which would come soon because the tundra had turned crimson and gold, some of it already browning. The country smelled like a winery from the fermenting blueberries and cranberries, and in the shaded parts of the lake, the ice lasted all day. It felt like full autumn, though it was barely September. One day, Roger buzzed in to the camp, and Flo was gone, suddenly back "outside," to civilization and that other world. I was glad I didn't have to leave the true world just yet.

I'd spotted a respectable bull moose from the top of the prehistoric Gwitchin graveyard above a series of low hills at the mouth of Old Woman Creek. The bull hung about the mouth of the creek, and he always seemed to be there when I climbed the hills and checked in the evening. His antlers spread about fifty inches.

I shot him opening morning. I sighted him from atop the hills and circled, stalking into a stiff west wind spitting snow pellets, and slipping through the willows to within a few yards to drop him. Later that day, I packed up my tent and gear, floated down to the mouth of the creek to set up camp, and then began boning the meat and packing it to the river.

It took three days to skin, quarter, bone, and pack the moose to the beach and hang it in the willows. Working on an animal pushing a ton in weight is a big job for one man. No one in his right mind would attempt to turn the carcass over, so I skinned it on its side as it lay. I removed the hide, then cut the quarters off as I went. Once I had the meat and quarters off on one side, I could flip the carcass and work on the meat on the other side. When I had all the meat stripped off the bones, I put it in cheesecloth bags to hang in trees. Over the years since, I've field dressed at least ten moose by myself. Sure, it's a big job, but a man can do it if he doesn't get in too much of a hurry. After you've done a moose or two, anything else is child's play.

SOLITUDE

Rick and I camped a mile apart, and I listened for his shooting. I didn't hear any, so I got comfortable, ate moose chops by the kilo, and ingested more blueberries than I should have.

Rick floated around the bend and into the eddy in front of my tent one sunny morning. He hadn't killed a moose. I hurriedly packed up the tent and shoved it in the raft, and we pushed off downriver, hunting moose and caribou as we floated. Toward evening, we found a good camp out of the wind behind willows and spruce, with a hundred-foot pingo just behind for observation where we could scan the vast willow flats and tundra hills. The hills behind were veined with centuries-old caribou trails. The camp became a regular stopping place on my river trips for the next decade.

Upriver, in the mountains, the black clouds had socked in the range. Happily, down in the foothills, the weather was ideal Indian summer. The days were sunny and warm, and the nights just cool enough to chill the meat well.

I started a fire while Rick pitched his tent. I then hung the meat from the willows, skidded the raft back up in the trees, and tied it off in case of a hard blow during the night. You can't be too careful four hundred miles from anything that might be considered help. I hadn't paid much attention to Rick while I gathered firewood. He'd pitched his tent near mine and tied off his raft, but he had left the meat inside it and hadn't hauled the boat out of the water.

"Best to take care of that," I said and nodded at the raft. "Bear might get into the meat and ruin your raft. The wind could come up, too, and other problems."

I turned my attention back to the steak sizzling over the coals and the water steaming in the kettle. The evening meal and the time by the fire were perhaps the best parts of the hunting trips. Take care of chores and then kick back.

During the night, I awoke to a new noise. I lay listening, then the sound shifted. Possibly the wind had turned, bringing new noises with it. Probably nothing to it.

When I crawled from the tent in the gray dawn to stir up the fire, Lowe's raft was gone. The river had risen more than two feet, and it now lapped at the rise where we'd pitched the tents.

THE DANGEROUS GAME

For a brief moment, I figured Rick had floated off downriver before I awoke, but then I realized his tent was still there and I would have heard him had he left. A stream flowed down through where the fire had been.

"Rick!" I called. "Rick!" He crawled from the tent in his long johns and rubbed the sleep from his eyes. "Your raft is gone! Didn't you haul it up?" I knew it was a stupid question and wondered why we sometimes ask such things when we already know the answers.

"Huh?" he asked, trying to shake himself awake. "What?" Then it sunk in. He stared at where his raft had been. He'd tied it off but had chosen a dead, brittle willow branch, and the pull of the current had snapped the branch. The lighter wood of the break told the story.

I started a fire on the high ground. Rick dressed, then climbed the pingo with his binocular. No one spoke. We were too deep in thought. We both knew my small raft wouldn't carry the two of us and gear, and Rick was a big guy pushing two hundred thirty pounds. I'm not sure what conclusion Rick was coming to, but mine made me anything but comfortable. Still, I could see no way around it.

When he came back, I said, "I'm gonna leave you here," and watched for his reaction. "Both of us can't ride in my raft. If we tried, I'd have to dump half the gear and the meat, and we'd have a tough time getting through the rapids."

He shuffled his feet and looked at the ground. He couldn't come up with a better idea, but he didn't like the conclusion.

"I'll leave meat and other grub. You've got the rifle, and you can always shoot more meat. This is a protected camp, and there's plenty of firewood. A rescue helicopter can land on the pingo if it has to, but once the water drops, it can land on the beach." I didn't know who I was trying to make feel better.

Loaded with my gear and more than half the meat, I pushed off into the current. Lowe stood on the bank and looked low, no pun intended. "I'll shoot five times if I find the raft in the next few miles, then you can hike down and get it and float out."

I didn't really expect to find it in the flooded torrent. If it hadn't been sunk by the raging river, it was halfway to the

SOLITUDE

Porcupine by now. Miles later I found the raft and its meat circling endlessly in a big eddy under a cliff. I tied it off, though there was no place to beach it, and fired the .270 in the direction of Lowe's camp. I figured it was too far for him to hear it. Then I pushed off again. I told myself that he had nothing to worry about: He had food, clothes, and a tent, and all he had to do was sit back and wait.

 I felt guilty that I didn't feel too sorry for the guy. And I felt happy to get off by myself again. Yes, solitude is a fine thing. It's nearly impossible to come across solitude "outside," in civilization, and if you do, it doesn't last long enough. Silence is just as fleeting, and it is never pure because the unnatural noises we get used to in our routines—barking dogs, engines, the hum of appliances—are always present in the background. At the moment, I had both. Anyway, unless Rick did something foolish or ran afoul of a grizzly with piles, he'd survive until I could report the matter. After all, it was his own carelessness that had gotten him into trouble.

 That night I camped on a big sandy beach at a bend in the river. I pitched the tent on a rise high enough so water wouldn't reach it if the river rose. I dragged the meat and gear up, too. I built a fire on the beach, sat on a big piece of drift log by the fire, and watched the smoke drift downriver in the cooling air. All the while a big moose steak broiled and the tea pot whistled and gurgled. As I stood by the fire sipping hot cocoa in the last dusk, to my astonishment, Rick floated around the bend and into the quiet water of the beach.

 I didn't believe he could have heard the shots, and I was skeptical he'd find the raft if he did, so I was indeed amazed. He was in bad shape. The raft had eight inches of water in the bottom, and he was soaked. He'd sat motionless in the raft in the freezing air for hours. His lips were purple, and he shivered violently. I led him to the fire and tossed the deadfall I'd collected for the morning on the embers, then poured him a cup of steaming water. "Slowly," I said as he sipped and shivered.

 I dragged his gear and raft up onto the height of land, pitched his tent, and found his driest clothes (none of mine were big enough). I made him change by the fire and used some of the

THE DANGEROUS GAME

wet clothes to carry scalding rocks from the fire to his tent. I wrapped them in drier clothes and stuffed them into his sleeping bag, then led him to the tent. He drank two cups of hot cocoa and ate a moose steak. He was shivering less violently, and when the thermogenic properties of the red meat kicked in, he quit shaking altogether, especially with the hot rocks in the bedroll. I firmly believe he'd have died of hypothermia that night if he hadn't found my camp. He believed it, too. In the morning, we found the hot rocks had scorched completely through the first layer of clothes I'd wrapped them in.

We floated on from there. Rick didn't shoot a moose, but he no longer cared. He felt he'd been luckier than he deserved. There'd be another year for moose hunting. We were in no hurry. We weren't to rendezvous with Roger Dowding for another week, and the rendezvous was only two or three camps downriver.

At one camp on a big island, we got intimately acquainted with the largest wolf pack I'd come across. From the howling, we counted at least nineteen in the pack, all howling from different places and all within a half-mile of our camp. I howled back in response. One answered from just across the river, then another from two hundred fifty yards downriver, then another from behind, and more. I howled again as we sat by the fire. They answered again; then two came out of the timber on the other side, waded through the riffles downriver, crossed onto the island, and trotted up toward us at the fire. For the first time I thought about the rifle. I eased to the tent, slowly eased a cartridge into the chamber, and walked back to the fire . . . just in case, mind you, because I did not want to shoot a wolf. I did not want the meat, and I had enough trophies for one expedition. I howled again, and the two wolves on the island trotted purposefully toward us. More wolves howled from behind and up- and downriver.

The two wolves trotting toward us caught our scent and stopped. You could see them lift their snouts into the downriver breeze and pick up a molecule of human stink here, another there. They seemed more curious than frightened. They didn't run or slink off. We listened and watched the wolves howl until dark, then we crawled into our tents. The wolves cried throughout the night, so often and from so near that I found it tough to sleep.

SOLITUDE

It snowed three inches toward morning, and the day dawned scrubbed and bright, though the temperature didn't climb above freezing. We camped another day on the island before pushing off for the rendezvous that would bring that season's solitude to an end.

MORE SOLITUDE

I'd thought a lot about solitude that year. It was good having fine people to share the best country I knew, but it also detracted from the full feeling I got when traveling solo. Sure, I got away from those people for a day or longer, but I always knew I was coming back, and it's just not the same. Living in the bush alone with no one to know or care whether I showed up at the evening fire gave me a wild and glorious sense of freedom. I had no one to explain a damned thing to.

Being alone always gives me a satisfying sense of accomplishment because I am responsible only to myself and for my own survival. If I get hurt or sick, I will either get better or die. No one will rescue me, if that is even possible in a land without radio contact. Yes, I know plenty of readers will consider this a curious epistle written by an eccentric, and perhaps they're right, but I wouldn't have been considered quite so eccentric had I written this a hundred fifty years ago. Too often, even the best writers can't explain the truly intangible, and I'm not one of the best. Let's get on with the trip.

I compromised. That season I would trek up off the Sheenjek to the high country and hunt sheep for a month or so, then hike and float downriver to the Lobo Lake country to meet up with my longtime fishing, pheasant-hunting, and deer-hunting pals, Rick Lovell and Mims Barker. From there, we'd float downriver and rendezvous with Roger Dowding and his familiar Cessna 185. I planned to cover at least three hundred square miles alone before I had company.

Roger dumped me at the dry lake near Last Lake, and I sweated the gear across the tussocks to the river. I'd bought a new inflatable boat—a Riken fourteen-footer—with a rowing frame, cargo nets, heavy-duty whitewater oars, and big coolers that fastened underneath the rowing frame. I'd brought along

MORE SOLITUDE

the smaller Achilles raft, too, as well as the usual assortment of camping gear. I made more than twenty trips toting gear back and forth between the dry lake bed and the river. After sunset, I inflated the Riken and floated the gear downriver to the stream from which I would hike up into the sheep country. It was early August and it did not yet get fully dark.

On the evening float, I spotted two bands of caribou bulls, three moose, one grizzly, and a wolf. It felt so good to be home again, I couldn't even explain it to myself. It was the same feeling I'd first felt on the Coleen River years earlier.

I camped on a river bar that night and listened to the wolves howling. In the morning, I deflated the raft and stuffed it and all the gear into steel drums for protection against grizzlies. I sprayed the drums with oven cleaner to give any bear that took a bite a nasty surprise. I didn't want to give the bears enough time to figure out how to get into the drums. Fresh bear tracks crisscrossed the beach.

In the morning, I stuffed the tiny tent into the backpack, shouldered the .270, and started up. I made it to the now-familiar campsite by afternoon, after sweating through the muskegs in the bottoms and then up through the spruce forests into the barren, alpine tundra country. I forded the same numbing, waist-deep streams. Early on in the trek, a very light, almost-white wolf that barked like a dog kept pace with me a hundred yards off. I'm sure he was curious and equally sure he'd never encountered man.

After pitching the tiny blue tent, gathering a panful of blueberries, and filling the jugs with spring water, I hauled willow deadwood from the creek bottom. As I sat by the fire that evening, listening to wolves howl far up the creek and sipping cocoa, I was content. Of all the camps in that country, this was my favorite. It was very open, the tallest vegetation being nine-foot willows along the creek. Elsewhere, the tallest growth was the thigh-high dwarf birch, and there wasn't much of that. The site was remote and inhabited by more wildlife than a game park. Mostly, though, I prized the absolute solitude of a bare tundra bench in the broad, U-shape glacial valley.

Sheep season didn't open for a few days, though the idea of a set date to begin hunting seemed as absurd as anything else we do

THE DANGEROUS GAME

"outside." That idea was right up there with giving governments money to do things we had no use for, spending most of every day in odd clothes, working so we could say we were happy, and paving over the wetlands and other places so we could run the race faster. In the solitude and absolute clarity of the Far North, none of it made sense. "Outside," we went through the motions without thinking too hard about why. If we ever stopped and took the time to think, we wouldn't persist in our trivial routines.

That first day, I hauled firewood and loafed. The sun burned through the Indian summer haze, and I lay on the dry tundra and read and dozed. In the afternoon, I awoke to stare at a bull caribou staring at me from twenty-five yards. Finally, unable to deal with the question, he reared and then cantered off in a half circle. Then he trotted back to look from another angle. He repeated the maneuver half a dozen times before he caught human scent. When he did, he reared a bit higher, trotted off, stopped, and then stared again. It's comical how game animals react to a man when they have never seen one before.

The next day, I scouted for the huge ram I'd seen the season before. I'd dreamt of him both while awake and while asleep. During the year he'd become an obsession, and I meant to collect him now that I was certain truly big rams wandered in the Brooks Range.

I trekked up to where I'd seen the big ram, but I didn't find him. I spotted a band of rams in the canyon I had named Trophy Creek after killing my first sheep there. The rams grazed the still-green tundra below a nameless col, and I only stalked them close enough to satisfy myself that the big one wasn't among them.

I hiked to another canyon the next day, with a lunch and a binocular. I spotted four rams—one was much better than any I'd shot and would probably tape thirty-eight inches—but I did not see the big male. I spotted a sow grizzly with a couple of two-year-old cubs across a stream, two bands of bull caribou totaling forty animals, a cow and newborn calf moose, and two flocks of ptarmigan. I wasn't close enough to determine if they were rock or willow ptarmigan, but I'd never seen either that high.

That evening, as I ate a concoction of grayling and rice, a chocolate-brown grizzly grazed on lowbush blueberries behind

MORE SOLITUDE

the camp. When I noticed him, he was busily stripping the bushes thirty yards away. He didn't see me slink to the tent for the rifle. I chambered a round, then let out a war whoop. The bear sat on his haunches and looked around in surprise. I whooped again, and he lumbered across the flat and straight up the mountain. He didn't slow until he crossed the skyline a thousand feet above.

Sheep season opened, and I journeyed up to glass the north side of Black Mountain, the peak I'd named two years earlier. I found the tiny, dirty-white specs of sheep high on the tundra slopes below the cliffs and scree. The sheep were safe from wolves there.

I crossed the big basin and forded the stream, which was swollen from earlier rains, then sweated up the shoulder of the mountain to the first sheep band. All were rams, but none was good enough, none worthy of obsession, though every one was bigger than the two rams I'd killed in early years.

I eased back out of sight and stalked around the shoulder of the mountain to the second band of sheep. Two or three pushed forty inches, but none was my grail. The rams spooked and raced into the cliffs, looking like dirty-white insects on a dark wall. Others followed, and I eased away and upward; I'd seen two more sheep away from the individual bands. Though they were both good trophies, neither was what I wanted.

I came back three more times to the same basin to search for my ram. Some of the big sheep had left the basin, but others had stayed. I didn't see a ewe or lamb in the area.

Late one morning, I climbed an avalanche chute up the north face of Black Mountain toward a small band of rams. When I had climbed hands-and-fingers over the cliff and onto a tundra bench, the rams had moved on. But then I glimpsed one on a cliff above. If things worked out right, I would climb out of the avalanche chute fifty yards away before he could scent me.

It worked out, though *four* rams stood and stared. I recognized one of them, the ram with the exceptionally wide-flaring horns that was with the big one the year before. He had a lot of annual rings on his horns, too. I settled the cross hairs on his brisket as he stood on a ledge just above and touched off. He disappeared at the shot, but a little puff of white fur floated off in the wind. He'd dropped without knowing what hit him.

THE DANGEROUS GAME

I'd given up on the monster ram a day earlier without really realizing it. He'd been a Methuselah the season before, and the odds were slim he'd survived one more tough Arctic winter.

The ram I collected was twelve years old. The horns pinched into the cheeks, then flared out; they later spread on the tape thirty-one inches. The curl went thirty-eight inches. Almost as important, I had the best of red meat. I caped the ram, skinned the rest of the carcass, and quartered it, laying the quarters in a cold, ice-filled cave. I'd pack it out the next day.

Clouds rolled in over the divide, and by the time I crawled into the tent that night, rain and snow pelted the fabric. The clouds lowered, the rain turned completely to snow and sleet, and the tent, slapped by the wind, was like a mainsail in a gale.

The next morning, the heavy weather had quit, though the mountains still hid in the clouds. I shoved the sharpening stone, saw, and knife in the backpack and hiked up to retrieve the mountain mutton. I startled a very blond grizzly from the creekside willows, and I circled well up the bare hill and away, since I didn't carry the rifle.

Partway up the avalanche chute, I heard a clatter above and a sharp crack like a rifle shot, and then another crack, and another. I stopped and looked up, but I knew what it was. I stared up at the puffs of rock powder hanging in the air where the boulder had hit as it blew down the channel. The walls on either side were unscalable—I couldn't escape that way, even if I had time. Against the broken-rock scree, I could not see the rock hurtling toward me in the shadows, though I saw the rock powder hanging in the air. I ducked just as the boulder rocketed past with an audible *whoosh*. It was three feet in diameter and would have taken off my head. I sat on a boulder and watched my hands shake before I resumed the climb. Even if the rock had only broken a leg or hand, I wouldn't have made it out.

I happily hauled the meat back to camp without further incident and crawled into the tent as content as possible. I loafed the following days along the bench, eating sheep meat and watching the game move about. When I'd eaten enough meat that I wouldn't have to carry too much down to the river, I trekked out and down to my cache. I loitered more days fly-fishing for grayling, then pushed off downriver for my rendezvous with Mims and Rick.

As I waited on the river beach near Lobo Lake, I watched for caribou. I thought it would be nice to have red meat for the guys when they came in, and the sheep meat was just about finished. Some cows and small bulls had migrated through, and two moose browsed in the willows just across the river. I fished and wandered.

The big bulls came at night. I crawled from the tent in the dusk of early morning to see them spread across the tundra in back of the tent. They'd just swum the river. I dived into the tent and grabbed the rifle, half-laced my boots, and stalked in my long johns toward the grazing caribou. I picked a good one and fired, and when the bullet hit, a great burst of water splashed from the sodden fur. He dropped, and I picked out another good bull—in this unit, the limit was five—and fired. That one wobbled a few yards and dropped. The first bull got to his feet, and I hit him again. He went down. I raced across the bogs in my long johns and sloppy boots. To my astonishment, I had three dead bulls. The one I thought had gotten up was really another bull. I had the meat of three bull caribou to take care of, all within two hundred yards of the tent.

The bulls were all good ones. The first had long beams, heavy double shovels, long points, and upper palming. The second was freaky, with a twisted, very odd main beam and short points sticking out of unusual places. The third bull was just an average, mature trophy. I had all the meat and antlers into camp by nightfall.

In early September, the nights were shorter and colder, while the days were usually sunny and hazy. The gold-and-crimson tundra smelled of wine from the freezing and fermenting blueberries and cranberries. The willow leaves along the river had been stripped by the winds, and the peaks just north were dusted white with the first snows. The bull moose across the river had cleaned the velvet from their now-white antlers. The caribou had begun to shed their velvet, too, and it hung in bloody tatters. The geese and swans and ducks from the north slope had flown into Lobo Lake, and the cacophony woke me

THE DANGEROUS GAME

three or four times each night. But I wouldn't have quieted the celebration if I could.

One evening as I sat by the fire, Roger's blue-and-white Cessna roared low over camp, banked upriver, and flew low over the beach, which was different now after high water. Deciding against landing on the beach, Roger flew downriver a mile and landed on the higher and drier beach there. I rowed across the river and hiked down to help haul the gear up to the raft.

I ate most of the dozen donuts Rick and Mims brought and half a head of lettuce—irresistible and exotic foods that I'd forgotten about in the bush. I then broiled a big mess of caribou steaks for the guys.

The hunters, Rick and I, rode in the big Riken inflatable, and Mims floated in the smaller Achilles. Rick wanted to shoot a big caribou, while Mims was along for the ride and the fishing. We fly-fished from the rafts in the big river eddies. We released most of the two-pound grayling we caught, and once Mims hooked something off the bottom—probably a pike—that took out the line but never showed itself. We floated around a bend one evening, and a herd of caribou bulls grazed on the tundra along a low bluff. Antlers bobbed above the scrub, and Rick and I both knew they were good.

I had voluntarily put myself into noncombatant status and wasn't shooting. It was just as much fun stalking game when someone else had the rifle. We rowed cautiously into the bluff and tied the raft to the willows. The wind drifted into our faces as we stalked first through the willows and then onto the open tundra. Mims rowed to a beach across the river and watched as Rick and I crabbed through more willows to close the distance for a better look at the herd of bulls. Rick knew which one he wanted, one with upper palming and long points. He killed it with one shot at sixty yards with his 7mm Remington Magnum.

We quickly caped and quartered the bull in the evening, loaded it into the boat, and pushed off to find the camp just downriver. I'd named it Rising Water Camp after the mishap the season before.

After the chores, I climbed the pingo behind camp to glass for game; I would take a good moose if I could find one. We stayed at Rising Water Camp for two days while Rick worked on

MORE SOLITUDE

the cape and the meat. We spotted caribou, wolves, and moose from the pingo. We floated more days down the Sheenjek, loafing and fishing for grayling along the way. Though Rick had a moose tag, he was content with the caribou. I felt the same. We spent one day in the tent out of the wind and rain and played matchstick poker, then floated down the river to the rendezvous beach. It took Roger two trips to get our gear back to Circle.

On the drive down the gravel Steese Highway to Fairbanks, I pondered solitude. Too much of it makes you a hermit; too little makes you anxious and cranky. The amount for each man varies. Some can survive with just the solitude they find on a toilet seat. Others need a month or more. But we all need it. Finding the right balance is the tough part.

CALL OF THE SHEENJEK

The rest of the year was pretty much aimed at getting back in the bush again, and not just any bush, but *the* Brooks Range bush beyond the Arctic Circle. A day didn't go by that I didn't remember the howling wolves, the big rams on black-rock peaks, the grizzlies that always made the heart jump, the caribou pushing southeast, and the moose. Mixed in were the dusk campfires with caribou steaks or grayling sizzling over the coals, or the ptarmigan stew cooked in gravy, or wild cranberries so sweet they dissolved in your mouth. Indian summer afternoons on the colorful, wine-scented tundra flats picking blueberries were part of it, too, along with that quick turn from Indian summer to late autumn, the new snow dusting the gray peaks and the wind stripping the last brown leaves from the riverside willows as big chevrons of geese from the Arctic Ocean winged their way south. These visions filled my town-bound thoughts through the winter. Everything else seemed pale and prosaic.

Gathering gear and tweaking were part of it, too. I scoured the catalogs for whitewater goodies, tried out rifle cartridges, and visited sporting goods stores to check out the latest backpacking stoves. I figured I was the richest man alive to have the liberty to return to the wild each year, and I couldn't fathom weighing myself down with a job that wouldn't allow me two months in the Arctic bush and at least that much more at my cabin on the Yukon. Thirty-year mortgages and fine pickup trucks never intended to haul venison would strip away all that wealth, and I would become one of the masses with no sense of freedom—after all, they *had* to work to maintain their establishments. It's a freedom that rises from a sense of confidence in having the ability to rely on yourself, to survive in true wilderness where no other help or support exists. The wild country and that sense of freedom, the same that Colter and Bridger and Smith knew in the Frontier West, kept me alive through those years, completely alive, like nothing I've known since. I was richer than Bill Gates or the Bush Dynasty, back then.

* * * * *

When I first journeyed to Alaska in 1981, I met a petite blonde on the shuttle bus in Denali National Park. I was on my way to photograph in the Outer Range, and she was touring with her sister. She lived in Michigan. She would visit me in Utah, and we phoned for a while, but then another woman came along, and that was that. Half a dozen years later, I got a postcard from the blonde, and we started writing and phoning and visiting. To shorten the story, one April she quit her job and traveled to Alaska with me.

Roger flew us to the upper Sheenjek in July, and we floated, camped, and just looked around. Then we floated downriver to "my" sheep canyon, cached the gear in the steel drums, and trekked up to camp. We stayed weeks before the sheep season opened and just enjoyed the scenery. Cheri fell in love with the country—with its isolation, its wildlife, its silence, and its stark and stunning beauty.

We didn't collect a ram that season though we hunted hard, often staying out thirty hours straight because it did not get dark that early in the season. We saw young rams, but nothing with any heft. The failure made me edgy. I was unused to the continuous company, and I got anxious about that, too. But she put up with me.

As important as the lack of trophy was the lack of meat. I caught grayling along the river on tiny dry flies, but fish doesn't satisfy like red meat, and Cheri wasn't a fish-eater, anyway. Since we camped across the river from Lobo Lake, I climbed the cemetery hill often to scan for caribou. But I found none, and I got more worried. They'd either already left the country or hadn't yet migrated through. Both of us were meat-hungry and wearied of the dwindling dried foods. If we didn't get meat to supplement what little we had left, we might get into trouble.

THE DANGEROUS GAME

The thought that the country might not provide what we needed had never crossed my mind before. It crossed it then. We would have to continue surviving on grayling and berries, rationing the little rice, flour, and other civilized foods we had.

But the country had *always* provided. In the frozen dawn, "she"—the land, the country, nature—dropped a gift right into camp. I heard them clucking in the dawn, and they seemed close. I stuck my head out of the tent, expecting to see some off in the willows or down the beach, but there they were, right in front of the tent, between the sleeping and gear tents and behind us. I pulled my head back into the tent, dropped a shell in the Harrington & Richardson single-barrel shotgun, and then eased the flap aside, lining up the bead on one bird head and another just beyond. Both dropped at the blast and beat the tundra in their death-fluttering. I shot two more on the ground—when you're meat-hungry, you don't worry about sport—and then one more before the rest of them walked back into the willows. Both Cheri and I giggled with relief.

In the cold and wilds, two people can easily eat half a dozen ptarmigan a day. We ate three that day and saved the rest. But the next dawn, the ptarmigan came again, and when the breeze blew away the smell of gunsmoke, we had seven more. We immediately cooked up six of them in cranberries we'd picked behind camp, and it was impossible to remember anything else that had ever tasted so good.

The birds flew into camp each dawn. Apparently, we had pitched our tents on gourmet bird gravel. We shot what we needed: The birds kept as well as in a refrigerator during the cold nights, and we moved them into the shade during the day. We eventually pushed the Riken raft into the current and floated downriver. We camped at Rising Water Camp the first night, and I told Cheri of Rick Lowe's misadventures. We scanned for game from the pingo, though moose season wasn't open yet, and we lazed about the pleasant camp, eating ptarmigan and grayling and needing no justification to do anything else.

We finally found caribou at the next camp. The first evening there I saw a big bull asleep on the edge of the river, and Cheri and I stalked to just across from him on our side. Cheri sat and got comfortable, and I told her to hit the bull just ahead of the shoulder and under the drooping neck to take out the heart. She did, but the bull leapt straight into the river and plunged across in his last, urgent death rush. I plunged into the frigid evening river water to grab the bull before he floated off downstream. I grabbed an antler, but the bull made one last lunge, pulling me off my feet and underwater. When I got my feet on solid ground again, I pulled the feebly struggling bull toward shore. I dragged him onto the beach and coughed up a pint of river.

Once we'd hauled the bull well away from the river, my lips turned purple and I started to shiver in violent bursts. My wet hair froze into a helmet. In camp, Cheri stirred up the fire and put water on to boil while I changed into dry clothes and tried to quit shaking. She poured four cups of steaming cocoa into me and fed me hot soup before I could stop.

The next day we climbed the bluff and hiked out toward a distant band of caribou we'd spotted through the binocular. Toward midday, I killed a bull with thirty-six points, quartered it, and began packing the carcass to camp. I packed the rest of it the following day, and we finally had more red meat than we needed.

One morning, we pushed off into the current again and floated a day downriver to a pleasant place I'd found in earlier years. I'd named it Bluff Camp after the big bluff across the river where I'd sit and spot game. The camp was on a dry spruce bench, just above a black-sand beach and a big, deep pool that was always good for grayling on dry or wet flies. We spotted moose, caribou, and grizzly from the bluff, and I caught two-pound grayling in the big pool. Moose season hadn't quite opened yet, so I did not think of shooting one . . . though in the country, what could it have mattered?

We floated another day downriver and camped on a sandy bluff above the current. We heard moose battering saplings in the forest, but the season was still not open. For two days we sat out a windstorm that permanently bent the rods of the heavy-duty expedition tent. If I had not raised a log barrier, I doubt the tent would have withstood the gale, which was strong enough to throw softball-size rocks across the beach.

THE DANGEROUS GAME

When the wind stopped, we floated another day downriver and camped on another sandy hillside above the river. Behind camp, a slough flowed sluggishly between us and the willow flats and spruce forest beyond. Rapids raged down in front of the camp, and caribou and moose tracks cratered the sand. The spoor said the caribou had already migrated out of the country, and moose season still wasn't open. That anxious feeling was returning because I'd promised my Gwitchin neighbor Lucy Roberts a supply of "Indian meat," and I didn't have enough for both of us yet.

We climbed a high, timbered bluff behind the camp and scanned the vast willow flats for game. Mostly we saw nothing except a lone fox or a raven flapping listlessly through the spruce. Late one afternoon, as we sat by a fire and watched, we spotted a lone bull caribou trotting north a mile from the river on the other side. I could see through the binocular that he was good, but he was far away and going farther. He was also traveling in the wrong direction, away from the rutting grounds in the Ogilvies to the southeast.

For no reason I could see, the bull suddenly turned ninety degrees and made a beeline in our direction. If he continued in a straight line, he'd hit the river a half-mile above us. We'd never make it through the willows in time, so we sat and watched. He hit the bluff just where we'd thought he would, then, without reason, he again turned down the bluff until he was exactly opposite us. The bull plunged into the deepest current and swam across until he stood directly below us to shake the water off. But the willows were too thick to shoot into. He trotted into the timber below and a few minutes later climbed the steep bluff and stood just ten yards away. I killed him in his tracks. To our surprise, instead of tumbling down the bluff, which probably would have shattered the big antlers, he lay down and balanced precariously on the edge. Then and there I named the place Surprise Camp.

I tied the bull to a sapling with my belt so he would not crash down the seventy-five-degree slope; then I quartered the carcass, removed the cape, and cut the head free so I could pack them onto a flat piece of tundra. We hauled the bull into the camp the next day.

CALL OF THE SHEENJEK

We now had no reason to worry over meat, even if I did not kill a moose. So we pushed out into the current again and floated downriver to the rendezvous spot where Roger would pick us up, a place where he had cached fuel in blue plastic drums.

The weather had been gray upriver in the peaks, and I half-expected the river to rise. That first night on the rendezvous beach, I heard the change in the water. At first it sounded subtle, as I lay in the sleeping bag in the dark and listened. (When sleeping in the wilderness, it's necessary to sleep with one ear awake to listen for a small sound that might indicate a grizzly or something else nosing around.) I heard something else, then—something wet and rushing—and the sound changed as I lay there. I was suddenly out and pulling on hip boots. Water surged across the place where Roger would land. The tent was, for the moment, safe on a small rise, but we threw the camp in whitewater bags, untied the raft, and jumped aboard. Before we launched, I rushed back and rolled the fuel drums to the highest bit of ground and left a note in a plastic sandwich bag for Roger, indicating he should look for us downriver.

By that time, the gravel bar was almost completely underwater. As the water continued to rise, it hissed through the hot coals of the fire. We floated through the night and toward dawn found a high bluff that we thought might work as a landing strip. A trapper cabin lay beyond it, along with a cache full of exotic foods like raspberry jam, peanut butter, syrup, and cans of greens and peaches and apricots!

I know I shouldn't have, but I raided the cache. Appetites leaped to the surface that had been sublimated for seven weeks. We gorged on the preserves and the canned fruit and vegetables. Sometimes, appetites build so strongly there is nothing we can do but indulge them. I indulged. I ate an entire tin of raspberry jam as I sat by the fire one evening. I ate tins of salted nuts, indulged in hot soups, and sucked down syrupy apricots. I vowed to run down the trapper that had the local trapline and repay him somehow.

We spent the better part of three days clearing the logs and debris deposited by spring flooding on the rocky beach. I was glad I'd brought the double-bit ax. As I cut through the big spruce logs, Cheri rolled them aside, and then we hauled away spruce and poplar drift logs and filled in the low places with rocks. I paced off the landing strip and found it was long enough, with a little to spare.

Roger flew over from upriver one morning. The flow had dropped again to normal levels, and he had landed and found my cryptic note: "Look downriver, W.P." He flew low to check out my makeshift airstrip, swung lower yet to check again, and then circled to make a final approach and land. I was very proud of the ax work and the finished airstrip.

"The strip's not long enough to get you guys and the meat off," he said.

We pondered the alternatives: use two costly flights to get us out, use two flights to a beach downriver and then take all of us and the gear from there, or float farther downriver. In the end, Roger said, "Let's try it. If it doesn't look like we'll make it, I'll shut her down."

Bush pilots aren't noted for longevity, and I could see why. We loaded up.

Roger taxied the 185 as far up the beach as he could get. He revved the engine and held the hand brake before he released it, and we bounced and lurched and bounced some more down the beach. The time between bounces got longer, and as we got close to the end of the beach, we all watched without breathing. Evidently, he'd made up his mind to go though with it. I grasped the sissy bar and held tight. We bounced once more, just feet from the end, and sailed out through the willows, the twigs slapping the wheels and strut. The plane sailed out over the water for a moment and then dropped six feet before the Cessna leveled off and began to climb.

Roger Dowding and Joe Firmin were the best bush pilots I'd flown with to that time, and I'd flown with a number. But if Roger skirted this close to death often, he was pushing it. Flying, like everything else in the wilderness, is full of close calls. Death might come from crashing a plane or from drowning when a raft hits a sweeper hanging out over the current. Death might come from a boulder taking your head off in an avalanche channel. It might come from a bear mauling, an ax injury, or a fall from a bluff. It might come from a ruptured appendix or an allergic reaction to a bee sting. But it's the challenge of surviving in the face of these dangers that makes the country so healing, so rejuvenating, and so attractive. Once you are bitten by the wilderness bug, you can do nothing but return—the call becomes irresistible. Civilization, with its seat belt and helmet laws and enforced safety, seems a pale existence in contrast. Up in the bush, nothing is sanitized.

    I turned to look at Cheri stuffed in between all the gear in the back. All I could see was her face, but from the smile I knew that she'd been bitten, too. Roger understood, too, or he would not have done what he did. I saw the grin when he banked and dropped low to look over a sixty-five-inch moose on a willow flat. We knew there were few of us left, and maybe that was for the better.

IT CALLS YOU BACK

Cheri was as anxious to get back as I was, but somehow we'd gotten corralled into guiding a bunch of friends through the Sheenjek country. Of course, all of them were the best of people, ones who could appreciate the last great place in the United States.

Flo Krall, my former professor whom I had taken on an earlier expedition with me, and her fiancé, philosophy writer and professor Paul Shepard, were coming in first. Later, Pete Spear, my college buddy, longtime friend, and hunting pal, would fly in when Flo and Paul flew out. Colorado rancher and genuine buckaroo Herschel "Bud" Hendrickson would also fly in, and the four of us would float-hunt down the Sheenjek. Though the expedition seemed too complicated for my tastes, it proved interesting.

Cheri and I flew in first to the upper Sheenjek, well above Last Lake. Roger dropped us with our rafts and gear and food on a river bar. I inflated the small Achilles raft and then shot half a dozen ptarmigan for Cheri's supper before floating off downriver (Cheri would stay to meet up with Paul and Flo later in the day). I also pitched the expedition tent because it looked like rain, knowing that if the country weathered in, Cheri might be without company at the camp for days. I left her the single-bore 12-gauge H&R for security.

I floated downriver well into the evening; then, instead of camping at "my" creek, I cached the gear in steel drums and hiked up the canyon toward sheep country. Later, I would rendezvous with Cheri, Flo, and Paul at Lobo Lake. Cheri and company would take the Achilles raft downriver with them, and I would cut cross-country from the sheep camp to Lobo Lake. I was looking forward to the trek because much of it was through country I hadn't walked through yet.

Cheri had named our sheep canyon "Walt's Creek," and that worked for me. I made good time, pushing up through the bottoms

IT CALLS YOU BACK

and muskegs, then into the higher spruce forest. I climbed onto the alpine tundra, through the rushing streams and bogs, and on up. It was late July, and it did not get fully dark, so I could travel for as long as I had energy. I pushed straight to the bench where I had camped when hunting sheep. After I pitched the tent, I crawled into the down sleeping bag, pleasantly weary. I had made it to my sheep country two days earlier than I'd hoped.

The hunt turned tough. I hunted sixteen hours a day and saw, on average, two or three small rams a day. I watched the usual grizzlies, fewer than usual caribou, a moose here and there, and a few wolves. The summer had been dry and warm, and the smoke haze from the big fires along the lower Sheenjek, in the Yukon Flats, and over in the Old Crow country blew into the high canyons. I was out hunting longer than I had planned. Probably the dry summer had something to do with it, and the rams had stayed where the feed was better.

Late one day, as I made my way into the head of Trophy Creek, I thought about all the walking I'd done hunting sheep. Great fun, I guess—at that point I wasn't sure—but with zero results. I slid down shale scree then across a bottom and looked up the tiny rivulet. The sun was about to drop behind the ridge, but when I glanced up I saw a big ram.

It wasn't that old ram of a lifetime I'd seen a few seasons earlier, but it was a good one—certainly the best I'd seen this trip. He lay facing into the sun, his lemon-peel-color horns pinching in close before flaring wide like an argali's. The bases had plenty of heft, too. He lay a scant hundred yards up the creek, and I figured in the right position I might just be able to put the slug in the back of the neck. However, by the time I sat, the ram was out of sight behind the curve of the slope, and it was too risky a shot to make offhand. He was with another good ram, too, but it was not quite as good.

I dropped to my belly and crawled across the shale and through the rivulet until I was out of sight. I then double-checked the wind and hurried up the slope, still out of sight behind the curve of the shale slide. The stalk was textbook perfect, and when I eased into position, fifty yards from the rams, both stood and stared incredulously for a moment.

THE DANGEROUS GAME

Sheep do not like danger above them. If a wolf shows below them, they are not unduly alarmed because they know they can outrun any wolf alive uphill. But they panic if one gets above them.

Both rams whirled and trotted up the shale until they stopped at my elevation. I settled the cross hairs of the 7mm-08 just behind the shoulder of the big one and touched off. He dropped at the blast, kicked once, and lay still. The second ram, which was a bit smaller and had a broken back left horn, stood wide-eyed, and he continued to stand and stare as I made my way to the trophy ram and dragged him into the bottoms. He was still staring while I took photos. Finally he turned and walked down the canyon.

I crawled back into the downy comfort of the sleeping bag very late in the day. I climbed back up in the morning, boned out the meat, sawed the horns free from the skull, cleaned the cape, and started back for camp as happy as is possible without sinning seriously. I further fleshed the cape the next day and hung the meat in cheesecloth in the creekside willows, then propped the cape up to dry in the wind on the dwarf birch bushes. Of course, I couldn't carry salt on this kind of expedition, but wind drying worked as well. The problem comes with wet weather; then again, if it is wet, it is usually also cold, so the cape won't spoil, regardless. I cut the backstraps into chops, then propped the horns against a rock and admired them.

I planned to rest and then hit the trail for the Sheenjek rendezvous the next day. I'd push down the canyon, cross over into a nameless drainage behind Brushman Mountain and hike south, then cross down into the main Sheenjek valley and traverse the foothills, tussocks, and muskeg bogs, ultimately meeting up with everybody on the beach near Lobo Lake. It would have been much easier to hike down to the cache and float down from there. But I wanted to see new country.

Things didn't work out exactly as planned. Maybe I ate too much fresh sheep meat that day, or perhaps I'd gotten some bad backpacker food. I got so sick that night that I vaulted from the tent naked into the rain. I was so sick there on the tundra in the rain that I barely had strength to crawl back into the tent. At dawn, I was far too weak to think of leaving. I lay in the tent sipping water, and my strength slowly came back. By afternoon, I thought seriously of trying it. I could always camp where I was if I became sick again.

I packed up camp and walked down to the creek to retrieve the boned-out sheep meat, which led to a further surprise. During the night, a sow and two big cub grizzlies had raided the cache. I looked at the mess, and then I looked around carefully before backing onto the bench where I had the rifle. Armed again, I walked cautiously back down and retrieved what little meat I could.

I walked slowly down the stream, keeping clear of the willows and keeping an eye out for the bears. I angled up the slope that dropped into another nameless stream that poured into Walt's Creek farther down. I forded the rushing, waist-deep, cottonwood-fringed water. With the big cottonwoods and the other vegetation, the place looked like a Wyoming canyon, not a place a hundred miles north of the Arctic Circle. I climbed a ridge and dropped into another canyon, working along a stream and an old, well-trod caribou path, smooth as a graded Park Service trail. I sat and rested and watched a big sow grizzly and a yearling cub cavort in a beaver pond downstream, then I climbed above them to get clear of any potential problem. High on the next ridge, I saw the Sheenjek winding through the burgundy-and-gold tundra far below. I camped in the river bottom and pushed to the rendezvous the next afternoon.

I got a hero's welcome, of a sort—the "hunter back from the hill" and all that. I cleaned up, Cheri fixed hot grub at the fire, and we all admired the great, golden ram horns. With the horns in camp, the illness seemed insignificant, and I didn't say anything about it. The labor of the sixteen-hour hikes through the high peaks and tundra basins seemed unimportant, too. In the end, I told of the late sun, the fine-winey smell of the tundra berries, the golden-horn ram in the afternoon, the big mountains, the silence, and the solitude.

When my college buddy from my Utah State University wildlife science graduate school days flew in, Flo and Paul flew out. Pete Spear had been writing to me all summer at my house in Circle,

THE DANGEROUS GAME

mostly about gear. I'd urged him to get a good inflatable boat, or a raft if preferred, because getting out depended on it. Besides, if he shot a moose, he'd need a big raft for the meat and trophy.

You'd have to know Pete: He's such a miser that he holds onto a nickel so tightly it screams. He's developed the art of not paying for anything into a science, and in the old days at the Cactus Club, he was always the last to buy a round. Predictably, he'd bought a smallish, department-store raft, and I vowed not to bail him out of any trouble he got into because of it. Though Pete's a likeable guy, he takes some getting used to.

Bud Hendrickson, the Colorado buckaroo, flew in with Roger the next day. I'd hunted on Bud's ranch, down on Mesa Creek, for mule deer several times. He had plenty of deer, though none was large, but I kept hunting there because Bud was one of the good ones. He is a dreamer, the kind who gets a distant look in the eye when you talk about the Far North.

We camped on the beach for two days to allow Bud and Pete to get their bush legs, then we shoved off into the current. Bud was properly outfitted. He was friendly with the manager of a big, Grand Junction sporting goods store, and the guy knew what was needed. Bud bought a good fourteen-foot raft with a proper rowing frame and accessories. He had the right clothes, too. Pete, on the other hand, came on a bootstrap. Each was supposed to bring in food, and we'd pool resources. Pete brought ramen noodles and oatmeal, while Bud spent a small fortune on gourmet, dehydrated backpack foods.

I planned the first camp at Rising Water. Pete wanted to shoot ptarmigan and moose, and a few hours downriver we got into thousands of the tasty birds. Without exaggeration, Pete shot up a hundred shells and didn't kill a single bird. (I wrote of this in "The Great North Ptarmigan Shoot," in my book *The Hunting Adventures of Me & Joe*, Safari Press, 1995, and at least one book critic called it a "yarn.") Absolutely true, and Pete was a great sport about it. The long and short of it was that after all the sporting clay competitions he'd bragged about, he couldn't hit a real bird. I could not stop laughing on the shoot, and toward the end, I guffawed each time he shot. I shot half a dozen birds at the end so we would have supper that night, and

IT CALLS YOU BACK

I did it with my bush shotgun, the old H&R single bore, which by that time had its fore-end duct-taped to the barrel.

At Rising Water Camp, Cheri pitched the tent while I dashed up to the pingo observation place to scan for moose. The moose season had opened, and we starved for red meat. We hoped someone would collect one on the big willow flat across the river. Pete hiked out south toward the big plateau to scout for caribou, and I gave him a warning not to shoot a moose so far from the river or he'd have to carry it out. Bud and Cheri wanted to shoot moose, too, so with all the moose hunters, I decided not to shoot.

We could scan four or five miles of river-bottom willow flats from the pingo, but all we found in two days of watching were small bulls. We watched a few more days, hoping a good one would show, but none did. Red meat was becoming an obsession because we'd been surviving on grayling and backpack food. One morning as Bud and I watched a two-year-old bull browse just across the river, Bud said, "I need a steak. Let's get that bull."

I rowed us across the river, and we stalked to within thirty yards. Bud shot it twice with the .270. He was awed by its size—nearly fifteen hundred pounds on the hoof. We spent the rest of the day boning and packing the meat to the river, then floating across in the raft.

"I wanted a big bull rack to hang on the porch back at Mesa Creek," he said as we sat by the fire that evening, slicing into steaks too big for a normal plate, "but I sure am happy we got this here little, good-eating bull." Even though we all wanted a trophy bull, Bud really shot the small moose so the party would have meat. It was just like Bud to do that, too. The rest of us could hold out for our trophies.

We floated on from there and stayed at Bluff Camp. There, Cheri killed a good bull with a fifty-four-inch spread, taking three long shots from the .270. When we'd taken care of the meat, we floated a long day downriver to Surprise Camp.

Pete had been trying for moose and caribou with a bow without luck. As he sat up on the bluff behind camp while the rest of us enjoyed the evening fire and moose-steaks for dinner, we heard a bull grunting from the far willows across the river. I

THE DANGEROUS GAME

did my own impression, "*OOOoo-ghk, OOOoo-ghk,*" and the bull answered back. I called, the bull called, and I answered. In the meantime, the bull cut the distance until he stepped from the willows onto the open bluff just across the river. Keep in mind, Bud and Cheri had already collected their moose and I wasn't hunting them, so I was calling just for fun.

"*OOOoo-ghk, OOOoo-ghk,*" I called again, pinching my nose to give the call a more rasping, guttural sound. I put real emotion into the call, too. The bull answered and then waded into the rapids. When he climbed out of the water on our side, I scraped an old caribou shoulder blade on nearby brush. The bull thrashed willows with the big antlers only yards from the tents. He grunted again and then walked slowly toward us in that rutting-bull side-to-side swagger. The bull was providing us with good after-dinner entertainment, and I called again to see what might happen.

He battered a willow with his big antlers, then stepped to within one yard of Bud's tent. I got worried. I slinked to the tent for the rifle, then shouted to scare the moose. If he was frightened, he didn't show it because he turned and walked around the camp. I yelled again and he smashed at another willow, and then he stepped back into the river with a nasty look back over his shoulder. On the other side, he disappeared into the brush without a hurry. A moment later, Pete ran into camp and said, "Give me your rifle."

I rowed Pete across the river, then I rowed back to camp. Half an hour later we heard three shots, and a half hour after that, Pete showed up on the bank. He'd killed the bull, and we butchered and packed it out the next day. Surprise Camp lived up to its name one more time.

Everybody now had a moose. We floated down to the rendezvous river bar, and Roger flew us all out in three or four shuttles. Bud and his wife, who'd driven up to meet him, stayed at Circle before they drove back down the Alaskan Highway.

In a sense, I felt as though I'd fulfilled a social contract, the obligation to other *Homo sapiens*. I'd shared the fine country with a few of the very best of the species, the kind that would not exploit the land in any manner. I'd done my duty. And while it

IT CALLS YOU BACK

hadn't been unpleasant, it hadn't been the same as when we were alone. Cheri felt the same.

"I missed the solitude," Cheri said one evening as we sat in front of the window and watched the Yukon River.

"Me too," I agreed, even though I'd had those weeks to myself hunting the big ram. I glanced at the golden horns propped against the wall and smiled. "Me too," I said again.

LEANING OUT

You get mentally and physically sloppy back in town. Some never get out of that state, so they don't know what it's like to "lean out," or get lean—physically, mentally, or spiritually.

The sloppiness varies. I get sloppy in Circle—working on the cabin, cutting firewood, and floating on the Yukon River—because I know that if I take off two toes with the scalpel-sharp, double-bit ax someone will get me into Fairbanks and the hospital, a hundred seventy miles away on the gravel Steese "Highway." I am not worried about survival, so I am more careless. This explains why I injure myself more often there than in the bush, where I could easily drown, get mauled by a bear, fall from a cliff, or experience any of a number of otherwise minor disasters that wouldn't be fatal near civilization.

Here I am, again, trying to explain the intangible, when the only way to understand it is to experience it. I've tried for decades to clarify the subject, but the only ones who get it are the rare trappers or hunters who spend time in true wilderness and do it alone, at least on occasion. Oceangoing sailors sometimes get it, especially if they sail alone as I did for a year or two in the Caribbean. I remember long conversations in bars on Cay Corker and Grand Bahama and beside campfires on uninhabited islands. While the sailors tended to be more verbal than the hunters and trappers, it was all about the same thing—independence, awareness, and responsibility to yourself.

Bush pilots sometimes understand it, too: They have to stay alert, not only to the mechanics and handling of the plane, but to the weather, to obstacles such as the six-inch spruce spike sticking out of a beach landing spot, and to nuances of wind on taking off or landing. Most, though, don't get the solitude part, and some panic at the idea of going down in the wilds alone.

LEANING OUT

Roger Dowding flew us for years in his Cessna 185. Roger and Joe Firmin partnered for a time, but when Joe wrecked a plane and insurance premiums rocketed, they went their separate ways to run their own companies. They remained great friends and helped each other out whenever possible. They were not only our business associates—one or the other always flew us into the Arctic bush—but they became fast friends. Whenever they flew up the Yukon in the vicinity of Circle, they'd land and visit us at our cabin.

One particular season, Cheri and I planned to spend the whole season alone, expecting to live in the bush for eight weeks. We took enough gear and food to make the stay comfortable—a case of champagne, folding camp chairs, and more canned food than we'd used in earlier years when space and weight were important considerations. We had planned too much gear for Roger's 185, so we booked Joe's 206. The bigger plane could carry all the gear we wanted, as well as both rafts. The big, fourteen-foot Riken could carry everything, and if we got too much meat and too many trophies we could employ the smaller boat, though the Achilles would mostly serve as an emergency spare.

The only place Joe could land and take off again with the 206 was the dry lake bed near Last Lake. He dropped us off, and we made plans to meet him on the big beach at the confluence of the Sheenjek and Porcupine Rivers in two month's time. If there was too much snow then or the weather was bad, we'd simply float another day down to Fort Yukon, and he'd fly us back to Circle from there. When Joe took off, I felt, at long last, the elation of coming home again to peace and solitude. I saw from her smile that Cheri felt something as pleasant, but we didn't discuss it. Sometimes it's too easy to talk a thing away.

It took us nearly seven hours to pack all the gear across the tundra to the river. It took more time to inflate and assemble the Riken, load up, and then float off. We floated three hours to the mouth of Walt's Creek, delayed in part because we spent an hour watching wolves feed on a caribou kill on a gravel bar, and another half hour watching a grizzly strip soapberries from riverside bushes. The wolves knew we were there but ignored us, and the grizzly was so busy eating he didn't sense us.

THE DANGEROUS GAME

We camped that night on the beach, starting the long pull up to the sheep camp the next morning. Cheri carried a bee sting kit now, after having a bad allergic reaction to a hornet sting the previous season. We also hauled the H&R 12-gauge with buckshot loads so that Cheri would have some protection from a curious bear if I were off somewhere. Most grizzlies ran, but there was always the odd one that didn't. The only thing predictable about a grizz is that you never know what he will do. After considerable experience over the years hunting not only in North America but also in Africa, I've come to the conclusion that a grizzly will charge unprovoked more readily than any other beast. But, then, you could argue that surprising him was provoking him, or even that wandering through his territory was infuriating to him. Anticipation is the only way to survive in the wilds.

We hunted hard for two weeks without luck. Once we stalked rams on the steep north slope of Black Mountain, but the winds shifted and the sheep bunched; I couldn't get a shot as they huddled a mere thirty yards below. Soon after, they bolted straight down an avalanche chute, and the next time we saw them, they were far across the canyon, a mile away. We stalked two other good rams on one other occasion, but they made us out and ran for it before we could get close enough for a shot. We were nearly out of the grub we'd hauled from the cache on the river, and I'd already caught all the nearby grayling.

One morning, I looked out from the tent and was hit in the face with a big raindrop. The clouds had lowered to above the tent, so with the sheep hunting over for the day, I decided to hoof it down to the river and the cache and pack up a load of food. To save energy I didn't carry the rifle. Cheri decided to relax and do some reading, so she stayed behind.

I laced on my Vasque Sundowner hiking boots—the best boot I've come across (and I've tried more than I can remember)—fastened up the gaiters, and shouldered the empty pack. I made it to the river in surprising time. Of course, it took longer trekking back up with a pack full of food.

Before I'd climbed above the forests, I noticed big bear scats full of red soapberries. (I never could figure why bears love the

LEANING OUT

red berries—I've tried them, and they are bitter as alum—but they are an early and midsummer staple for the bruins.) Now, rain can make even old spoor look much fresher than it is. These scats looked fresh, but I hoped they weren't.

As I walked on, I noticed, suddenly, that I was in a big soapberry patch along the creek. It had been a good year for the fruit, too. I wished I were somewhere else, especially since I hadn't hauled the gun. The droppings were everywhere, and I noticed clearly older droppings, so the bears had been working over the berry patch for some time.

I heard a low growl just as I neared the upper limit of the berry patch. I stopped and looked around carefully, again wishing I'd brought the 7mm-08. I heard the growl one more time but didn't see anything. I backed slowly toward the nearest spruce tree, fortunately one a bear wouldn't be able to knock over with a single swat.

The bear stood up from the soapberry bushes twenty-five yards away. I backed until I felt the tree against the pack, then I reached for a branch just as the bear started toward me. The branch broke with a loud snap, the bear stopped a moment, and I found another branch, hauling myself up in a shower of twigs. It's surprising what adrenaline can do for arm strength. I climbed as high as I could, but it was only ten feet up a spindly tree. The bear walked to within a dozen feet from the tree, and stood and stared up at me with a look I'd anthropomorphically call "quizzical." The hair on his shoulders stood up as if he were full of static electricity.

I cussed at the bear in the best fashion of a shore-leave sailor. I cussed until I went hoarse. The bear was little fazed, though the hair on his shoulders and neck was no longer rucked up. He finally tired of the whole event and wandered off. I waited in the tree for an hour. When I finally climbed down, I hurried to the high and open country, not feeling any relief until I walked into camp and had a rifle at hand again.

A week later, we climbed toward the head of Trophy Creek where I'd killed a nice ram the season before. Boulder-hopping up the creek and through the cliffs, we rounded a bend, and I looked up to see two rams. We backed quickly down the stream

THE DANGEROUS GAME

before they had the chance to see us; then, as quietly as possible, we climbed the scree. The wind was perfect.

When I bellied over the low ridge, eight rams lay in the shale along the ridgeline, dreaming of past loves and ruminating. Cheri crouched below, and I motioned for her to crawl up to watch. All the rams were mature, but one stretched out on a black outcrop caught my eye. The horn tips climbed well above the snout line before they began to flare. From the steep uphill angle, they seemed to drop to the jaw line, too. It seemed a fine head. I touched off when the cross hairs settled nicely on his shoulder. He leapt straight off the cliff and skidded to a stop in the scree.

The other rams stood and milled about. One I hadn't seen stood on the skyline, and through the scope I saw the heavy bases and the better-than-full curl, the left horn broomed well back. The ram was at least as long as the one I'd killed, but much heavier. As I watched through the scope with the cross hairs on the big ram's shoulder, I can't honestly say I wasn't tempted. I remembered Isak Dinesen's character Charles Bulpett saying, "The person who can take delight . . . in a magnificent head of game without wanting to shoot it has not got a human heart." I flicked the safety back on and stood. The rams gawked a moment before stampeding over the ridge.

As so often happens in this country, the beasts had gotten to the carcass by the time I returned to pack out the meat the next day. This time it was eagles and ravens. They'd eaten a lot and had fouled more. I boned out and cleaned up what I could and hauled it to camp.

We lazed around the camp and watched the migrating caribou. Ninety percent of them were bulls, and we saw some astonishing heads. But though the season was open, I didn't want to pack that much meat down to the river. The days had shortened, and the nights were long enough that we now had several hours of dark. We listened to the wolves howl in the night. One morning, I climbed from the tent to startle five wolves a few yards away. The last wolf, an adult, carried a plastic bag with a sheep roast I'd cooked the night before. Another adult trotted off, followed by three young pups. I had to laugh, though I had been looking forward to sheep meat for breakfast.

LEANING OUT

The living in the high country was too good to leave, but another part waited below on the river. We hiked down and out, floating down to Lobo Lake and hunting ptarmigan along the way. Bird numbers were up, and we had plenty to eat when the sheep meat ran out. We often polished off ten ptarmigan a day, so hunting them was a regular and pleasant routine.

When the Arctic Ocean sea ducks began leaving Lobo Lake, we figured we should, too. We camped first at Rising Water Camp, as usual. The day was cold enough that on the way down we stopped at a black-sand beach at the bottom of the big rapids to warm up with a big fire and a lunch of ramen noodles and hot cocoa. We didn't find a big moose there, but we watched caribou cross the river and hoped for a big one. A very blond grizzly grazed on blueberries a mile downriver nearly every morning. We weren't hurried.

The routine was firm now, established through experience on the river. We knew where we'd camp each evening, at least on the upper half of the river, and we knew how long it would take to get to each site. We beached at the bottom of the rapids at Bluff Camp late one afternoon and saw a cow and calf moose trotting up the beach. On the day's float, we'd seen two wolves, a score of caribou bulls (including a big one I couldn't get a shot at), and a decent bull moose I didn't try for because he was in a bad spot. We also saw a grizzly swimming in the river right in front of us, and he almost did us in.

The current pushed us toward the bear in the river, and I heaved against the oars to avoid hitting him. No telling what would happen if I did, but at the least, he'd send us to the bottom with a swat or a bite into the rubberized raft material. We might get to shore, but most of the gear wouldn't, and we would have a hard time surviving, let alone traveling out to the rendezvous two hundred fifty miles downriver. Cheri slid the rifle from the soft case and cranked a round into the chamber. The grizzly still hadn't seen us, but the current swerved the raft on a collision course in spite of my fervent upriver rowing.

I shouted. The bear rose to hind legs and stood against the current. The water came to his neck, and he grunted. Cheri took the oars, while I grabbed the rifle, aimed in the water

THE DANGEROUS GAME

alongside his head, and pulled off. At a low angle, a bullet makes a hell of a racket and impact when it smashes into water right next to your head. The bear lost balance and fell back, tried to regain his footing, and then swam for the far shore. He climbed onto the rocky bank, stared as we floated by, and then started back into the water. Evidently, he figured he could eat us. I put another slug into the water alongside him, and he bawled and swatted at the splash before turning his attention back to us. I shot into the water a third time, and both of us shouted as loudly as we could. He turned reluctantly and climbed the low bluff, then turned again to stare. I shot into the water again, and he sat back, pivoted, and lumbered off.

We didn't find a big bull moose at Bluff Camp, but we got other action. A trophy caribou crashed right through camp, followed closely by two wolves. I mean, this was right *through* camp, too. All of them jumped into the river and swam across, the bull gaining a bit. Eventually, we found a nice caribou, without so much competition, while glassing from the bluff across the river. We collected him, then pushed off into the current again.

We floated another long and cold day in the wind and mush ice in the river to Surprise Camp. This was the best camp for getting a moose. Something always surprising happened here, and, so far, the surprises had been pleasant.

In the heavy frost of the first dawn at Surprise Camp, I crawled from the tent in my briefs and T-shirt to answer the call of nature. As I always did at that time of the morning, I paid my respects to the sun rising in the southeast and took a look around. The last place I looked was right behind the tent, where, to my astonishment, a tremendous bull moose stared at me not two yards from the tent. I lunged for the rifle just inside the tent flap at the same time the bull pivoted and crashed off through the willows. I yanked on the pacs and raced after him . . . *in briefs and T-shirt.* I plunged through the slough, the water drops freezing on the hair on my legs, and charged through the willow brush and down into the next slough. But I didn't catch him. Surprise, surprise! I climbed back into the tent, half frozen and shivering so hard I had a tough time pulling off the pac boots. I didn't warm until the sun climbed well up and warmed the tent. The hot cup of cocoa laced with J&B helped, too.

As we watched for moose across the big willow flat across the river from camp, we saw a nice bull walk out of the spruce timber. Through the binoc from a high bluff a mile away, you couldn't really count the points, but you could tell he spread better than fifty-six inches or so, and that's a good bull that far north. Another bull stepped from the timber, then another, and then another, until we watched seven of them browse and push each other about. One bull's spread was better than sixty inches. Another didn't quite have that spread, but the palms were longer, broader, and more even. The other bulls were all fair to good for Arctic country.

We slid down the bluff and walked back to camp. Cheri kicked up the fire and started supper while I rowed across and tied off the raft to a strong willow. As I pushed through the trees, I spotted the sixty-inch bull staring at me from thirty yards. As I put the cross hairs on his chest as he stood head-on, another bull pushed through the willows right next to him. The bulls engaged antlers and shoved at each other. (Sparring allows bulls to sharpen reflexes, strengthen neck muscles, and judge the competition.) The second bull got the better of it, and though he didn't have the spread, his antlers were altogether better anyway. Not too serious, the bulls disengaged and browsed side by side. The rut hadn't quite started—if it had, they wouldn't have been so amicable.

I settled the cross hairs behind the second bull's ear as he bent to browse, and touched off. He collapsed but stood up again and lunged into the willows before I could shoot a second time. I ran across the creek and around the willows, and he stood there along with the sixty-inch bull, twenty yards away. I put another round into the chest, and he collapsed. I had my moose meat . . . but it wasn't over yet.

The other bull stared at me as if I'd killed his best buddy. Within moments, the other five bulls half-surrounded me and stared. I shouted five or six times before they would leave. I walked to the downed moose, propped the rifle against the willow, and put my foot on the antler lying on the tundra to measure the spread of antlers with my arms. That's when the bull jerked his

THE DANGEROUS GAME

head and threw me right over him. I landed on my back, eight feet away in a clump of dwarf birch. The bull staggered to his feet, lost his balance, and nearly fell on me. I raced to the rifle and finished him off. *That* surprise wasn't so pleasant.

We spent the next day skinning, butchering, and packing the meat to the river to float it into camp. We had so many white game bags hanging from the trees and scrub that it looked like a rookery of white vultures surrounding the camp.

We celebrated that night with a bottle of Mums champagne; a pile of moose tenderloin steaks; a rice dish made with moose blood, moose lard, and mushrooms gathered from the tundra; and a chilled dessert made from sugar, blueberries, and lowbush cranberries. I built a huge, roaring fire, the flames leaping a dozen feet in the air. How could it get better? We already missed it, though we still had a good week's travel downriver.

We'd float out for a day and camp at a new spot each night. Finding the right spot was sometimes a challenge. The country flattened, and the river turned on itself like a great snake. Often I had to row against the wind, downriver, to make any progress at all. If I didn't row, the wind blew us back upriver against the current. We watched closely for sweepers—big spruce trees whose root systems had been undercut from the river, causing them to fall into the water while still anchored to the bank. Some hung horizontally just above the water, some just beneath the surface, and others at the surface. They'd dump a boat, if the pilot was careless enough to hit one.

I'd learned about sweepers the hard way, as we all do the most important lessons that stay with us. Years earlier I was floating through this same wild country in the little Achilles, and I wasn't paying attention. The raft floated into a sweeper before I realized what had happened. The current flipped the craft, and as I was heavily clothed against the cold, I sunk straight to the bottom, along with much of the gear. Somehow, the boat cleared itself of the sweeper and floated downriver, dragging the tie line tangled in antlers. As the antlers went by, I grabbed them and pulled myself up the rope and onto the raft.

Very fortunately, most of the gear was secured in cargo nets, though I lost my ax and some other equipment. Two waterproof river bags containing the tent and cooking gear had floated off downriver. Luckily, I found them a day later bobbing about in a big eddy. Since that time, I've been jumpy around sweepers, and the lower Sheenjek is full of them.

Late one afternoon, I rowed to shore to find a camp spot, searching a camp or two up from the Porcupine River. I waded ashore in the hip boots, climbed the bluff to the flat and the spruce forest, and then walked around through the trees looking for a site big enough and flat enough for the tent. Cheri waited at the oars. As I pushed through the timber, the twigs made a racket against my hip boots, but over the racket I heard something that I couldn't place. Then I heard a great commotion from behind and whirled to face a grizzly charging straight at me, its canines glowing ivory in the dusky woods, and its shoulder fur bristling as it grunted and charged.

"Get the gun!" I shouted.

We've all felt it sometime—the knowledge we will, without a shadow of doubt, crash as the sedan skids out of control on an icy road. I had no doubt whatsoever that I was a nanosecond from getting mauled by an enraged grizzly, and I had already bent my knees and crouched to face the impact of four hundred pounds of meat grinder.

Cheri shouted something back, and to my surprise, the grizzly skidded to a stop behind a bush. Without another thought I sprinted for the river, dived off the bluff, landed in the raft, and nearly bounced out again while shouting, "Row! Row!"

Cheri leaned into the oars, and a moment later we'd caught the current. A moment after that, the grizzly was searching the bank for us. I dug for the rifle buried under the tarp—a bad place for it—with full intention of killing the bear in revenge for the fright he'd given me. I didn't find it before the bear disappeared back into the timber. The incident turned part of my beard white—no kidding. And I learned, again, never to walk into grizzly country unarmed.

We floated to the Sheenjek's confluence with the Porcupine and camped for two days before Joe and his 206 showed up to whisk us across the Yukon Flats to Circle. I came away from this trip knowing I'd been too sloppy; the close encounters with the

THE DANGEROUS GAME

grizzlies were the results. That first time, I should have backed out and away from the soapberry flat as soon as I discovered myself there; better yet, I should have carried the rifle. I should have carried the gun the second time down on the river, too. Fatigue was no excuse, not if you want to live out there. If nothing else, once I learn a hard lesson, I don't forget. I wouldn't make the same mistakes again. Then again, I should not have made them in the first place, and I am lucky to be alive.

WAITING FOR CHRISTMAS

When I was a kid waiting for Christmas, the first part of December was at least six months long. The big day would never come. As an adult, that's what the summer became to me, an endless time when all I could do was think about my remote North Country. I remembered the taste of caribou chops broiled over spruce coals, the floats along a sapphire river under a sky of the same color, the pleasant wine smell of frosted blueberries, and the howls of a hunting wolf pack.

We followed the same routine, flying up in Firmin's 206 with our pile of gear. We had especially enjoyed the season before and the profligacy of all the gear and food. I felt guilty about all that gear because, in a sense, it insulated you from the country and its hardships. But it was enjoyable to have the campfire chairs, the champagne, the canned foods. We had hauled in every bit the previous season.

You know the routine by now, so I will eliminate some of it. Up in the sheep mountains, we hunted hard and didn't find much in our favorite places like Black Mountain, Dark Basin, or Trophy Creek, so we worked northerly into Grizzly Creek and Sheep Ridge. (Remember, you won't find these names on a map—I devised them myself in earlier years.) We hunted in the Caribou Walk drainage, too, but game was scarce. We saw only a few bears, wolves, and caribou, and even fewer moose.

One day, as we started up for the day's hunt, I noted a grizzly on a slope half a mile from camp. I cussed at him with the idea of scaring him out of the vicinity and away from where he might do mischief. He'd been lying down, but now he sat up and stared straight at us from three hundred yards away. Though grizzlies are reputed to have poor eyesight, he clearly responded to our movement at that distance. I shouted again, but he just sat and stared.

THE DANGEROUS GAME

I put a round from the 7mm-08 over his head into a rock behind him. He merely turned and looked at the rock powder. He was directly downwind of camp, so he knew where it was, and it hadn't alarmed him. I fired two more shots, spaced with choice profanity for good measure. He merely watched us. Of course, leaving camp wasn't an option now, so we returned over the short distance we'd come and awaited further developments.

We'd no sooner gotten to camp than the bear climbed onto the bluff a hundred yards downwind. I fired a bullet at a rock nearby. Again, he merely looked at where it had hit. I fired another round. This time he growled, then disappeared into a depression as he walked closer. He had no fear of our scent, our voices, or our gunshots. It looked like a showdown.

I told Cheri to break camp as I watched with the rifle. I didn't want to kill the bear if I could help it, and it looked like I'd have to if we stayed. He edged to fifty yards, then pretended to eat berries as he sidled closer. When he had worked up to forty yards, he stopped behind a watermelon-size limestone boulder. I fired at the rock, and the impact kicked rock shrapnel in his face. He sat back on haunches and growled. But he didn't retreat.

The bear lunged toward us twice, and I held the cross hairs below his hump, keeping my finger on the trigger. He lunged again, and I nearly pulled off when he stopped at twenty-five yards. I prepared myself to kill him. I'd marked a particularly crimson dwarf birch bush seven yards away, and if he passed that, I told myself, I'd shoot.

Out of the corner of my eye, I noticed aluminum pans by the campfire ring. I sidled over and lifted them, and then banged one down hard against a rock. The bear stopped sidling and looked. I banged the pan again. He stared, then walked broadside to the camp over to the edge of the bench, dropping over the edge out of sight.

"Hurry," I told Cheri, moving to get between the camp and the point where the bear had disappeared. Just then he climbed back onto the bench, standing there and staring at us. I chose a rock six yards off, and decided that if he approached closer than that, I'd shoot to kill.

WAITING FOR CHRISTMAS

Finally, Cheri had the gear stuffed into backpacks. She shouldered her pack, and I shrugged into mine while she covered us with the shotgun. We hurried up the main drainage. When I turned to look back from half a mile up the slope, the bear was nosing around our campsite. We pushed on, and a mile later I looked down and back. The bear had followed our trail, his nose to the ground like a Walker hound. I got a chill. Though I'd encountered hundreds of grizzlies at close range, none had acted this way. He methodically followed our trail. I fired again just in front of him. He stopped a moment, then kept coming.

We hiked on, watching the backtrail and the bear. He closed the distance to a quarter mile. We pushed northwest, and when we crested a ridge, the bear was *still* coming. I made up my mind to pitch the tent in the next creek bottom, and if the bear kept coming, I'd kill him. I'd done everything possible to avoid a fatal confrontation.

We climbed into Sheep Creek and set up camp in the open so we'd spot the bear in time. Cheri rummaged in the packs for a lunch. I swept the ridgeline above with the binocular and spotted his head above the ridge. He watched for some minutes before he walked along the top, gave another look down, and then turned back. Perhaps we'd moved into another bear's territory. I hoped so.

I slept little that night. We stayed at the campsite the next day just in case and glassed for rams from the ridge. We didn't hunt far from the tent for three or four days, until I was relatively certain the bear wouldn't bother us again.

A week later, we climbed into the headwaters of Old Woman Creek, and while Cheri ate lunch on a ridge, I hiked higher. Midway up the higher ridge, I spotted three rams. Two were younger, probably eight or nine years old, but the third had heavy bases, lots of annular rings, and a horn that was broken back. The bases looked as if they'd go at least fourteen inches, and the entire horn looked to be about thirty-eight. He was better than anything we'd seen all season. I motioned to Cheri down the ridge for her to climb up so she could watch the stalk.

I slid down the talus into the bottoms, crossed a ridge, and then dropped into a deep, ragged gully before working up another

THE DANGEROUS GAME

slope. When I looked over a ridge, the three rams were grazing slowly up a barren hillside. I could see no way to get closer without their spotting me. Sheep that far north have had no experience with man, but they have evolved as prey animals, so they spook at the unknown, especially if it is above them.

I scrambled farther down the ravine, out of sight behind the slope. When I climbed back onto the small ridge, the sheep were well above me, but I couldn't see a way to approach closer and remain hidden. *OK*, I reasoned, *you're below them and they're calm, so just approach in the open, and don't sneak or rush.* I'd used the same tactic before, and once, while photographing in the Alaska Range, I had worked literally into the middle of a ram band with the nearest grazing three feet away. I crossed my fingers while I crossed the ridge.

The rams didn't make me out until I was halfway down. The two younger rams stared while the older one took one look and continued on up and away until he reached the other rams. One resumed grazing and the other still watched as I stalked across the slope and into the canyon bottom with an apparent lack of intent. I wanted them to think I was only another beast, one of those caribou noted for doing odd things.

In the steep, rocky country, I closed in slowly. I used the curve of the slope as I worked up a creek and got out of sight, and then hurried to close the distance. When I came into view again, I moved slowly and seemingly without purpose. Then, when I was out of sight again, I sprinted. The big ram had moved farther up the talus, but he was not alarmed, merely cautious. When I dropped out of sight again, I ran up the gully and gained a good hundred yards. The ram still fed slowly away. The two younger rams stared, walked, fed, and stared some more.

I knew I couldn't get closer when I climbed from behind the last boulder. The cross hairs met the top of the ram's shoulder as he climbed stiffly through the rocks. He limped, and, judging by appearances, he would not survive another winter. He collapsed at the shot.

As near as I could figure, the ram had been more than three hundred yards off. He was ten or eleven years old and had heavy bases. He was probably the same big ram I'd seen the season before.

WAITING FOR CHRISTMAS

We stayed at the camp, eating sheep meat and resting after the long and grueling hunt. When we trekked out, we found bear tracks at our first campsite. We hurried along, both with guns at the ready, and made it to the river after sunset. We floated a long day to the Lobo Lake camp and hunted ptarmigan and fly-fished for grayling. We stayed at the same familiar camps along the upper Sheenjek but didn't shoot. The days were sunny but cold, and mush ice began to show in the river.

The big surprise at Surprise Camp was the boot tracks in the mud. I knew it was inevitable as we'd noted kayakers and rafters in previous years, usually early in the season. They were few and far between, but still, in earlier years there hadn't been as many. It made me understand that it was coming to an end—our solitude, the peace, the hunting, the expeditions, the independence.

One evening, as we wandered the moose meadows across the river from the camp, we heard clattering antlers. No one had to tell me that two bull moose were sparring. We stalked toward the noise, keeping to the spruce on the bluff. We stalked almost a mile before we found them.

Three bulls sparred, three hundred yards ahead. We ghosted through the spruce on the bluff. Don't let anyone tell you that moose have poor vision. These moose spotted us within a hundred yards. The biggest bull was alarmed, so I lay on the tundra and held behind the shoulder with the little 7mm-08. I heard the loud *crack* of the shot, and the two smaller bulls trotted off into the timber on the far side of the big open meadow. The big bull stood—he wasn't going anywhere—and he showed no sign of going down. He wasn't weaving as he would if he'd been lung shot. I walked to within fifty yards, and he still stood and stared. I shot him through the shoulder, and he collapsed. The first bullet had skimmed beneath the brisket and broken the off foreleg. Apparently, and surprisingly, animals as big as moose can't walk on three legs.

We had a long day of packing the moose meat a mile to the raft and then floating across to the camp. We again celebrated with a bottle of Mums and a big meal, but it was more subdued this season. A lone wolf howled from off toward the Yukon, and the moon climbed from the Old Crow, flooding the spruce forests and tundra with cold, silver light.

THE DANGEROUS GAME

A few days later we floated out. The Indian summer had turned into hard-edged late autumn, and the winds had stripped the willows and cottonwoods and birch of leaves. The tundra had turned to gray. One day, snow spat out of a north wind and the Sheenjek spewed us into the Porcupine River. We camped two days at the confluence before Joe flew us back across the Yukon Flats and the Black River, over the Gwitchin village of Chalkyitsik, and across the Yukon River to the dirt strip at Circle. Joe and Cheri unloaded the 206 while I walked slowly to the cabin for my truck. Coming back was more somber than usual, and I could think of nothing in civilization that I had missed.

APPENDIX

Over the years my quest for big game has taken me to many places "off the beaten track." I have had some exceptional hunts, and I have also had some that have left me feeling angry and frustrated. Based on my experiences, I consider the following outfitters, guides, places, books, and accommodations to be the best.

AFRICA

Outfitters:
- Pro-Guiding, Namibia, PH John Wambach. Contact *proguide@iway.na*
- RMT Safaris, Zimbabwe, PH Russell Tarr. Contact *rmhunts@ecoweb.co.zw*

Guides:
- Willie Phillips (retired), Botswana
- John Wambach (see above)
- Russell Tarr (see above)

Places:
- Okavango Delta, Botswana
- South Masailand, Tanzania

Books:
- *Flame Trees of Thika*, Elspeth Huxley
- *Green Hills of Africa*, Ernest Hemingway
- *Horn of the Hunter*, Robert Ruark
- *Out of Africa*, Isak Dinesen
- *Safari: A Dangerous Affair*, Walt Prothero

Concierge/Accommodations:
- Afton Guest House, Johannesburg, R.S.A. Contact *aftongh@netactive.co.za* or phone 011-27-11-391-7625. (The very best at getting things done and making you comfortable; includes meet and greet.)

THE DANGEROUS GAME

Restaurant:
- *La Gondola*, Raffaele Granaudo, 4 Monument Road, Kempton Park, Johannesburg, R.S.A. Phone 011-9752216 or 011-9754412.

ASIA

Outfitters:
- Yuri Matison, Badakshan Expeditions (hunts in Tajikistan for mid-Asian ibex and Marco Polo sheep). Contact *pamir@orc.ru*
- Vladimir Treschov (hunts throughout Asia, specializing in sheep). Contact *tmarina@online.ru*

Guides:
- Dovelat (Tajikistan)
- Taktamat (Tajikistan)
- Yuri Matison (Tajikistan)
- Jumaa (Turkmenistan)
- Vladimir Plaschenko (eastern Siberia)
- Vladimir Treschov (see above)

Books:
- *East of the Sun and West of the Moon*, Theodore Roosevelt
- *Man-eaters of India*, Jim Corbett
- *The Great Arc of the Wild Sheep*, James Clark

NORTH AMERICA

Outfitters:
- Escalante Safaris, 557 Lakeview Dr., Elk Ridge, UT 84651
- Kibler Guiding, Box 667, Roosevelt, AZ 85545 (480) 200-7791
- R&R Guide Service, Rob Jones and Rod Schuh. Contact *rrguide@gci.net*.
- Boyd Warner, Box 1407, Yellowknife, NWT, Canada XIA ZPI
- Wade Lemon Guiding, Holden, UT (435) 795-2299

Guides:
- Jaypatee Akeeagotak, Grise Fiord, Nunavut, Canada
- Mike Fisher, Orem, UT
- Jon Kibler, Roosevelt, AZ

APPENDIX

- Rob Jones, Anchorage, AK. Contact *rrguide@gci.net*
- Sam Kapolak, Bathurst Bay, Nunavut, Canada
- Scott Ruttum, Anchorage, AK
- Wade Lemon, Holden, UT

Books:
- *Hunting American Lions,* Frank Hibben
- *Sheep and Sheep Hunting,* Jack O'Connor
- *Tales of a Big Game Guide,* Russell Annabel
- *The Hunting Adventures of Me & Joe,* Walt Prothero

Taxidermist:
- Taxidermy-Art Studio, Yuri and Natashe Rulin, 7600 South Redwood Road, Salt Lake City, UT 84084, (80l) 255-4754
- Atcheson Taxidermy, Butte, MT

Hunt Broker/Booking Agent: (Worldwide)
- The Hunting Consultant, Vance Corrigan, Livingstone, MT (406) 222-0504 or *huntfind@wtp.net*